John Matthias was born in 1941 in Columbus, Ohio. For many years he taught at the University of Notre Dame, but also spent long periods of time in the UK, both at Cambridge and at his wife's childhood home in Hacheston, Suffolk. He has been a Visiting Fellow in poetry at Clare Hall, Cambridge, and is now a Life Member. Until 2012 he was poetry editor of *Notre Dame Review* and is now Editor at Large. Matthias has published some thirty books of poetry, translation, scholarship, and collaboration. His most recent books are *New Selected Poems*, (2004), *Kedging* (2007), *Trigons* (2010), *Collected Shorter Poems Vol. 2* (all verse) and *Who Was Cousin Alice? And Other Questions* (2011) (mostly prose). In 1998 Robert Archambeau edited *Word Play Place: Essays on the poetry of John Matthias*, and in 2011 Joe Francis Doerr published a second volume of essays on his work, *The Salt Companion to the Poetry of John Matthias*. *Collected Longer Poems*, is the second of a projected three-volume edition from Shearsman of Matthias' complete poems.

Also by John Matthias

Poetry
Bucyrus (1970)
Turns (1975)
Crossing (1979)
Bathory & Lermontov (1980)
Northern Summer (1984)
A Gathering of Ways (1991)
Swimming at Midnight (1995)
Beltane at Aphelion (1995)
Pages: New Poems & Cuttings (2000)
Working Progress, Working Title (2002)
Swell & Variations on the Song of Songs (2003)
New Selected Poems (2004)
Kedging (2007)
Trigons (2010)
Collected Shorter Poems, Vol. 2 (2011)
Collected Shorter Poems, Vol. 1 (2013)

Translations
Contemporary Swedish Poetry (1980)
    (with Göran Printz-Påhlson)
Jan Östergren: Rainmaker (1983)
    (with Göran Printz-Påhlson)
The Battle of Kosovo (1987)
    (with Vladeta Vučković)
Three-Toed Gull: Selected Poems of Jesper Svenbro (2003)
    (with Lars-Håkan Svensson)

Editions
23 Modern British Poets (1971)
Introducing David Jones (1980)
David Jones: Man and Poet (1989)
Selected Works of David Jones (1992)
Notre Dame Review: The First Ten Years (2009)
    (with William O'Rourke)

Essays
Reading Old Friends (1992)
Who Was Cousin Alice? and Other Questions (2011)

Collected Longer Poems

John Matthias

Afterword by Mark Scroggins
Monotypes by Douglas Kinsey

Shearsman Books

Published in the United Kingdom in 2012 by
Shearsman Books Ltd
50 Westons Hill Drive
Emersons Green
BRISTOL
BS16 7DF

Shearsman Books Ltd Registered Office
30–31 St. James Place, Mangotsfield, Bristol BS16 9JB
(this address not for correspondence)

www.shearsman.com

ISBN 978-1-84861-240-2

Acknowledgements
An earlier version of the 'Afterword' previously appeared in *The Salt Companion
to John Matthias*, edited by Joe Francis Doerr (Cambridge: Salt Publishing 2011).

The poems in this volume were first published as follows:
Crossing (London: Anvil Press Poetry 1979);
Northern Summer (London: Anvil Press Poetry 1984);
A Gathering of Ways (Athens, OH: Swallow Press 1991);
Pages. New Poems & Cuttings (Athens, OH: Swallow Press 2000);
Working Progress, Working Title (Cambridge: Salt Publishing 2002);
Kedging (Cambridge: Salt Publishing, 2007).

'After Five Words Englished From the Russian'
was first published in *Huffington*, issue 1, 2012.

Contents

In Memory of My Friend Jay Walton

(who preferred my shorter poems)

Facts from an Apocryphal Midwest

For Michael Anania and i.m. Ken Smith

I. Seven Moves Toward Embarkation on the Local River

*Nous embarquâmes le troisième Decembre
avec trente hommes, dans huit canots*

*& nous remontâmes la rivière des Miamis
faisant nostre route au Sud...*

—Fr. Hennepin

•

Overheard on Riverside cycling toward
the bridge and U.S. 31:
Look, he says, *if things had turned out*

*differently a long time back,
not just you, but everybody on this
river might be speaking French*

& trading otter skins or beaver pelts.

•

1 arpent: 160 *pieds de Roi*
84 arpents: say about one league
28 arpents, then, to the mile

But distances are tricky
and it often takes
you longer
than you think.

•

Four thin men, two white, two black
stand fishing near the Farmer's Market
where the Amish come to sell

their vegetables and breads. It's early
afternoon in heavy, muggy August.
The river's low & stagnant for ten miles.

Catchin' anything? Jus' tin cans an' tires
Four thin fishermen—
and no Miamis, not a Potawatomi in town.

•

Oui-oui-la-Mèche
L'Espérance de la Brie

Père Gabriel
Père Louis
Père Zénobe
René Robert Cavelier (Sieur de la Salle)

•

Measurements of distance "There were several varieties of league; but the one that Hennepin undoubtedly meant was the ordinary league of 84 arpents. That will give 3.051 plus 5220-5280th statute miles. You need have no hesitation in assuming Hennepin's league to be 3.052 statute or English miles."

"We embarked on the 3rd of December with thirty men in eight canoes, and ascended the river of the Miamis, taking our course to the south-east for about twenty five leagues. We could not make out the portage which we were to take with our canoes and all our equipage in order to go and embark at the source of the river Seignelay, and as we had gone higher up in a canoe without discovering the place where we were to march by land to take the other river which runs by the Illinois, we halted to wait for the Sieur de La Salle, who had gone exploring on land; and as he did not return we did not know what course to pursue."

Lost in nature or attacked by nature —Fr. Hennepin

10

2. Five Maps, a Medicine Bag, and a Myth

•

Carte de la Nouvelle Découverte

Illuminations of the priests haranguing Indians.
Much conjecture. Crudely drawn Ohio
and Missouri and Wisconsin…
Père Marquette's route back it's got
entirely wrong.

•

Carte Généralle de la France Septentrionale

The Ohio's called the *Ouaboustikou.*
Pictures of the creatures
native to the Mississippi's western plains
include a camel, ostriches, giraffes.
A monster seen by Père Marquette and Joliet:
Horns of a deer, beard of a tiger,
face like that of a man—Also
many nasty scales
and a long tail wound around it.

exageration
for what?

•

Carte de Jean Baptiste Franquelin

La Salle's Starved Rock, a natural fortress
all but inaccessible a hundred feet
above the Illinois, the little colony below.
La Nouvelle France: Penobscot
to the south of Lake Champlain and to
the Mohawk near Schenectady
and then where Susquehanna rises
and the Allegheny past the south of Erie
on to Southern Michigan & then
northwest to Mississippi tributaries.

La Louisiane: The Mississippi valley,
the Ohio valley, Texas.
Rivière Colbert. Grande Rivière des Emissourittes.
Rivière des Illinois, ou Macopins.
And down below Starved Rock the colony:
Shawnees, Ouiatenons, Miamis,
Piankishaws, Illinois, Kilaticas, & Ouabonas.
3,900 warriors huddling
under *Le Rocher* & trembling for the Iroquois.

•

Carte de M. Mathieu Sâgean

a society
of upside down
thoughts ideas,
practices, and
creatures

The nation of the Acanibas, towns and castles,
King Hagaren, Montezuma's kin.
Women riding unicorns. Bricks of solid gold.
Caravans of horsemen
and a thousand oxen bearing priceless treasures.
Everyone polygamist.
Perpetual summer there, a cool breeze.

•

Rand McNally Atlas, 1985

The old Sauk trail, they say
still runs under U.S. 12
north from Niles to Detroit.
U.S. 20 takes it west through
Rolling Prairie to Chicago.

You can drive a car that's named
for Cadillac up U.S. 12
to Ypsilanti, turning north
at 94 to a port named for the Hurons.
You can even drive
your Pontiac to Pontiac.
But only trickster Wiske's brother

Chibyabos ever drove
in a Tecumseh to Tecumseh.

•

What's in your medicine bag, Neshnabe?
Gifts from Wiske? Toys?

A skunk's bladder. Ear of a bat.
Three fat joints and a switchblade knife.
Pussy hairs from Mama Chickie's whores.
What's in your map, little Frog?
If I drop this at your feet, it will explode.

•

The story goes that poor and feeble Tisha had a vision. A stranger dressed elaborately in clothing he had never seen before appeared and said he'd build a boat for him to travel over land and sea and rivers in if Tisha showed him just how big it ought to be. Tisha then took twelve enormous paces, smiled at the solemn stranger, waited. Suddenly a ship appeared the likes of which he'd never seen or even dreamed of. It had thin tree trunks planted vertically upon its decks, it had white sheets attached, it had nine great guns. Boat-Maker and Tisha climbed aboard and sailed over land and sea and rivers. They met and took aboard a mighty seer, a mighty hearer, a mighty eater, a mighty runner, and a mighty maker of wind. These were Boat-Maker's friends.

Pirate ship

capt.

One day after many travels they arrived at the camp of evil Matjimanito. He and all his friends were cannibals, and many bones lay all around. Matjimanito challenged Tisha to a contest where he'd gamble for his life. When Boat-Maker saw poor Tisha trembling, he insisted on a game which Matjimanito had never played before. When Tisha shouted *now*, Wind-Maker blew the ship up in the air above the village shouting out: *everybody's bones get out of here!* The nine black cannons fired, the dead all came alive, and Matjimanito and his men all perished when the ship came down and crushed them. After that, Tisha was a famous man. He travelled all the world over with his elegant protector and his friend. Eventually, Boat-Maker taught him how to speak his language. It was French.

He is the one to pay attention to

3. Copper. South from Lake Superior

...and down the old Sauk trail
although there were then, three and more millennia
before the French, no Sauks....

mother nature

The trail itself was there, and those who mined
the copper, *they* were there,
and those who came on urgent journeys from

the lower Mississippi & the Gulf to lug it back
were there, and leaned into
their labors in the mines and on the paths.

time

Mounds at Moorhouse Parish, at Miamisburg,
tumuli along the northeast
of the marshy lake between the Kankakee and

Portage Prairie with its recent graves & glacial
memories of mastodon & mammoth spit up
needles, chisels, knives & awls in fine profusion—

time connects to every era

& when Bernal Díaz entered Tuspan with Cortez,
he found that *every Indian had,*
besides his ornaments of gold, a copper axe,

very highly polished, strangely carved.
The copper came from west and north
of Mackinaw, Sault Ste. Marie, & Whitefish point.

from Minong where ten thousand men once mined
the copper for a thousand years
but left no carvings, writings, signs, nothing

even if we cannot see it

but their simple tools. Their dead they
buried elsewhere. Jacques Marquette was first to put
the island on a white man's map....

modernization makes us forget the interconnectedness of things

If the copper came by water to the forest paths,
it came by long canoe along the shores
of Huron into Lake St. Clair and then Detroit

where the trail curved into Canada.
Was Father Claude Allouez, the Jesuit, correct
who said of them who called

themselves *Neshnabek* and the other
tall Algonquins at Green Bay that golden copper
shapes were manitous, that queerly

wrought and efficacious metals were the secret
household gods of Potawatomies
who worshipped, like grave alchemists, the sun?

4. Saint-Lusson, Green Bay

The King of all these Frenchmen *was* the sun,
or so he liked to say, and Saint-
Lusson's vain oratory blazed with a brightness

at Green Bay outshining any local *kiktowenene's*.
But did he know to whom he spoke? Did
he know the phratries and the clans? Who was Bear

and who was Wolf or Bird, Elk or Moose or Fox?
He knew less of them than they knew
of the ones who built the mounds and made the trails

and mined the copper glowing in their lodges.
Chaskyd the ventriloquist? Wabino
eating fire? What was sleight of hand & superstition

to these soldiers of the King who sang *Vexilla Regis*
and the Jesuits who dreamed theocracy
and sought to make of these great lakes a Paraguay?

Nicholas Perrot, himself a spirit-power
said every Shaman there, assembled lines of Winnebagoes,
Potawatomies, Menomonies and Sauks before the *engagés,*

and cynical *coureurs de bois,* before the priests, before
the silken Saint-Lusson. *Vive Le Roi,* he said,
picking up a clod of earth and brandishing his sword...

Did Wiske smile on these transactions, throw
tobacco on the fire? And did his brother Chibyabos chant
beyond the sunset names that sounded there

like Onangizes and Onontio? *Vive Le Roi, and hail*
the highest and most mighty monarch and
most Christian King of France and of Navarre

for whom I take possession of this place Sault St. Marie
and also lakes Superior and Huron also
Manitoulin also all the countries rivers lakes and

streams contiguous adjacent thereunto both those dis-
covered and the ones we will discover
in their length & breadth & bounded only by the seas

declaring to the nations living there that they
from this time forth are vassals
of his Majesty bound by laws & customs which are his.

Then Allouez harangued them about Jesus.
Francis Parkman writes: "What remains of sovereignty
thus pompously proclaimed?

Now and then
the accents of some straggling boatman or
a half-breed vagabond—

this and nothing more."

5. Making of the Rivers and the Prairies

Before that rhetoric, that epigraph,
gushing of the ancient, unheard waters all along
the terminal moraine. Before the melt,

Maumee ice flow inching toward a Wabash
where no water ran, a Saginaw
into a dry Dowagiac. Before an unbound Kankakee,

glacial borders pressing ice lobes out
to flood the valley where no valley was, to spread
the drift two hundred feet and more above

Coniferous, Devonian and Trenton rock.
Before the flood, copper manitous locked up in stone
on distant islands not enisled

before the miners who would dig for them
where no mines were and build the pregnant mounds
by forest trails that were not blazed.

Before the forest trails, before the oak & ash,
path of the moraine: sand & boulders,
quartzite, clay and till...

Before the Potawatomies. Before the French.
Before the Studebaker &
the Bendix and the Burger Chef....

                    •

                    10,000 years ago
the Erie ice, the Saginaw,
the Michigan converged just here.

Hills and ranges fixed the contours then.
Basins formed, and runoff made
two rivers wider than the Mississippi.

Tributaries broke through lateral moraines.
The Elkhart and the Yellow rivers
drained away the last of Maumee glacier—

no waters yet could run off to Desplaines.
When they did, the two great rivers
slowed—silted up their valleys with debris

and changed their names.
Turning on itself, Dowagiac became its former
tributary, flowing to Lake Michigan.

Kankakee at flood time
emptied into the immense abandoned channel,
flowed on to St. Joseph, left

an ice gorge, then a sand bar and a bluff
here at Crum's Point.
Drainage opened to the east

all the way beyond the lakes to the St. Lawrence.
Water levels fell, channels
slowly narrowed, and the River of Miamis

took its present course. Curving to the south.
Flowing to the north.
Rising where it fell in the beginning.

So Crum's Point burst its ice-dam and
the Kankakee flowed mostly with the stronger
new and narrow river now.

Silted up to fourteen feet, the site
of a confluence sealed itself with rock
and sand and soil: made

a watershed on the continental divide.
Above, the level sand plain. And below, the marsh:
Seignelay south-west, & Illinois.

From a millennium of glacial drift, the prairies
now had formed: Portage, Palmer
Sumption…

Terre Coupée,…

•

But on these waters:
Could you sail a ship?
And on this land: *Found an empire now*

surrounded on the north and east by oak & hickory? On the south
adjoining: scattered clumps of alders, willow bushes native to these soils.
The prairie reached from portage landing two and one half miles, three
& more from the nearest eastern verge. To the west & south, the vast
expanse of grass and marsh appeared as one great plain. Deep into the
west, a stretch of rolling timber.…

6. The Boat-Maker's Tale

He'd sent the Griffin on back to Niagara
loaded with the furs he thought
would play his debts…
                    Colbert walked in shadows

at Versailles, the river to be named for him
named otherwise by Onangizes, called
himself, like Colbert's king, the shimmering sun.

Frontenac, Onnontio to Green Bay's Ouilamette
and all the rest of Gigos clan,
dreamed a map of colonies and little forts

stretching from above St. Joseph on the lake
down the river of Miamis
to the marshy waters of that languid

tributary to be named one day for Seignelay
whose own necrology of ships
made him Minister among the idle admirals

in the shipyards and the ports of France.
Stretching farther still…
Stretching well beyond that river to the one

that only Joliet and Père Marquette
among the French had ever seen & named & spoken of
saying that *no land at all no*

country would be better suited to produce
whatever fruits or wheat or corn
than that along this river that the wild cattle

never flee that one finds some 400 in a herd
that elk & deer are almost every-
where and turkeys promenade on every side.…

Prom the day a man first settled here
that man
could start to plow. . .
      But Cavelier, La Salle,

had sent the Griffin on back to Niagara.
He'd build a second ship
to sail down the rivers he would find.…

For he himself had said in Paris, sounding
just like Père Marquette, *it's all*
so beautiful and fertile, free from forests

full of meadows brooks and rivers all
abounding there in fish & game
where flocks and herds can even be left out

all winter long. All winter long!
And it was nearly winter now in Michillimackinak.
The King had said to him *We have received*

with favor a petition in your name and do
permit your exploration
by these presents signed with our own hand

but now he was in debt. Migeon, Charon—
they'd seized the beaver pelts
and even skins of skunks—Giton, Pelonquin!

Names of enemies. But there was Henri Tonty here;
there was, indeed, Count Frontenac.
These he'd name against the plotting creditors.

The *ship will fly above the crows,* he'd said,
his patron governor's heraldic mast-
head besting Jesuits in a Niagaran dream of power.

He had his Récollets to do whatever of God's work
there was. Hennepin, who strapped
an altar on his back and cured the fainting

Father Gabriel with a confection of hyacinths!
and Gabriel himself; and Zénobe.
They'd sung *Te Deum* well enough upon the launching.

He'd have them sing a good deal more than that—
Exaudiat, Ludovicus Magnus!—
once they'd reached the Colbert's mouth, the sea.

The ship *had* nearly flown across the lakes.
In spite of an ungodly pilot
and in spite of god knows dreadful storms

she'd been the equal of the Erie and the Huron.
How she'd sailed out beyond Niagara!
Her canvas billowed & she fired her five small guns

to the astonishment of Iroquois along the banks.
Then a freshening northwest wind.
Down the lake and to Detroit's narrow straights

she sailed until she met a current there strong
as the bore before the lower Seine—
and twelve men leapt ashore to pull her over, through.

They marvelled at the prairies to the east & west
and stopped to hunt, and hung their
guyropes full of fowl and drying bearskins.

From wild grapes the priests prepared communion wine.
Then they were in Huron where the gale
attacked them and they brought down mainyards, tacked

with trysail, then lay long to the till.
The pilot blasphemed damnably while all the rest
cried out to Anthony of Padua

who calmed the winds and brought the ship to port
at Michillimackinak beside
the mission of St. Ignace, Père Marquette's fresh grave.

That was in the early autumn when the Ottawa
and Huron fishing fleets
were strung across the lakes from Saint Marie du Sault

to Keweenwa, from Mackinac to Onangizes' islands
in Green Bay. He'd worn his scarlet coat
with its gold lace and flown the banner of the king

while all his men fired muskets & he stepped ashore.
That was autumn, when the sun
still burned their necks & missionaries harvested.

But it was nearly winter now and he would be he said
in Illinois country when the rivers froze.
Heavy clouds blew in from Canada on northern winds.

The ship had sailed away. And so they
set forth on the lake in four canoes: fourteen men
who bore with them a forge & carpenters' &

sawyers' tools to build the Griffin's twin
beside a fort they'd also build on high ground near
the navigable lower Illinois.

They cried out to each other in the dark.
For it was dark before they were across the lake.
It stormed again as when the Griffin

rocked and shook on Huron, waves against the fragile
birch bark, rain in their red eyes.
Anvil and bellows, iron for nails and bolts,

pit-saws, arms, and merchandise for gifts
and trade when they had reached the Illinois town below
the portage weighed them down.

Gunsmith, blacksmith, joiner, mason, master-
builder Moyse Hillère—
they paddled for the further shore with Cavelier

and three priests and the guide. Half of them
were cousins to *coureurs de bois*
and would desert. Two of them were felons.

All of them washed up together with the breaking
waves beside
the mouth of the Miamis

and gorged on grapes and wild haws & on the carcass of
a deer that had been killed by wolves.

Here they stayed for twenty days, and built a tiny fort, and spiked the hill
they built it on. They took nine soundings of the river's mouth, marking
out the passage that a ship might take with buoys and bearskin flags. The
first brief snow blew in across the lake well before December and ice
began to form along the river's edge. Occasionally, La Salle's Mohegan
guide could find a deer to kill, or bear, and brought them meat; but food
was scarce and all of them began to urge La Salle to press on to the
portage and to Illinois or Miami camps where they might find, in covered
pits, a gleaming hoard of winter's corn. When Tonty finally came with

men who had been sent ahead from Fort Niagara but had scattered in the woods, the party numbered thirty-four. Four were left behind with messages and maps for those who would arrive to reinforce them when the Griffin sailed back past Michillimackinak and down Lake Michigan & anchored here. If the Griffin wasn't lost. If the furs to pay off creditors had not been stolen by the pilot and his men. If all of them had not sailed straight to join the outlaw trader Dan Du Lhut at Kamalastigouia up in Thunder Bay.

Nous embarquâmes, wrote Hennepin, *le troisième Decembre. Avec trente hommes… Dans huit canots.* They were John Boisrondet, L'Espérance de la Brie, La Rousselière, La Violette, Picard du Gay, Etienne Renault, Michel Baribault, Bois d'Ardeene, Martin Chartier, Noelle Blanc, the nailer called La Forge, the Indian guide they called Oui-Oui-La-Mèche, and those with names now known to all or names now known to none. They took up paddles once again, prepared to travel on, to shoulder their canoes along the portage trail if they could find it. Had it been spring, had it been high summer, the fields and woods that lined the river's channel would have blossomed for them, fruited like the prairies on the east and west of the Detroit straights when they pulled the Griffin through to Huron and the priests made wine. And when at last they reached the portage, they would have seen tall cedars, oaks, and water-elms; in a ravine declining from high ground they would have seen along the curving trail splashes of the reds and blues of wild forest flowers; flocks of plovers, snipe, might have flown above the trees to land beside the standing cranes in fields of wild rice in fens the far side of the watershed across the prairie with its elk and deer and buffalo which traders would begin to call one day the *Parc aux Vaches.* But it was winter; they saw none of this. They saw the skulls and bones of animals, a bleak gray plain; they lugged their eight canoes and forge and iron and anvil up the hill and then along the portage path behind La Salle who brooded on the Griffin in the melancholy, willful, isolated silence of his mind, La Salle whose men, with five exceptions, would forsake his vision and his surrogate at Fort Crèvecoeur—39 degrees and 50 minutes latitude exactly on his fine Parisian astrolabe— and daub in tar-black letters on the planking of the half-built river boat: *Nous Sommes Tous Sauvages.*

The man who followed him in many ways was like him, and read his words, and read the words and followed all the trails of others who had passed this way before he did himself, but after him who was the first to come and was the object of his search. Charlevoix he read, and La Hontan. Tonty's own account, and Hennepin's, and all of La Salle's letters both to Canada and France. Transcripts, depositions. He too knew about insatiable ambition, pride and isolation, subduing all to an inflexibility of purpose. When his chronic and mysterious illness made his head swim and his joints swell, made his eyes so sensitive to light he could not read, his nights so sleepless that he could not even dream his shattered double's thousand mile trek from the lower Illinois back to Montreal, he had his friends read to him, tried to comprehend their strange pronunciations of the language of the texts and maps and manuscripts *de la France Septentrionale* which he followed to the Kankakee or Seignelay and then beyond....

Terres tremblantes, sur lesquelles on peut à peine marcher he read, and wrote how "soon they reached a spot where oozy saturated soil quaked beneath their tread. All around were clumps of alder-bushes... pools of glistening water *une espèce de mare* and in the midst a dark and lazy current, which a tall man might bestride... twisting like a snake among the reeds and rushes and... *il a faut continuellement tourner...* They set canoes upon this thread of water and embarked their baggage and themselves and pushed on down the sluggish streamlet looking at a little distance like men who sail on land... Fed by an increasing tribute of the spongy soil it widened to a river *presque aussi large que la Marne,* and they floated on their way into a voiceless, lifeless solitude of boundless marshes overgrown with reeds....

At night they built their fire on ground made firm by frost
quelques mottes de terres glacées

and bivouacked among rushes..."

7. Convergence... & Dispersion

Behind La Salle, before his blinking chronicler,
these others came. They came
to undo all designs of Tisha and his friends,

all designs conceived by Jesuit or Récollet
or empire builder in Quebec
or dreamed beneath Starved Rock among the Illinois.

25

These others came on urgent journeys of unmaking
and from very far away
but very fast and very quietly and no one knew.

They travelled not so much by river routes & streams
as by the trails. They came
because the French and their Algonquin allies

were establishing an iron monopoly
on furs which handsome ladies like Madame d'Outrelaise
and Madame Frontenac—*les divines*

they called them at Versailles—liked to drape around
their pink & chilly shoulders
when in Paris they would hear, at Arsanal,

the private recitations of Racine and Molière
or walk the Louvre along Perrault's
great colonnade, or walk le Brun's new gallery nearby.

These others walked the narrow trails
from Mohawk lodges on through busy Onondaga country
to the Senecan frontier—

These others were the Iroquois.
And when LaSalle objectively took note of 1680's comet
wondered at in Paris and the calculated

object of Sir Isaac Newton's will,
Increase Mather wrote upon the theocratic tablet of his soul:
A Portent! Well, it may have been.

Trade among the openings of oak and on the open prairie
would be anything but free.
And so they leaned into their journey, east to west,

and put a price upon it.
Over trails between the rivers flowing to the lakes
& those that flowed into the Susquehanna south—

then across the Seneca & north beyond Cayuga
to the watershed between Ontario and Erie, to Niagara.
Canadasegy, Canadaragey, Canawagus—

villages on ley lines into which their dancing feet
trod magic from the Hudson river west
and to Detroit....

•

Behind the Iroquois,
the English and the Dutch.
Behind the Dutch and English, the Americans.

Braddock, Washington. Clark & Wayne & Harrison.
The Iroquois trails and the Sauk
widened to accommodate the marching of militias—

For convergence of new peoples in procession
down new roads, dispersion's
an express condition, and diaspora's required....

Pontiac's conspiracy. Tecumseh's genius
and the wild hallucinations of the Shawnee prophet
in his Prophetstown. Black Hawk for an hour.

All the rest is trade—wagons made
by Clem and Henry Studebaker in a town Coquillard
founded for the Astors.

Oh, and Cooper's wooden Indians.
Standing near the banks of local rivers in his book
of 1848, they decorate a prairie

modelled now on European parks mown by gardeners
who themselves become like trees
on the green & flowering stage which they prepare

a decade after the removal of the Potawatomis.
They stand there like Pokagon, last
okama of the lakes whose little band did not accept

the Treaty of Chicago engineered by Billy Caldwell
but remained in his protection
and in his most pious Christian prayers, and even

in his fiction ghosted by a local lawyer's wife
whose husband pressed his claims
in every court. Cooper's stagecoach, meanwhile,

clatters past the Walker Tavern on the old Sauk trail
that's become the route of Western's
bright red buckboards & their Concord Coaches from Detroit.

The aging author whose new book will be dismissed
for tedious didacticism & a meager plot
engages Mrs. Martineau from London in a civil conversation

interrupted by her not infrequent jottings in a diary
about how wisely planned
and prettily she finds this road from Niles

which the Iroquois took to slaughter Illinois women
at Starved Rock and which, from
Ypsilanti down to Edwardsburg and then beyond

80,000 western emigrants began to stream by 1838 or 39.
We cross St. Joseph's River,
Mrs. Martineau observes, *upon a ferry towed by ropes.*

And as the clever horses pull us up the bank
we find ourselves in Indiana territory. She glances up
at Cooper who, in turn, acknowledges her smile.

The stagecoach travels on. Arriving from Fort Wayne,
and heading north & west along
what still they call the Dragoon Trail, the U.S. mail…

while ahead of it, turning just in front of Cooper's
coach on Michigan, honking Studebakers
and the children marching smartly off in little groups

before the dignitaries—councilmen & mayor
& some Elks & Shriners dressed to look like Potawatomi
and Illinois elders—

and everybody smiling at the camera
as if this were
some kind of local pageant

·

& they gathered near the portage trail
to commemorate La Salle in a depression.
Hoover, says the Mayor, will employ honest citizens

to build a great historic monument. A corner
stone is laid. Massed bands of high school students play,
choirs singing in the cold... *Semper Fidelis.*

December 5, 1679. *Queleques mottes de terres glacées.*
Eight years later and
La Salle was murdered by conspirators in Texas.

A bell tower rises, in a man's imagination,
some two hundred feet. (The monument was never built.)
On the river, down below the pageant,

in a man's imagination or before him on his page
Now and then
the accents of a straggling boatman

or a half-breed vagabond
this &
nothing more...

Northern Summer

For Joseph Buttigieg and Vincent Sherry

The flight of sentimentality through empty space.
Through its elliptical hole
an heraldic blackbird's
black wings, yellow beak, round eyes, with the yellow
ring, which defines its inner empty
space

—Göran Sonnevi

I The Castle

                    Occupies
a picturesque
commanding strong position
on the summit of a cliff some forty
feet in height
the base of which is covered
up at flood tide by the waters of the Forth.
Large, magnificent, commodious
with rock nearby and wood and water to afford
the eye a picture of a rare
and charming beauty
forming a delightful and romantic spot
the sight of which
could not but amply compensate et
cetera
                    the language of a tour book
threading aimlessly
through sentimental empty space.

Or build on, say, an Edward's language
to his dear and faithful cousin
Eymar de Valance
like a second generation builds upon
the ruins of a first?

                    finding not

in our
Sir Michael Wemyss

good word
nor yet good service and
that he now shows himself in such a wise
that we must hold him traitor
and our enemy we do command you that ye
cause his manor where we lay
and all his other manors to be burned his lands
and goods to be destroyed
his gardens to be stripped all bare
that nothing may remain
and all
may thus take warning—

Language
moving upon consequence
Consequence
upon a language: Flight
of an heraldic bird
through space that is inhabited.

Some say Bruce had raised his standard here.

II Pied-à-terre

I live between the castle and the coal mine
in a folly. It's the truth.
They put a roof on it last year. I have
a room, a window on the sea.

                   Strange to say, I
haven't seen my host yet,
Captain Wemyss.
He's holed up in his castle in this awful rain.
I'm holed up in my folly with
my pads and pens.
If the sun comes out this month, maybe yet
we'll meet
a-walking in the garden O.

"Baron Wemyss of Wemyss"
all the old books call
his many forbears.
Do I just shout out *hello there*
Wemyss of Wemyss?
Seven centuries of purest Scottish pedigrees,
says Mr. F., the Edinburgh historian.
Twenty-seven generations.
I can offer
just one eighth of watery Kirkpatrick.

The flight of sentimentality through empty space!
A rhetoric, at least; (an awkward line).
The flight of Sentiment
is through a space that's occupied.

This space is occupied, all right,
and I am guest
of both the present and the past.

                    The past
begins in caves,
the Gaelic *Uamh* soon enough becoming Wemyss.
James the Fifth surprised
a band of gipsies in one cave, drinking there
and making merry. Though he
could join them incognito in his famous role
as Godeman of Ballangeich
and share their mad hilarity, James the Sixth
would only shout out *treason*
when he panicked of a sudden, claustrophobic,
in a *Uamh* become a mine.

Above the caves and mines they built this house.

And put a chaplain in it! I find there was
no piper here, and worse, no bard—
But Andrew Wyntoun, a prior of St Serf,
wrote a family chronicle in verse
& praised

An honest knycht
and of good fame
Schir Jhone of Wemyss by his rycht name.

Well, if I'm the guest of absent hosts
the cost of lodging here a while
is neither waived
nor anywhere within my calculation—
(the flight of Sentiment
is not
through empty space)

Did Mynyddog Mynfawr, camped along the Forth,
feed the brave Gododdin mead and wine
a year
a year
a year?

Or did he send them sober down his mine?

III The Mine

The flight through empty space of Sentiment
—mentality! There's nothing
sentimental
within sight of this abandoned mine.
From where I stand
I'd talk about dead gods, I think.
                              From where I stand on this
deserted beach
between the castle and the mine
I think I'd say the legates
of the dead god Coal
had built his image here to look
exactly like a gallows made of iron & alloy
high enough
to hang a giant from—

The tower's erect upon the hill, but nothing moves.

Who worked here once?
No Free Miners from the Forest of Dean
have hewn the coalface down the ages
here at Wemyss from when
the coughing grey-eyed servants
won the coal
for monks at prayer in freezing Dunfermline
but virtual slaves. No *gales,* no lease
for them.
                    "Coal beneath the soil
shall be inherited with soil
and property." The lairds of Fife could pack
a Privy Council and by act of law
reduce a man to serfdom. He
was bought or sold
along with his equipment. His child
went underground at six
to earn an extra seven pence
lest he sail to Noroway with Sir Patrick Spence.

The tower's erect upon the hill, and nothing moves.

When fire leapt down the tunnel, forked and dove,
an age had come and gone. The
nation voted Labour
but the coal board blundered here in Wemyss
at once.
                    The lift plunged down
through all that soaring iron and alloy, down
to where the caves and tunnels
smoulder uselessly and spread the fire
on inland through
bituminous rich veins. It could burn
a hundred years. It could burn as far as London.

Miles of heavy cable lie around me
on the beach. Almost ankle-thick, it unravels
like a length of rope left over

from a hanging. It raised and lowered the lift.
The lift descended with amazing speed.
With amazing speed
the fire leapt down the tunnel, forked and dove.
Everyone, I think, got out.

A tanker steams across the bleak horizon.

The tower's erect upon the hill.

IV A Queen

John Knox said the visit of the Queen
had raised the price
of wild fowl sufficiently
that partridges were sold at half a crown.
He was not a sentimental man.
Of the Regent's coronation
he'd remarked: "Seemly
as to put a saddle on the back
of an unruly cow."
                              O belle
et plus que belle crooned
Mary's friend, Ronsard. Better him than Knox
for gentle conversation?
Better all the Medicis & better maybe
little sick king Frank
whose inflammation of the middle ear
and abscess of the brain
were dear to Calvin.
                              And yet her keen eyes
danced out of a window here
in February, 1565.
It was cold that year in Fife.
Every fireplace here at Wemyss was blazing
full of fine Wemyss coal
when Mary gazed at Charles Darnley riding by.
Yesterday was warm & bright
when Peggy, who's the cook, pointed

38

out the window, showing me
where Darnley had dismounted. I had come
to get a pan to heat some water in.
He had come to woo a queen,
win the Matrimonial Crown and full equality
of Royal right, make every kind
of mischief in the realm. The empty space
between the window and
the place he stood beside his horse
in sexy tight black hose was filled at once
with Feeling—

Darnley sang a song more serious than Ronsard's
and Bothwell entered in his
little book that Kirk o'Field's convalescent
suffered from *roinole* and not
petite verole—
                    syphilis, not smallpox.
But that was later on.
At Wemyss it was a sentimental morning.

V A Prince

Or talk about Charles Edward then.
Charles, Edward, Louis,
Sylvester, Maria, Casimir, Stewart.
The Bonnie Prince himself,
the grand Chevalier. To the Forty-Five
this castle sent Lord Elcho.
Kindred of my own kin's forbears, my
brooding and attainted
absent host,
                  he gazed from Holyrood
through gilded ballrooms & out casement windows
at the gillies & the pipers & the clans
weighing odds, meditating
languages—Gaelic, French, the
lisped Italian English of his Regent Prince.

The King enjoy his ain again?
Doubtful, but for honour
one must risk in any case this autumn theatre
although it issue
in a winter's desolation....

Claymore!—
                (or is it *Gardyloo?*)—*echoes*
even now from Holyrood
through Fife. Beneath those Strathspey
dancers' feet when Elcho's mother
led off celebrations
of the rout as Prestonpans,
history smouldered with surprises
older than the coal fields
on the Wemyss estate.
Language moved upon inconsequence
and consequence
at once: *Will you see me*
to my quarters? and
                    No quarter...

as if you'd hear two voices whispering
behind you while you stared
down Royal Mile thinking of the sheltered hollow
under Arthur's seat....

The empty space between the window
framing Elcho and the place the clansmen camped
filled up in time with sentimental tales
and the progeny
of all those partridges
whose price the visit of the Scottish Queen
had raised, said Knox, to half a crown.
And yet his line of vision then
was tangent to
the flight of an heraldic bird
whose spiral into time
was on a furious northern wind—
vehement,
and with a terrifying sound.

VI A Voice

I hear my mother's voice reading Stevenson—
or is it Scott? Someone's wandering lost
among the heather. I must be eight or nine.
I know I should be reading this myself,
but when I read the words the voice I hear
ceases to be hers....
                                    There is a space
I have not learned to fill
somewhere between printed marks and sounds
and I am lost in some way too
among the heather, frightened of the distances
when all I want to do is drift on lang
uage into dream....
                                    "Cha n'eil Beurl' agam..."
someone says, but I follow him
in any case on hands & knees in terror.
Have I got the silver button in my teeth?
Am I papered for the murder of that
Campbell back in Appin? We're through
the cleft, the Heugh of Corrynakiegh,
and now the moor: it's black and burned
by heath fires. Moorfowl cry.
The deer run silently away from us....

Or am I underneath the castle of my enemy?
And is my enemy my only friend? I hear
the sentinel calling out in English
All's well, All's well
but we crawl off toward a hovel
made of stone & turf & thatch. There's
a fire inside, and over it a small iron pot.
The ancient crone who's stirring it
offers me a boiled hand
                                    to steal away
some gentleman's attention
from his Ovid... and pack him off to bed
with images to mingle
with his dreams, said R.L.S. to Baxter.

And Scott: that "laws & manners
cast a necessary colouring;
but the bearings, to use heraldic language,
will remain the same,
though the tincture may be different
or opposed...."

Bearings... tincture...
Theft and Dream,
flight of an heraldic bird through language,
and my mother's voice.

Who are the Kirkpatricks? where is Abbotsford?
How can poor sick R.L.S., listening with
his Hoosier wife, hear off in Samoa "beaten bells"
from just across the Firth?

For a moment, laws and manners seem no
more than colouring. Charles Edward back in Paris
casts a medal of himself—*Carolus Walliae
Princeps*—and the future hangs
on messages delivered by the likes of
Alan Breck from men like Cluny
in his cage—
language moving upon consequence....

                    But time has gone to live with
Waverleys and Balfours, with townies
like Rankeillor and his lowland lawyer ilk.
I am awake in Fife. I hear
the distant echoes of my mother's voice reading.
Sentiment's transfigured into history,
and history to sentiment.

VII Kirkcaldy

In Kirkcaldy one considers economics.
We need a dozen eggs. I leave my folly, catch
a bus near Wemyss, and walk around
this "old lang toun" that bears the name

of Mary's last defender.
Loyal old Kirkcaldy, last
support and stay of an unlucky queen,
scourge of Bothwell, keeper
of the craggy rock in Edinburgh
out of which your one-time friend John Knox
would pry you even with his
final fetid breath—
                                    Linoleum?
In June
descendents of those Covenanters Cromwell shot
treat their jute with linseed oil
where William Adam, stone & lime Vanbrughian,
built in Gladney House
a Netherlandish lesson for his sons
and Adam Smith returned in early middle age
and wrote.

Did Elcho see young Robert Adam on the castle wall
where John Knox saw Kirkcaldy? each one
moving through the crystal chambers
of his mind to build more perfect measurements
before the cannon fired
of distances heraldic birds might fly,
language moving upon consequence
to say *Nobility,*
Salvation, Space?
                            When Adam left
Kirkcaldy grammar school
for Edinburgh, Smith enrolled at
Glasgow, never mentioning (when he
returned at forty-five) the Forty-Five.
"The workmen carry nails instead
of money to the baker's shop and alehouse.
The seat of empire should remove itself
to that part of the whole
contributing the greatest share to its support.
In sea-port towns a little grocer
can make forty-five percent upon a stock. Capitals
increased by parsimony

are diminished by misconduct, prodigality...."
And not a word about the bonded miners
in the collieries & salt pits.

Economies! Those workmen died
in nailers' dargs to earn a casual footnote.
That parsimony made a bigot certain he was saved,
his neighbour rightly damned.
That seat of empire never moved;
its rebel colonies themselves became imperious.
Those country houses made by Adam and his sons
rose up with fortresses
they built at Inverness on orders straight
from Cumberland, which bled.

The smell of jute on linseed
stinks of deprivation: linoleum peels off floors
of little grocers in this town
where faces in the baker's shop and alehouse
thirst for darker oils
sucked up Shell, BP, and Exxon rigs
from underneath the bottom of the sea.

The Regent dragged Kirkcaldy from his rock
and hung him on the gallows Knox prepared him for:
face against the sun.
His blinded eyes beheld a crazy German
sitting firmly on a Stuart throne.
History gave William Pitt *The Wealth of Nations*,
the brothers Adam peel-towers & Fort George.

Beggared sentiment flew straight into the hills

VIII Ossian, etc.

And metamorphosed there in Ossianic melancholy.
James Macpherson heard, he said,
the howling of a northern wind; he heard old men
chanting through the night about the woods

of Morven; Selma filled, he wrote,
with names & deeds—Fingal's, Oscar's, Gaul's—
but language threaded aimlessly through empty spaces
& through languorous dreams, *with rock nearby*
and wood and water to afford the eye
a rare and charming beauty, the sight of which
could not but amply compensate
admirers of the sentimental and the picturesque.
Where better read a "forgery" than in a folly?

And shall I like these poems
that David Hume defended when he found
the heroes' names authenticated
by an inventory of all the Highland mastiffs?
Napoleon did, who never heard of Dr Johnson,
but who carried *Fingal* into battle
imitating, now and then, with relish,
the Ossianic style in his memos & dispatches.
And Goethe, caught up in the turmoil
of his *Sturm und Drang*, built
the European Zeitgeist from a massive
mountain sadness caught in far Temora.
Staring at Macpherson's book,
they filled the emptiness before their eyes
with what they were.
                              It was an age
of forgeries & fakes: Pretenders
old and young, gothic ruins in the garden,
memories of casket letters, padded
coats and powdered wigs. And while Macpherson
roamed the hills in search of Gaelic bards,
a London dealer named Buchanan
sold the Earl of Wemyss a phony Venus
signed *Van Dyck:* "the sight of which could
not but amply compensate," etcetera,
Buchanan whispered softly in the noble ear,
and rubbed his hands, and grinned.
Staring at the canvas on his castle wall,
the Earl filled the emptiness before his eyes
with what he thought he saw.

"The Erse Nation may be furious with Lord North,
for even Fingal tells him so,
but adds: 'And yet, my Lord, *I* do not
desert you.'" Walpole, 1782.
Macpherson travelled south & changed his style,
learning, it appears, a language moving
upon consequence, and consequently moved among
the circles of the powerful & into spaces
occupied by EICs and Nabobs. With a pamphlet
written for Mohamed Ali Chan, he scattered
all the nouveaux riches in London.

      To my surprise,
I find I rather like him,
this child of the Macpherson clan
who came to be MP from Camelford and drive
a private coach, though it's true
I cannot read his book for very long.
Who can say what spoke to him
in Ruthven, tiny village on the Highland Road
near Perth where plowmen unearthed shards
of Roman bowls & where the farmers
scratched St Kattan's name as *Chattan*
on the Druid stones. Here he saw
an end that emptied the entire north
of ancient feeling. The broken clansmen
staggered to his very door. It was
the Highland Army's last assembly; Cluny had
a price upon his head; Macphersons fled,
then hid him; Charles was somewhere
in the islands or in France. The barracks
where Macpherson played a soldier burned,
and he was nine. Then enormous quiet.

I close the book and walk out on the shingle
staring into low wet fog upon the Firth
that rolls against the rocks like spindrift.
The beach is empty, save for one old man
and one black bird that's flying toward the mine.
The limbs of trees are heavy, drip—
as if with melting snow.

When old men faltered
in their songs
Macpherson squared the widening empty circles
with what came to hand: with rocks,
with fogs, with dripping trees, deserted beaches
and old men by which heraldic birds
were briefly lured to perch
on names like *Fingal, Oscar, Gaul*
as if on severed limbs upon a field of slaughter
the sight of which did not appal
the rock nearby or wood and water which afforded
the clear eye a rare and charming beauty
where the Erse Nation was not furious with Lord North.
Seeking to fill emptiness, Macpherson
marked its boundaries,
surveyed & gerrymandered sentimental space—

Samuel Johnson filled that space
with rage, Napoleon with a military will.
They too longed for grander feelings; an actual object
and a cause. Heraldic birds appeared
on the horizon, flying north.
Macpherson travelled south.
The Earl of Wemyss stared happily upon his Venus
signed *Van Dyck*.

IX

And I stare quizzically at what I've written here,
at language that has used me one more time
for consequential or inconsequential ends that
are not mine. Can I tell which (& where)
by making declarations: the one? the other, now?
By speaking Edward's language
to his dear and faithful cousin, Eymar de Valance,
as a second generation speaks
the ruins of a first?
                              by finding not
in our

Sir Michael Wemyss
good word? or occupying picturesque positions
on the summit of a cliff?

Can I tell which (& whose) by calling points
that mark the intersection of some arbitrary boundaries
castle, queen, and *mine?*
boundaries of a space by no means empty
where the cost of lodging
is exacted by a pile of books, by *castle, queen,* and *mine,*
attainted absent lord, and black heraldic bird?
I close the book and walk out on the shingle
staring into low wet fog, etcetera.
I never closed the book. I never left the room
to walk along the beach.

                        Tourist? Paying guest—
of language of
the place, but heading farther north
and pledging silence.

I've heard a scholar filled his empty life
by tracing down a thousand plagiaries from eighty
sources in MacP. I've heard the casket letters
occupied a thousand scholars who had emptiness to fill
for half a thousand years. Otherwise,
who knows, they might have filled those spaces
with the motions of a Bothwell or a Cumberland
through whom the language of the place
spoke itself to consequence.

I've heard a man found Waverley "so colourless
and unconvincing as to be
a virtual
                        gap on the page."

And where are you, Kirkpatrick? (& Matthias)

Or you—
                whose little ship ran battle-scarred

before the wind to Norway, piloted
by Hanseatic sailors well past lowland Karmoi.
Did you follow then the rocky coast to Bergen?
and from there a black heraldic bird
to Copenhagen, Malmö? Did you sail north from Orkney
shouting into gales, spoken for by oaths,
language howling you to silence deep as Dragsholm?
Did she say, whose French was not
Brantôme's, whose verse appalled Ronsard,
l'oiseau sortira de sa cage? And did she say, before
Kirkcaldy chased you through the mists
around the Orkneys, *Sonnets in italic hand
conjure you to Scania....*
*You'll crawl in squalid circles for eleven years & more
widdershins
and widdershins, weeping....*

So Bothwell's route is mine. I'll stuff my mouth
with herring, think of Anna Throndsen,
and not return to Fife either with the Maid of Norway
or the Duke of Orkney's head.
My bird of Sentiment took flight from Inverness.
Tangent to our Baltic steamer's course, he's plighted
to a Hanseatic taxidermist who will stuff him
for an øre—
                    Or: *l'oiseau sortira de sa cage?*

Old Bert Brecht, wily exile,
fleeing just ahead
of the Gestapo,
making for L.A. by way of Finland,
did you really see "High up in Lapland
towards the polar arctic sea,
a smallish hidden door"?

Through that door *black wings, yellow beak
round eyes...*

                    appear a moment, pause

                         & disappear

The Stefan Batory Poems

for Cynouai and Laura

One: Hacheston, Suffolk

To begin with a name—
Katarsky—
        To begin
to leave with a name, Polish,
for a Polish ship named
for another, for Stefan Batory.
                Name of Katarsky.
Name of Stefan Batory.

To begin to leave this place
I've lived that's no more
mine than his, Katarsky's,
a village near his farm,
a land that's rich with legends
not my own, not his.

Name of Katarsky. Names
of his twins, Andrzej & Zbyszek.
Slid down haystacks with
my wife, these twins, when
she was five.
             Andrzej & Zbyszek.
Katarsky.
          After the war
when hay grew again
into haystacks, when the Poles
in England, some of them,
went home…

Katarsky, says the lady in
the shop Oh Well Katarsky sir
I'll tell you what I know
about Katarsky and that farm
and how he might as well have
gone on home the Russians *or*
the Germans and I
have to interrupt, say

no, oh stop it now
I only wanted
a Polish name for a poem:
only wanted a way to say goodbye.

Two

> I wake up having dreamed of whales
> To find my family sleeping in
> Their berths. The breakfast menu
> Is under the door: delicious
> Smells in the pasageway...

I can have Soki, Zupy Sniadaniowe, Jajka, Omlety, Ryby, something from the Zimny Bufet, Przetwory Owocowe on my bread, Sery, a hot cup of Kawa bez kofeiny (coffeinevrije: decaffeinated). Or mint tea and compote. The day's program includes Holy Mass in the Cinema, a matinee concert of chamber music (Vivaldi, Handel, and Telemann), afternoon tea, an American film with dubbed-in Polish, cocktails, bingo and dancing. Wife nor daughters stir. I open Mickiewicz....

"Ye comrades of the Grand Dukes of Lithuania, trees of Białowieża, Switez, Ponary, and Kuszelewo! whose shade once fell upon the crowned heads of the dread Witenes and the great Mindowe, and of Giedymin, when on the height of Ponary, by the huntsmen's fire, he lay on a bear skin, listening to the song of the wise Lizdejko; and, lulled by. the sight of the Wilia and the murmur of the Wilejko, he dreamed of the iron wolf...." What an Invocation! Comrades and trees! The trees are important.

Last night as we passed Land's End I spoke for hours with a couple from Newcastle leaving England to emigrate to Canada. They stared hard, saying goodbye, looking into the darkness for a last flickering English light. They're sorry to leave but can't, so they told me, save a sixpence in a year. I wished them luck in Canada. And comrades. And trees.

I decide to go on deck.

Three

You, Batory, an *elected* monarch.
You owed it all to Henry de Valois.
Lithuania backed the Russian Tzar,
The Church took the Archduke; the
Anti-German *szlachta* was for any
Anti-German. You from Transylvania.
But leave it to the French:
Ambassadorially, the Bishop of
Valance distributes rings to
Get the throne for edgy de Valois.
Who took one look and fled:
Brother Charles croaked
And he (Valois) was Henry Three
Sipping port in Paris.
The horsy gentry blinked and summoned—
Married you to Royal Anne Jagiellon.

How much did you know? Not as much
As Canon Koppernigk who made
His measurements at Frauenburg (which
He called Gynopolis) pretending in
His *Revolutions* that he stargazed
On the Vistula away from battlefields
And Teutonic Knights. Not as much
As Koppernigk whose system, Prince,
Because he longed for Cracow
And his youth, would run your ship
If not your ship of state aground,
But this at least: How to maintain
Access to the sea; how to use
A chancellor's advice. And how
With Danzig yours to drive with
Peasant infantries the Russian Bear
Beyond Livonia to the Pope.

The cavalry was not deployed—
Horses in their stables, and at hay.

Four

A day passes, the weather is rough. We meet Poles, Englishmen, Irish, Americans, Czechs, Swiss, Frenchmen, Germans, Russians, and two Japanese. Diana teaches Laura how to approach a new friend: *Was ist Ihre Name, bitte? Was ist Ihre Name?* It turns out to be Alma. Laura is delighted. Cynouai is seasick and goes early to bed. It's my night for the movies.

The Cinema is down a flight of stairs outside the dining room—and *down, low,* so very low in the ship the room should be some kind of hold or place for ballast. In the middle of *Little Big Man,* I realize with a start that I am actually under water. If we spring a leak, this theatre will instantly fill like a tank, the watertight door will be closed by a panicky steward, and there we'll be—each of us holding his nose and floating to the ceiling as Dustin Hoffman shrieks in Polish and tomahawks fall from the sky....

Was ist Ihre Name, bitte?

Was ist Ihre Name?

Five: The Library

I

The weather improves. Serious now,
I attend to correspondence.
Here they read the news and study
Not Mickiewicz or the other unread
Poets on these shelves
But ups and downs of stocks
And the extraordinary language
Of my President reported in the
Daily Polish/English mimeo gazette.
The banalities and rhetoric of power
Dovetail with the mathematics
Of the market: Soon the brokers,
As in 1929, will sail nicely
From the upper stories
Of the highest buildings in New York,
Their sons will pluck the feathers
From their hair and look for jobs
A thousand miles from the ethnic
Bonfires of their dreams, the
Poor will stand in bread lines,
And I, a curio from 1959, will find
My clientele reduced to nuns
And priestly neophytes. I return
To Indiana—the only place
Save Utah where the Sixties,
Though Peter Michelson was waiting,
Failed to arrive.

II

I am, as Peter thought I would be,
Going back. But slowly.
The journey takes nine days.
Unanswered letters—his and Ernie's,

Kevin's, Mrs. Harris's—
They weigh on me.
My friends, my gifted student,
My daughters' much beloved nurse.

"Too much mopin' now," says P.,
"And many mumblin's…
But you *will*
Be coming back because although
You think yourself no gringo, John,
You are: and this is where
The gringo fighting is.
Or gringo baiting.
Or: whatever the conditions will allow.
I'll expect you here in August."

And Kevin writes: "I'm scared
Of everything and wholly lack
Direction…
Plus, of course,
I'm personally responsible
For all of human misery: the
Shoeless Appalachians, every
Starving Indian. And what
I like to do is eat, talk to
Charming educated people, drink
Good wine, read the best
Pornography, discuss at leisure
Every new advance
In Western decadence."

E. has written to me once a year for eight years straight. This year it's about my poems. And his. His muse grows younger (he is over sixty-five) as mine begins to age. My attraction to quotation, commentary, pastiche: exhaustion? or the very method of abstention that he recommends? Many days I'd be a scribe, a monk—and I, like monk and scribe, am permitted to append the meanings that my authors may have missed. "He abandoned himself to the absolute sincerity of pastiche": on Ekelöf, Printz-Påhlson, Otherwise? Poets know too much. We bring things on us. There is always an extra place at the table: the poem, as Ernie says, arranges it…

With total serenity
He abandoned pastiche for patchouli
For patchouli and panache
He abandoned his panto-panjandrum
With utter contempt for panache
He abandoned patchouli
He abandoned himself with unspeakable simplicity
To pastrami.

Inventions organized to dance
A variation of our lives?
Or simply evidence?
Or letters to and from our friends?
Here, the doctor said, is your scarab.
Prospero whispers in one ear
And Lenin in the other.

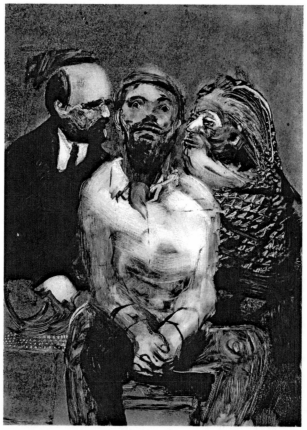

Six

Familiar, the dull rattle
and buzz of screws
abates; we glide....

A hundred yards away
Gothic dips and spires—
St Brendan's "floating crystal castle."

Calving from some ancient
ice sheet, pinnacles around a central
mass like sails,

it makes good time: radar brought
back only sea return—echoes from the waves.
A spotlight caught it in the fog.

Late, late...
Are we in Brendan's time?
We suffer sea return.

The ship will tilt on its keel,
roll on the last wave
over the edge of the earth.

Seven

The Batory, a passenger says, once belonged to the Holland-American line; it was, indeed, the famous "Student Ship." If this is true, my strange sense of *déjà vu* is explained by more than the simple fact of my being, after sixteen years, at sea again. Can it be, in fact, that I am on the "Student Ship" once more? which flies the colors now of Poland?

Every detail has seemed so extraordinarily familiar: the location of rooms, the structure of the decks (did I kiss that girl from Georgia *there,* just *there?),* the clever organization of space which makes what is tight and constraining appear to be comfortable and larger than it is. The same ship! I was on my way, eventually, to Turkey, where I thought to save my small-town childhood love from becoming an adult. She had spent a year in Istanbul with her parents; her letters had grown sophisticated and knowing; I was afraid. Seventeen and virginal, I sailed from New York thinking I was Henry James and clutching to my heart every available illusion about myself and the world.

Ghosting on the bridge or in the engine room, hailing Flying Dutchmen or staring darkly at the sea, any foolish sentimental shade aboard is mine.

Eight

Two violins, a double-bass,
Drums, piano, and trumpet—
Accordion, of course:
A curious sound.
For our tea they play us schmaltz
And polkas.

At night, the same musicians
Are transformed: they make
A fearful frantic jazz-cum-rock
With other instruments
And sing a polyphonic polyglot
Appropriate to
Mid-Atlantic revels.

On a sleeve, four gold rings of lace, an anchor above; on another, three gold rings. I point out the captain and his second officer at an adjacent table. Cynouai: "Then who's driving the boat?" Laura: "It drives itself."

Over cakes, I polish my translation from the sixteenth century Polish of the famous Jewish Cossack, Konrad Konrad. He is not, unlike Michelson, Matthias and Sandeen, altogether serious in his treatment of the terrifying retribution falling upon the unfortunate bard as a reward for the practice of his craft. Thus I render the piece for a vanished upper-upper British accent and into an idiom which I think would not displease, say, Edward Lear.

Nine

Edgar Allan Poe
Wanted to go
To Poland.
So, probably, did Lafayette.
In 1830 he was too old.
James Fenimore Cooper
Cried: "Brothers!"
Everyone remembered Kosciuszko.
In Paris, Mickiewicz
Was eloquent: "The West,"
He said, "It dies of its doctrines!"
With Michelet and Quinet,
They cast him in bronze.
Of Lamennais: "He weeps for men."
Of Napoleon: "Come!"

Divination by Jacksonian Hickory:
Buchanan liked his ambassadorship,
His high teas with the Tzar.
In spite of Samuel Morse, that
Established Gomułka.
Churchill said: "It's no
Time for quarrels…"
Sikorsky crashed in his plane.
"Hel falls," said Hemar.
"Assassins steal our Westerplatte."

Batory, they've thrown your best
Philosopher out of Warsaw.
The one who stenographically took
The Devil's report.
I don't think Rosa Luxemburg
Would be pleased. She,
Like you, was a fighter & proud.

I like to think of Rilke's Angels
And his loving explanations to von Hulewicz.

I don't think about Esterhazy
Or Chopin. I think of Hass's poem
For his Polish friends in Buffalo.
Hass—who reads Mickiewicz
For his mushrooms.

I think of Jean Rousseau: "At least
Do not allow them to digest you!"
I think of Kazimierz Stanisław Gzowski—
Knighted by Victoria, founder
Of the city of Toronto.
I think of Materski in the forests
Of my native Ohio: "Send no
Exiles inland." Ohio—unaware
Of 1830, of 1848.

Calling for my gambling debts,
The learned Purser
Quotes for me a famous
Unacknowledged source in Yiddish:
"Oh, frayg nit: 'Vus iz it?'
Los mir gehn zu machen Visit."

We approach the Gulf of St Lawrence.

Ten

The long aerial of Alma's German radio brings in, at last, the news. The C.B.C. is pleased: Nixon quits. That man named Gerald Ford is president. "An honest Nixon," someone says. "A sort of Hoover type." A little late, I think, for Hoover now. But we are on the river, the sun will surely rise, and very few are interested in politics. An age of boredom dawns. New Poland steams toward Old Quebec.

> I gather friends around me in
> The eerie morning haze:
> "Sea hunger," I say, "has gripped
> The West. It will hack its way
> To the Atlantic." Friends,
> I'd have rather written that
> Than take the town. There died Wolfe
> Victorious. "Let us build," said
> Eisenhower, "a canal!"
>
> "*Franciscus Primus,*
> *Dei Gratia Francorum Rex.*
> What, bearing such
> A cross, did Cartier observe?"

Indians, I suppose. Exotic birds. Looking for Cathay, he didn't hear, his German aerial extended to its length, such twitterings as these: 'I want to talk with you about what kind of line to take: I now what Kleindienst on it—It isn't a matter of trust. You have clearly understood that you will call him, give him the directions. I don't want to go off now to get us: ah! To maken ani deeeeeeeals.'

Indians. And exotic birds. At sea there is no time, and therefore do ye joke about solemnities. Therefore do ye sip Courvoisier or ponderously lie, or sleep with other people's wives. But on a river? On a waterway that Eisenhower built? *Was ist Ihre Name,* after all? Open your Mickiewicz. Abandon your panjandrum. Suffer, when the hum of screws abates, your sea return.

On one arrival here the crew abandoned ship: engineers and deck hands diving through the portholes, swimming toward the haunted isle of Parkman's Marguerite. Thévet the cosmographer at Natron heard *her* tale. Polish seamen didn't. Instead of *Little Big Man*, Warsaw played *Dziady* on a Forefather's Eve. George Sand had found it stronger stuff than *Faust*. Gomułka sent his tanks against the Czechs.

> Am I guilty of obscure
> Complicities, America? O Poland?
> The ugly birthright of
> My sinking class? Western
> Nations dress themselves
> To dream a dull apocalypse
> While I float down that
> River loved by old Champlain
> And every last Algonquin
> In his long canoe. I'm guilty
> And in luck in lousy times.

I walk the promenade deck, look at archipelagos and tiny fishing villages, return Mickiewicz to his shelf between the propaganda and the porn. I slip my bookmark, Jessie's letter dated just about a year ago, into a jacket pocket. Then I take it out and read I once again. "These few lines," she says, "to let you hear from me. I am up but I am havin trouble with my arm an shoulder pains me like before. But I was glad to hear from you and I am glad you all are well. I thought about you all because you did say you was

> Comin over before leavin an I
> Didn't know what happen. I don't
>
> Know whats wrong with people now an
> I'm afraid to set out on the porch
>
> Any more. Give my love to the girls
> An write me again some time. This
>
> Will be all for now. It's real
> Cold here. Love from your friend,
>
> Jessie Harris."

The Mihail Lermontov Poems

for Diana

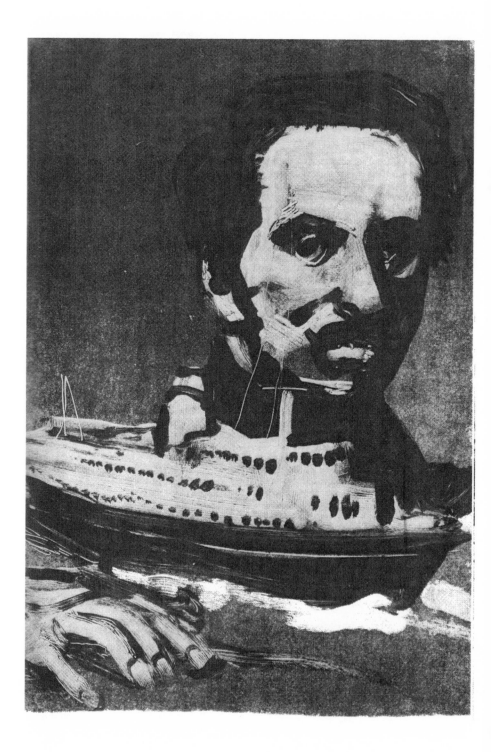

Dogeared Proem

in which I decide to change my name before returning to England on a Russian ship after two years of sincerely trying to come to terms with America

Once I had a Polish friend, Zymierski.
He changed his name to Zane.
Dane Zane it became. (It's Zane Grey I blame.)
Perhaps you've seen his ivory-handled cane
In the historical museum
In Barcelona, Spain.
I resolved, in disapproval,
Never to change my name—
Even for the best of reasons,
Even in the worst of times,
Even for the sake of love, the sake of fame.

Still, today I've heard it claimed
The Baltic Shipping Company's
Investigating all the old Decembrists.
Safety first, I say.
Anyway, like Pushkin,
I'm interested in my maternal side.
(My father's fathers I cannot abide.)
No curly hair, no swarthy
Abyssinian face, I can't embrace
An Ibrahim (Great Peter's Black,
In lace); nor, like his
Successor Lerrnontov, find
My line extends to Ercildoune
And gnomic Thomas with his elves.
But I can reach for names
That suit me just the same

Like old Arzeno, watchmaker
And jeweler, born in some Italian drain,
Republican and Methodist
(Rare, as the obituary read,
For one of his nativity)
Who, once he reached Ohio

"Enjoyed the largest gains
In all of Georgetown"—

And Kirkpatrick, Scottish-Irish Democratic
Miller who was Abolitionist before
The Civil War, him whose
Moniker my social-working Aunt
Still answers to
In hot unsociable and palmy
Mid-Floridian lanes.
Her Christian handle's Jean,
Not Jane.

Arzeno and Kirkpatrick! How happily
I'd hyphenate your names!
Great grandfathering immigrants
Might summon if combined
In just proportions
A Maternal Spirit
Powerful as any Abyssinian or Elf
To whom I would declaim
A strange refrain:

—"O wild Italian-Irish Lass & Muse
O take aim and snipe at
(If not slay)
The heavy and judicial German
In me called Matthias.
Protect with *sprezzatura*
And some Gaelic gall this voyager
His life
His children and his wife.
O help me put on my disguise.
Help to make me good
And wise.
I'll be to God and man
Jack Arzeno-Kirkpatrick
For an odd span
Of days
Of days and nights."

Two

I'm introduced to the distinguished touring poet. He's a grand sight, all right. I'm mightily impressed. Dark hair, dark complexion, dark and piercing eyes. His companion (from the Secret Police? is our artist on a leash?) remarks with irritation: "Watch him. He will gaze contemptuously at all around him. He will greet you," the companion maintains, "with an unfriendly stare; he will be rude, insolent, and arrogant; he will respond, if he responds at all, to any remark of your own, with a sharp retort." I look at him and say: "You happen in one hidden glorious hour to waken in the longtime silent soul once more mysterious virgin springs of power." He responds with a sharp retort. I say: "Then trust them not? nor let their song be heard? Veil them in dark oblivion once again?" *In measured verse and icy rigorous words: a sharp retort.*

So. We understand one another immediately. With a little quick maneuvering in and around the more exotic midwestern towns we manage to lose his shadow somewhere in the vicinity of French Lick, Indiana. We fall immediately into a discussion of his life and times. "Bad times," he says. "Hard life." "Boring," he says. "Repressive." I smile sympathetically. "Listen," he says. "Nicky the First, after all! The Gendarme of Europe, The Cop. I exist at the will or the whim of a Cop." I smile sympathetically. "Monroe," I reply, "and his Doctrine. It's late applications. Not to mention Tzar Andrew—his powers & pains." He says: "The elegant and Jacobin Spring of December failed when I was young." "Yes," I sigh. "I remember the weather." And he: "The face of Pushkin." And I: "The fate of Poe." He buys me a Vodka Collins. In my imagination we are transported to Tsarkoie Selo where the poet, Cornet of the Life Guard Hussars, entertains. Saber blades, as Viskovaty has described the scene, "serve as standards for the sugar-heads which, with rum poured over them, burn with a beautiful blue fire, poetically lighting the drawing room from which for the sake of effect all candles have been removed."

"I became famous in a single day," he tells me after a couple of drinks. "Anna Mihailovna Hitrovo—we knew her as *la lèpre de la société*— showed that angry poem of mine to the Tzar. 'Fuel for revolution' she told the greedy crew that round his sceptre crawled. They sent me to the Nijegorodsky Dragoons where I slept in the open fields to the howling of jackals. I ate *churyok*, drank Kakhetian wine, and dressed like a Circassian with a gun in my belt. Still, Bielinsky praised the 'iron clangour' of my mighty line, and the mountains were a consolation." Abruptly, he stops.

After a long and awkward silence, he blows out the sweet smelling and eerie blue-burning sugar heads of my imagination. "Do you like the sea?" he enquires. "You'll perish, of course, in a duel."

He heads east in a '73 Datsun. He turns into a ship.

Three

Ah, the stuff of greatness: Lermontov! Lermontov!
And the sources of greatness, Pushkin
And Byron. A lecture on greatness: by Olga
Our cultural commissar. An example
Of greatness, contemporary: our captain, Aram Mihailovich.
A great weight: the 20,000 tons of our ship.
A great mountain range: the Caucasus.
Great is the sauna, the caviar, the vodka
And the Volga: great is the Volga Boatman, the boatman
Himself and the song in his honour.
The bridge is great, the ballroom is great,
The bars are great (and the booze in the bars): also
The bilgewater is great and the bureaus
In the Bureaucracy: great are the drawers
Of each bureau, the pencils and papers inside,
The paper-clips and the pens.
Great is the promenade deck and the number three hatch.
Leningrad is a great city.
Moscow is a great city. The Odessa steps are
Great steps, especially in the film
By Eisenstein, the great Russian director.
A Russian passenger tells me
In the gym: "Our system is greater than yours!"
Great is the gym, the barbells and the jumping ropes:
These will make us strong! The waiter pours
Us at breakfast endless glasses
Of pineapple juice: these will make us strong.
Marx will make us strong. Lenin will make us strong.
Great & strong is the ghost of Engels
Far away in the ruins of Birmingham mills
And great is our chief engineer, Vasily Vasilyevich,
Who runs the engines turning propellers
Made by the great propeller makers of Leningrad.
Great is the Neva River and the drawbridge across it
The Winter Palace the Rostral Column the gate
Of Mihailovsky Garden the Admiralty the Palace Square
And Isaac's Cathedral, all of these sights

To be seen on a tour of the great city of Leningrad.
Great is cyrillic calligraphy
And beautiful too in the hands of ancient scribes
Who lived in ancient abodes before our own glorious times.
Great are our own glorious times
And great are the writers of our own glorious times
Their works and their days. Great is
The writers' union and Ivan Ivanovich its guiding spirit
And great patriotic example:
Great are his works:
Especially great are his volume of poems *Praise*
To The Combine Harvester and his novels
Bazooka and *Love in a Sewage Treatment Facility.*
Great is the port side of the ship
And the starboard, great is the fore and the aft,
Great is the bow and the bowsprit
And the bow of Rostropovich its resin and hairs:
Great too is Shostakovich, sometimes:
His greatness appalls us in his Leningrad Symphony
If slightly less in his decadent earlier works
And his very private string quartets.
Great without doubt is the Bolshoi Ballet all the time
And great are the fountains
Of Peter the Great who was certainly great
In his time
And in his time a progressive.
Great is my cabin
Cabin 335
Where I read an anthology
Full of English and American poems
In Russian
And find in juxtaposition
One by Kenneth Koch
And one by Stephen Spender
And think continually
And think continually of what is great.

Four

I

And I have broken my resolution to stick it out in America. I said I'd suffer sea return, abandon my Panjandrum. I made some very solemn public promises in *TriQuarterly* magazine, Number 35: Yes, Bielinsky, in the famous *Stefan Batory Poems*, written on another ship, heading in the opposite direction. Stern and manly verses, iron clanging, yea! in every line. Readers world-wide are asking: Did I ever see Mrs. Harris again? How is Michelson doing? What became of Kevin? Is Sandeen writing poems? How do I pronounce: Mickiewicz? *Mickiewicz?* And who is wise Lizdejko? And who is wise Printz-Påhlson? Have I been sued for plagiarism? Libel? I didn't, did I, change my name to Arzeno-Kirkpatrick for nothing.

> Dreary, gentle reader, were my days in Indiana;
> Drab beyond my dreams. Besides,
> My wife is British. She'd abandon me entirely
> If I didn't take her to England
> For the Bicentennial Year.

> Also, I've had troubles with a lovely lady student.
> Whose wrath, you see, I flee. *"vi sva-BOD-ni*
> *s'i-VOD'-n'e V'E-chi-rem?"* I asked, though in English. *What?*
> *"DAY-t'i mn'e vash A-dr'is."* Who?
> ("Possession of an innocent, an unfolded soul,"
> Says Lerrnontov's Pechorin: "Boundless delight!")
> "Maybe I'm too old for this," I told her in the night.
> "Hath delight," she cried, "its bounds and bonds?
> "Doth brilliant Abelard just fall to bits in flight?"

> "Which bits are falling?" I enquired.

England! Which bits are falling? *What?*
In Dunwich
And in Dunkirk.
What?
Will there always be an England
Now that Wilson's out
Now that there's a drought in Suffolk?
Sings Callaghan, P.M., waking up
At Number Ten to pour
The North Sea Oil on his Kraut:
God bless the god bless the godblessed Yanks.
O help us sell our tanks
To somebody, thanks!

We know the Saudis want the Tower.
Already
Arabs own the Dorchester
And Royal Kens-
Ington Hotels. They hold controlling
Interest in the Cotswolds
And the Fens.
Nigeria is going to want the Inns of Court.
Castles reassemble daily
In our dreams
In dirty streets in Cairo and Uganda.
Better they should grow
On rocky California coasts. Better
Move the Bank of England into Berkeley or Big Sur.
Better ship the Bodleian to Boston or New York.
Who, after all,
Saved the battlefield at Hastings? *What?*
Bought the bloomin' battlefield for Blighty. *What?*
Better that a worthy bridge
Should span a tract of Arizona desert sands
Than sink into the Thames
Or fall into the hands & vanish in the lands of

Libretto for E.P.

To Mister K said Mister Nix
I want to see a little symmetry of islands
in the sticks
both east and west of us.
I've got a little fix on certain stars
tells
which island, Baby,
maybe
's gonna be
of States the 51st of 'em
in one
nine seven
six.

Five

I carry with me once again: the mail.
There is, after all, nearly always
Mail to chasten or to cheer—(it reached me
This time in New York)—and there are two
Classes of friends: those who write
When one's away
And those who don't or won't.

Says Joe: "As an added attraction in my dreams last night, there was a letter from you at the end of which was an addendum in red ink. The writing was large, spacious, and very lucid. It was some sort of a note from your wife, but it was signed: 'Cissy' (?). Suddenly the three of us were in an open motorboat cruising through the Everglades, accompanied by a group of people called "The Mini-Multi Nations": Each person was dressed most luridly in his native garb, and each, in turn, sang the folksongs of his native land in native lingo. There was a German on board, complete with green Alpine cap and burly legs, on whom the whole group turned when it came to be his time to sing. As we proceeded up the river, another, smaller motorboat crossed our bow. There were two fishermen in it, and one of them, quite ugly, cast his line into our boat, dragging the German out of it and into the water. Anyway, I'm writing letters to graduate schools and wondering: Have I got a chance at Heidelberg?"

Was muss man tun um ein guter Seeman zu sein.
What to do to be a good sailor.
Wenn Sie sich unwohl fühlen, müssen Sie sich im Ferien in der
     frischen Luft bewegen, mit etwas beschäftigen, und wenn
     Sie irgend können—etwas essen.
If you feel ill, keep moving and busy in the fresh air; this will
     often drive away dizziness and save you the not so good
     experience of MAL DE MER.

From an anonymous informant: the news that, in my absence, I have been the victim of a parody and mock-panegyric by a certain (clearly pseudonymous) N. Talarico published in a local (to the bush) but most notorious little mag. I am sent quotations from the choicest bits of his encomium: 'To Matthias, as He Makes A Name For Himself.' He begins, himself, with a quote: "...not unlike Darwin playing the trombone to his French beans." My portrait ("Sir, the subject is mean—like Eustace Budgel who threw himself into the Thames") follows at once: "Weary hair that sprawls like a hanging garden of King Neb's grass, vaulted forehead, wrinkles, fluting, proud dripping eyes, the schizoid clergyman buried under one too many vows... nerves frizzing and popping like the ectoskeleton of some prodigious frying crustacean...." But I cannot go on.

Patty writes: "I told McMurphy and McBride I was going to invite you to become a Catholic and they *hooted*. So I won't but still I think it's what we have to offer. Phytophthora root rot infests your pseudopodium. I saw Solzhenitsyn on TV; it was apocalyptic. *I* was apoplectic, afraid for the first time. I have something wrong with a bone in my foot. Stop drooling in self-pity, I tell myself. Face it, this is your home. Why do you keep going away? Think of McMurphy and McBride. I wanted to hide and am hiding but now I want to be found.

> Who do you think has a death wish?
> Have a good year, boss, truly.
> Regards. The end.
> Olé.
> Patty."

Six

Around and about. With the girls, first,
For haircuts. Less is more, as someone said,
And Cynouai looks ravishing
And two years older with her long hair
Shorn by Russian barberesses & skinny male apprentice.
Laura watches skeptically, then
Wants short hair too.
Two babushkas, says a barberess, blushing.
We say thanks, *spasiba*. We pay in roubles, smile,
And walk the decks. At a kiosk: safety pins
And toothpaste. At a coffee lounge: espresso, strong.
Smooth sea, clear sky: you can see for miles.
I think to myself: I am happy.
It is not our lot to be happy. I say to
My wife: though you know that I know it is not our lot
To be happy, today, I say, I am happy.
Today, she says, you are foolish.
Propaganda shorts, punctuated by cartoons,
Begin in the Rainbow Cinema at ten.
Their approach is not unlike my own: This is
The city of Moscow. See the happy people. See them
Work and play. Though we know you know
We know it is not their lot to be happy, today, we say,
They are happy. Today I can almost believe it.
Olga says: Some of you on board
Do evidently take my elementary Russian classes
Lightly. Therefore there will be, she adds,
Examinations. Rossiya, we learn today,
Is from Slavonic
Rus or Ros
Which is from Rutosi which is Finnish
Meaning Swedes
A corruption for the Swedish Rothsmenn
Meaning seamen meaning rowers
Meaning rowers rowing
Seamen
Back to Rothsmenn

To Rutosi Russ or Ross
Slavonic Rossiya. We continue. We row on.
Though we're not permitted visits to the engine room
We are very welcome, thank you, in the galley.
Why, I wonder, as we gaze upon
The shining copper bottoms of the many pots and pans.
Our master cook is called Natasha. First assistant: Fred.
Says Natasha brightly: *SUP ni-da'SO-l'in:*
There is too little salt in the soup.
Gangs of rival youths, the spoiled sons
Of diplomatic families, East & West, cavort in narrow
Hallways, make a passage dangerous.
We disapprove of gangs of rival youths. We approve
Of peaceful placid crossings always in all seasons yes indeed
And fully air conditioned, stabilized.
We disapprove: of television, of atomic power,
Of planes. We approve: of solar energy, of poetry,
Of ships. Beep beeps of daily news
Are amplified through all the hidden speakers in the walls.
There's no escaping it, nor the *Aurora,* tabloid version
Of the same. Reagan shouts: Remember the Maine.
(Does he know about the Storozhevoy?)
In the Commons, fisticuffs; the Pound is down
To one point six. Carter's got his democratic delegates:
He'll win the nomination. Ford will have to fight.
We disapprove: of Carter, Ford, and Reagan. We approve:
Of George the Third and Pitt.
Up on deck again. Sea gulls off the stern:
There must be islands near. At our feet, heavy ropes
And chains for tying up in ports.
Cynouai sights serpent which she likens unto lobster.
Balistae, she has read, threw Regulus his army
At such an awesome shape as this.
She quotes us Olaus Magnus: "…rising like a mast
And eating sheep and swine disturbing ships
And snapping angry men from slippery decks…"
Cynouai's developed in the last two years
Some devastating Indiana playground jive—charms
And spells & incantations—which, lamentably,
She teaches gentle Laura. Their poetry

Is ancient and confounding: it ruins equally the
Innocent and guilty, wrecking the unwary.
They smile sweetly at the little boy at lunch
Who has expressed enthusiasm for his broccoli.
"So, so, suck your toe! / All the way to Mexico!"
He pales and expires in his parents' arms.
We vainly offer consolation.
Who among the passengers, we wonder,
Represents the K.G.B.?
Shall we forgive the K.G.B. its agent
On our ship? That wizard in the game room
Taking on all corners at the chess board,
That's the one. Or the strange aristocratic
Lady we discovered after midnight
On the upper deck where animals are kept in kennels
Who was feeding her pet bat.
I notice on a printout that the management
Declines to be responsible
For Acts of God or Piracy (that's fair);
Or for quarantines and seizures, strikes
And "latent vice." They reserve the right
To "land" us if the Captain thinks we are obnoxious
Or unfit. So says clause fourteen;
And I wonder how obnoxious we can get before
We're landed, how they make that nice
Distinction about latent vice.
After lunch, the girls swim.
I talk a while to Brad, a Unitarian from Cleveland,
About sin. I complete some customs forms
And see the big-armed baggage boss. I think of
Olga Korbut, do some exercises in the gym.
Deckspiele, Bridgespiele, if we want to play,
Can bring us prizes: Russian furs
And Balalaikas for the winners. Tea is in
The Vostok Lounge today. Dancing lessons are at four.
The little tailor promises to press
Diana's wrinkled evening dress.
Our Master, Aram M. Oganov, cordially invites us
To attend a formal cocktail party
In the Large Saloon where he will introduce

His senior colleagues late this afternoon. The orchestra
Will play, and Leonid Bozokovich will sing.
Mihail Lermontov, will they recite your poems?
I doubt it, friend. The Baltic Shipping Company and crew
Don't know your stuff, I fear, though
Curiously enough they still have uses for poet's
Name and legend in the end.
The legend is extreme.
When you died, the locals exorcized your house.
The incense suffocated every flea & louse.
Terrified,
They thought you were demonic.
But you were only just
                    a little bit
                              Byronic.

Seven

My sympathy extends to Lord George-Brown whose photograph is printed in *Aurora* having toppled over in the street outside the B.B.C. in London where he had appeared, more than just a little drunk, to be interviewed and to destroy, before the grinding cameras, his Labour Party card. He was very moved, he said, to do this thing. Then he slipped and fell.

Once I met George Brown, when he was Foreign Secretary, at a party given by my future in-laws shortly after I'd been smitten by the beauty, brains, and grace of a certain elegant Miss Adams. In heady company, in the middle of the mythic Sixties, a decade when intensities were commonplace and inspiration was the rule, my head made light, my tongue made loose by many minty gins, I asked Miss A. to marry me. That I had a wife at home already didn't, at the time, seem to be a complication. I was moved, I said, like Lord George-Brown, to do this thing. Then I slipped and fell.

A few months earlier, Diana blew her interview with MI5. What can you do, after all, with a degree in Russian from an English Tech if you're fastidious and will not spy? Her regular attendance at the London branch of the Russian Orthodox Church, as girl chorister, alarmed them as they positively vetted her. She sang, angelic, with a group of ancient (indeed Tzarist) emigrés she'd met at Holborn College. But, ah! who else, wondered MI5, might one meet at such a place of dubious repute and mysteries? Their suspicions ended abruptly what might have proved to be a distinguished career. Diana was a pious sort for a while, and took me off to what we later started calling "smells and bells." Once in an endless Sunday mass I scribbled in frustration on an envelope: "O Flaming Slavic God, I pray / Cooperate with me today / Undo this chastity, I say!" It was January, then, of 1967. It took Him roughly until May.... .

Eight

Hydrodynamics, brother:
waves, and what? makes? waves?
Who or how, then, poets,
oh! the ships. Of similitude
and crest lines, cusps:
We sing it, Mihail Yurievich,
together, no?
For English *scip*, sir,
German *Schiff*: all root-like *skap*
I deal I dig out *scoop:*
Scop, we say it, lad, and
ship-shape: poet!
who hath scope enough?
by means of which (of whom) doth
man contrive, convey himself & goods upon
the waves, who waves at
signals lovingly what wives
await returning man he
shanty sings of sea-born signs
Armada Ajax Agamemnon
lo! Renoun or Devastation, *ho*—
Potemkin Horner Mayakovsky
Virgil quote: "Then
first the rivers hollowed alders felt!"

But what? makes waves? components
of Resistance: poets
must, as ships do, dear, encounter
counter, count on it:
so resonant these waves
this hull our hallmark, helmsman—
Red or restive
forces vary as their masses
Newton said of similitude a principle
vouchsafe it I to
poets ships of state or captains
legislators unacknowledged

wonder (I do) *could* you, Lermontov,
have suffered out an exile
in "The West?"
In my America, "America"
in circumstances
we could hypothetically
imagine for you
tired and poor
and brave
and staring down some shitfaced
bureaucrat who couldn't
spell your name
on Ellis Island though it
wouldn't have been
Ellis Island then, not yet?
Instead of death at 26
an immigration
maybe
to ByGod ByGum
your ship against
our waves
your waves against
our shores
resistance or combustion and collapse?

Napoleon abdicates
and Washington burns down.
Clay, Calhoun
and Crawford clamour.
Madison makes war.
Who'd mediate with Castlereagh?
Who'd cluck: "The Tzar?"
Commission oh commissioner it's
Adams fast and far.
Francis Key goes spangley in a decent dawn.
Thornton saves the patents.
You blink
at Moscow midwives
and you learn to say: Tarhani.
Your generation's made superfluous

in Russia by
the poet-peacock's frenzy
of December '25: the profiles
of the hanged
bleed into the margins of *Onegin*.
As the dandy and the duelist
replace the likes of
Küchelbecker and Kondraty Ryleev,
the Masons go all misty
and Mickiewicz cries: despair.

Do I see you as a Locofoco candidate?
An alien—seditious Natty Bumppo
tough enough to topple even Tammany?
Or Bard of Biddle's Bank?
Cousin, your ambivalence about all things
matches even mine:—
You take, I think,
no Hannibalic oath with Herzen.

On the Wabash, maybe,
some reformer leads you
as a pre-pubescent
to anticipate Pechorin's adolescence
with the Shaker image
of a rehabilitated bum
coined in Owen's dialogues
with Adams & Monroe:
A Hero of Our Time in Indiana,
positive & realist,
wrought to win in 1841
the Brook Farm Fourier award,
wrought to win
the distant praises of Zhdanov.

"Oh the plundered plowman
and the beggared
yeomanry," quoth Jefferson
who never really cared about
the buggered beggars—

And old John Randolph said: "it's
a stinking coalition now
of Blifil and Black George!"
Bargain and intrigue, he meant,
between the Nullifiers
and the Feds.

Though you were only twelve,
who hath scope enough?
In time, perhaps,
you'd be a good Jacksonian:
A kitchen-cabinet member
cribbing notes from Crockett
pilfering from Poe
dreaming of Tecumseh's ghost
and Lake Ontario
as you give your arm, chivalrous,
to the blemished Peg O'Neale,
write your epic *Alamo*
and draft at last a swan song
in your famous
ode: "Hypothecated Bonds."

In 1837, with the Panic,
you take off:
The West! You write to Mme. Arsenieva
née Stolypin: "The Rockies
are my Caucasus in exile:
who hath scope enough?" And of
the river boats: *"The means!* by which
a man contrives—
conveys himself and goods
upon the waves…"
All the rest is lost in mountain mists
and in
the numberless lacunae
which I find
in Olga's reading lists.

Oh, you were born beneath a curious star.
Who'd mediate with Castlereagh
would cluck: "The Tzar."
I whisper in your dreamy ear
babushka
in your favorite hatch.

We heave most handily past headlands toward the Thames.

Nine:

A Conclusion of The Mihail Lermontov Poems beginning with documentation, paraphrase, and quotations taken down in the Revolutionary Reading Room from a fine old tome on the Thames by Allen Wykes and ending by way of a change, once again, of my name...

At the other end of the river, at the other end of time, they offer sacrifices to the Great God Lud: a bevy of virgins is flushed down the spring at Lechlade where the River God and his friends—who much prefer the virgins to the sheep and roosters which they sometimes get instead, a substitution which, as we can easily imagine, often leads to wicked floods in the Spring—run (says my authority) *a pumping station belching out the daily fifteen hundred million gallons of water* pouring toward us even now over the weir at Teddington as we flow west with the tide toward Tilbury. *Hic tuus O Tamisine Pater septemgeminus fons:* "Here, O Father Thames, is your sevenfold fount." Among the potamologists, in fact, there is no agreement as to exactly where it is. But Leche will do for us as it did for Drayton in his *Polyolbion*, as it did for his friend Shipton when he found in Trewsbury Mede that "no water floweth hereabouts til Leche, the onlie true begetter."

> *If to my starboard red appear*
> *It is my duty to keep clear;*
> *Act as judgement says is proper*
> *Port or starboard—*
> *Back or stop her...*

None of your *Wallala-leialalas* for us; that's a boatman's song with a social function to perform. Not so long ago the captains of ships mismanaged by members of the lively fraternity operating out of Gravesend under the Ruler of Pilots were encouraged to dispatch on the spot any incompetent or unlucky helmsman with appropriate ceremonials or without. We've flown our yellow Q and blue and orange stripes; we've blown an angry short and two long blasts on our horn and taken on our pilot from the pilot cutter. He sings his lonely song: *But when upon my port is seen/a steamer's starboard light of green. / For me there's nought to do or see/that green to port keeps clear of me.* So we are now in the hands of a specialist in rivers and can hope, muttering whatever spells or mnemonics we like, to reach our proper berth with no encounters along the way with any supertankers, QE2s, ghostly Kelmscott oarsmen, estuary chains, Gordon fortifications, sunken Armadas, lightships, sands, sheers, nesses, muds, or stone outcroppings along the Hundred of Hoo. The statue of Pocahontas, who never made it horne, stares at us through a Dickensian fog.

"His body doth incarnadine," remarked a jailor, "Thamesis to uncommon sanguine beauty." It was a notable execution. If Thames Head is hard to find—whether in the Mede or in the Leche or in the Pool at Seven Springs—the Thames heads are far too numerous to count. I see them vividly before me bobbing in our wake, all those lovely saints and sinners, chatting with each other about noble or ignoble deeds, drifting toward Westminster with the tide. That it should have been the *head* that always so offended! Why not, like Montezuma, pluck out hearts? No, the English god did not want hearts; you lose your head or mind in this cold country, or you hang. Your heart is yours for hoarding. Said the Virgin Queen, keeping hers to herself, red of wig and black of tooth, Tilbury protectress—"I have the heart and stomach of a king!" The pirate Drake prepared once more to burn the Spanish beard:—*with*
further protestatione that if wants
of victualles and munitione were suppliede we wold
pursue them to the furthese
that they durste
have gone ...
A less official pirate, late of Scotland, said most memorably upon espying, there on execution dock, a friend: "I've lain the bitch three times and now she comes to see me hanged!" Three tides washed the bones; then he waved for days from Bugsby's Reach.... Tippling pints in Whitby's Prospect or in Ramsgate's Town we think we'd like it better in till past. When they flushed the virgins down the drain at Leche, floated heads in rivers or impaled them ornamentally on pikes—when oh they hung the pirates low beneath the tide,
We'd drink we would we'd
go pursue them durste
supply the victualles and munitione
write immortal doggerel we'd fight for Gloriana
Boudicca Victoria Regina choose your time
by Kitchener do your bit
for Winston spot the doodlebugs and buzzbombs
pluck out mines off Cliffe
outfox De Ruyter beat that prick Napoleon

prop on some dark night
a poor unlucky scapegoat in the new foundations my fair lady
of the bridge
and bind him there
we'd set a man to watch all night we'd do the job ourselves.
But you do not choose your time.

Lucky, guilty—
exiled or pursued,
some can choose at least a place.
As the times impinged
obscurely, George Learmont abandoned Thomas Rhymer's tower and—
as mercenary, pirate—left his home and went to organize the cavalry in
Poland for a minor Tzar. His business there was doubtless foul. Later,
Mihail Yurievich would dream of heather, kilts, and thistles, dream of
George Learmont, dream of ancestors and Malcolm and MacBeth as
time—his times—impinged on him obscurely, making him superfluous,
sending him to the Dragoons and to the mountains where he prophesied
his end, with great precision, twice. He "eloquently yearned," a learned
scholar writes, quoting his worst stuff, "to fly to high and misty crags and
wake the wild harp of Scotland once again." But the Russian god, unlike
the English, wanted hearts, great hearts—Lermontov's and Pushkin's—a
nasty bullet through each one. The Russian god would make of both a
statue and a ship—machinery converting poetry to prose, roubles into
dollars, treaties into grain, and revolution into resolutions and détente.
Because of which we may avoid a holocaust and bore each other to our
graves.

> For my time, too, impinges oddly,
> painlessly, obscurely—this kind of inbetween—
> impinges surely
> this time of jokes & parodies, pastiches.
> An inbetween
> when I don't know precisely what I want to do in time
> but only where I want to go
> again—
> And so we're here and waiting
> for a berth
> to park a ship in—
> waiting in a time of waiting

A time of waiting for—
For semi-retired former semi-active veteran-volunteers
of oh our still belovèd
dear and hopeful
sixties
to arise again arise
again arise
For some kind fool to build the equestrian statues
and compose the elegiac songs.

Riding high and mightily on weary white lame mare
whose forelegs beat the air
and haunches heave
his head at a tilt, his purple plumèd hat all brandishèd
on high on high
on point of keen upraisèd terrible swift sword
Squadron Leader Jack Arzeno-Kirkpatrick
sings his able arias
in honour of Air Vice-Marshal Matthias-—
who has children
and a wife
who is middle class for life.

Said Marx (correctly):
men will make their history, all right,
but not exactly
as they think or choose.
(Even he had everything to lose
with that excuse.)

The signal flags unfurl and fly;
the lights flash on.
Down come blue and orange stripes,
the yellow Q:
Up go W and L, and
up goes V:
Have you got dead rats on board?
Answers ATI: *There is no cause for alarm.*
BCV replies: *Approved.*
Down come quickly *rats, no cause, approved*—

Up goes HKB:
Hello, Komsomolka: I want
to ask you a question. Is gallantry obsolete?
Flaps the dreaded Drake: *Think, by god,*
of the Queen. Down with HKB
and Drake, up with
M. Maksimich: *Was it the French who invented*
the fashion of being bored?
We fly the blue Pechorin: *No, it was the English.*
Taking our various oaths, we resolve
to be gallant again, and brave—
yes, Komsomolskaya—
and away with boredom, England!
We fly *The Plundered Plowman.*
We will not plunder—
we'll plow.
We fly *The Beggared Yeoman.*
We will not beggar
we'll yodel.
And there's a kind of waterish Tree at Wapping
whereat sea-thieves
or pirates are catched napping.

Oh, our resolutions are serious enough
in spite of the jokes
and in spite of our preoccupations
—the baggage, the passports—
and we really do propose to lead a better life this year
than last
though we do not tell ourselves exactly how.

Standing on the promenade
in attitudes
of suspicion, attention, or anticipation
hoping for some fine
benign surprise
each of us looks at the land
thinking still of the sea.
Each contrives
to be abstracted one last time in sea-thoughts

or in dreams
before the symbolical stranger
posing as a customs agent
or a clerk or porter in a small hotel or pension
asks the question symbolical strangers ask
which only actions answer

and each, I think, hums a variation
on the final chorus
of the tune
—changing names and faces,
touching all the graces—
that he's whistled up and down the decks
through afternoon & afternoon.

—O wild Italian–Irish Lass & Muse
protect with sprezzatura
and some Gaelic gall this voyager
his life
his children and his wife.
O help me take off my disguise.
Help to make me good
and wise.
I've been to God and man
Jack Arzeno-Kirkpatrick
for an odd span
of days
of days and nights.

An East Anglian Diptych

in memoriam Robert Duncan and David Jones

Ley Lines

I

... & flint by salt by clay
by sunrise and by sunset
and at equinox, by equinox,

these routes, these
lines were drawn, are drawn,
(force by source of sun)

The dowser leans by Dod-man's
ley alignment and
against some oak by water now.

II

By flint: the tools
By salt: the meats
By clay: the rounded pots

Along the lines, by sun-
rise & by sunset
and at equinox, by equinox,

the Dod-man's sighting staves,
one in each hand, is it,
of that scoured long chalk man?

III

Past Tom Paine's house behind the puddingstone
and castle there aligned
strategically along the Icknield way

Beyond the Gallows Hill
beside the Thetford tracks to Brandon
down the Harling Drove

Across the Brickkiln Farm to Bromehill Cottage
& below the tumuli before
the rabbit warrens and top hats…

Some burials, some dead,
and here their flinted offerings.
Seven antler picks,

A phallus made of chalk,
a Venus (did they call her yet Epona?)
and a tallow lamp…

Beltane fire line forty miles long?
Conflagration's law where energy's electric
down the *herepath*

if *Belus* is spelt *Bel*…

•

No bronze until the Beakers.
No phosphorus lucifers until, say, 1832.
Toe holes, ropes allowed descent

for wall stone you could antler out,
shovel with a shoulder bone—
Floor stone you would crawl for…

Between the galleries, burrows
narrow as a birth canal, as dark,
where some half-blinded Neolith first

nudged the Brandon Blacks & passed
those flints as far down time as Waterloo.
Weapons, tools. Ornaments as well.

Flushwork on Long Melford Church.
Flint flake Galleting on Norfolk Guildhall.
Jags by thousands of the calcined stones

for Queen Victoria's potteries.
Strike-a-lights required on Maundy Thursday still—
oldest flints ignite a young god's Pascal wick,

But first an edge to cut away the underbrush
down ley lines
long before the Beakers and their bronze.

IV

Ten days, twelve chapters, and the young man soon to die at Arras finishes his book, his thirtieth or so, on the Icknield Way. It's mostly about walking. He walks from Thetford where he thinks the Way begins coming from the Norfolk ports across the River Thet and Little Ouse. He's melancholy. The times are difficult, he's poor, he'd rather be a poet, his wife is desperate for his company, his children miss him too, a war is coming on, and, anyway, he's melancholy by nature. He has a friend who tries to show him how to tum his prose to verse. Hell have two years to do just that before he dies on Easter Monday, 1917.

But now he walks and writes. It is a job. They pay you for these nature books, these evocations, all this naming you can do along the road and through the villages and over all the dykes. They'll buy your eye even if they're deaf to all this balancing of consonants and vowels. He's melancholy. He doesn't really want to take this walk. He does it for the money. The times are difficult, he's poor, he'd rather be a poet, his wife is desperate for his company, his children miss him too, a war is coming on. Still,

It's better on a path than on a pavement.
It's better on the road than in a town.
It's better all alone to walk off melancholy
than to poison a companionable air
(or stare out of a muddy trench in France).

Home, returned on leave, exhausted,
bored by prose he's published only months before
and talking with a friend who'll ask:
And what are you fighting for over there?

hell pick a pinch of earth up off the path
they're walking and say: *This!*
For this, hell say.
This This This

For

      this

    •

This King Belinus was especially careful
to proclaim that cities
and the highways that led unto them

would have the peace
Dunwello had established in his time.
But no one seemed to know

the rules or lines whereby the boundaries
of the roads had been determined.
Neither Geoffrey, who, saying that about

Belinus in his book then consults the works
of Gildas, nor Gildas either,
nor Nennius himself in *Historia Brittonum.*

Before Belinus paved the road to "Hamo's Port"
with stone and mortar as he paved
Fosse Way and Watling Street, walkers who

brought flint, brought salt, brought clay,
paved the way in footprints over peat
and grasses with their animals before them

or behind. *By flint:* the tools;
By salt: the meats; *by clay:* the rounded pots.
By ley lines, flint and clay and salt

by sunrise and by sunset
and at equinox, by equinox, these routes,
these lines were drawn

(but no one seemed to know the rules
whereby the boundaries
of the roads had been determined)

force by source of sun.

V

They leaned into the journey,
east to west,
beyond Grimes Graves and through

the place that would be Thetford.
For every dragon heard to have been slain,
they found a standing stone....

Beside the Hill of Helith and then
along the river Lark
they left their weapons and their coins,

wondered at the headless rider
riding on the muddy banks. Cautious, curious
at the Swales tumulus, at

barrows north of Chippenham, they guessed
fine Wessex bronze lay gleaming
in the buried dagger there... and aged (grew young),

passed by Burwell church, passed by
Burwell castle too, spoke
of Anna and of Etheldreda, queen and saint,

at Exing, saw the horses race along
by Devil's Ditch to Reach, gallop through
the sainfoin which they gathered

in their hands as stone aligned with stone,
church with church, holy well
with holy well, pylon (in the end) with pylon.

Counting *one five four: four seven four:*
four eight six at Whittlesford,
brides among them turned their heads

to gaze at Golliwog, Sheela-na-gig.
Whose giggle, then, this
gog-eyed goggle goddess ogling back

above the portal near the Wandlebury
Gogmagog? *By air:* the zodiac;
By fire: the dragon path; *by earth:*

the tumulus, the barrow and the grave.
East to west
they leaned into the journey where

the dowser leans by Dod-man's
ley alignment and
against some oak by water now.

Rivers

I

By touch: his twig reveals the waters,
his sounding rod bites into chalk.
Matrona, Bel and Wandil gather in the mist

upon the hillside, lean into the journey:
moon by sun against the darkness,
sun by moon against the giant with a sword.

By air: the signal from the Gogmagogs
to zodiacs at Edmund's Bury and Nuthamstead.
Knight to knight come forth. By air

the still response: the bull, the lion;
the eagle & the bear. If Wandil stole the spring,
spread his frost along the ley lines,

now he strides as Gemini across the sky.
(Not two children, not two goats,
but eyes of Wandil rain down geminids

where ancient Dod-men lie....)

II

By water now. Along the Lark to Bury
where by air the constellations
blaze down on these figures born of earth.

Was it before Beodricsworth became
Saint Edmund's town & shrine
that Sigebert's forebears paced off zodiacs

from Abbots Bridge to Stoke-by-Clare
discerned as fit propitiation still
by him who led the garlanded white bull

to its oblation for the barren girl
between imposing portals
of the Benedictine Abbey on the Lark?

By rivers then. Along this quiet one
past Bury where it forms
the tail of Sagittarius and on by sting

of Scorpio, by tribute and by tributary,
portaging on over Virgo
north of Shimpling to Chad Brook. . .

Where the Stour flows by Long Melford
they leaned into their journey, rowed along
the belly of the Lion close by Clare.

If Wandil gestured to the west, they
travelled east toward Harwich, backs against
the morning sun, oars against the tide.

Underbrush along the banks at first
held only otters, then at Mysteleigh solemn men
sat fishing, men knelt making salt;

at Manningtree, a single lighter hauled
the heavy stones up shallow higher reaches
where a mason waited with his tools

and visions of a chancel in his brain.
Stoke and Wilford built their low stone bridges then;
other towns built locks; local wool

brought bricks and lime and coal.
West to east, they met the horse-drawn barges,
passed young woodsmen felling trees

to build the *Thorn*, the *Syren* and the *Terpsichore*.
Lark by Stour by Orwell; Scorpio
by Lion. Moon by sun against the darkness.

Sun by moon. A giant with a sword....

III

Or with a ship. A *Syren* or a *Terpsichore*. And if a giant, then a giant metamorphosed over time. The man who'll six years later paint the *Hay Wain* may not know his river rises as a tiny brook east of the Chilterns in the Gogmagogs. And yet he feels the giant in it, yet he knows its gods. Today he finishes his sketch of Flatford Mill—the mill itself, the locks, the barge and bargemen, and the small distracted barefoot boy on his horse. He'll work it up in 1817 for the Academy and no one will complain that it lacks finish. The sketch itself is rough. He adds an ash—his favorite tree—some elms, a broken oak. He shades in clouds he's come to study with a meteorologist's precision. Then he shuts the sketch book and trudges off toward Dedham, marking in his mind the river's fringe of willow herb and reed, the rising heron and the darting snipe and redshank in the sky...

He wants to marry Charles Bicknell's daughter. He wants to paint this river and these shimmering green fields. He doesn't want to quarrel with Charles Bicknell, with the rector of his village, or with Bonaparte. And he doesn't want to paint for money portraits of the rich or of their homes: Malvern Hall, Petworth House, East Bergholt. The ships that followed *Thorn* on down the slips at Mistly shipyards belched a thousand years of Beltane fire at French sails on the Nile. Martello towers rose at Shotley and at Walton Ferry... But here and now it's quiet, he thinks. Here and now it's peaceful and the air is pure...

> It's better to paint rivers than great houses.
> It's better to be married than alone.
> It's better with companionship to sit through winter nights
> remembering the Stour in springtime
> (or a cousin lying face-down in the mud at Waterloo).

> Here, returned from London, nervous and annoyed,
> bored by portraits that he's painted only months before
> and talking to a friend who asks:
> *And what are you drawing landscapes for out here?*
> he picks a pinch of earth up off the path
> they're walking and says *This!*
> *For this*, he says.
> *This This This*

For

      this

       •

This other ryver called of old time
Fromus maketh his beginning
near to Framlingham and then descendeth

close by Marlesford and so
southeast of Farnham entertayneth yet
another ryver called the Gleme

which cometh out from Rendlesham
thus passing forth to Snapebridge and
contriving then his course to Yken

dedicates himself into the sea
not very far away from where the Stour & Orwell
run together into Harwich harbour.

Frarnlingham: Framela's people: strangers on
the Fromus before Fromus became Alde.
Folk who'd become burgen-holders paying 5d tax.

On the bluff above the mere the Bigods' castle
glowers: Henry's castle glowers back
from Orford. Herrings, cereals, pottery from

Staverton passed through the town, began a journey
inland or a journey to the coast.
Scratchings on the nave in Parham church

show navigable reaches: ships of little draft
came all the way from Normandy past
Orford, Sloughden, Iken, down this stream

that flows
into a pipe below a petrol station
now

IV

...Men will number
what they value most
in wills: "To Robert Cook my scalbote,

my anchor and the things belonging to it and
my spurling bote: to George Clare
my fysher, fartle, makerel nets & warropes:

To John Weylonde: A manfare of haryngnetts:
capstaynes, skewers & my sparlyng netts
that hangeth in the low to the sea this yere

and when the sparlyngfare is done the netts
schal then be partyd to my children:
Thomas, Christopher, Erasmus: ships belonging

to the havyn to be sold at Aldeburgh church."
The men who made the wills were fishermen;
the others built their boats along these shores...

or sold them victuals, or worked upon the land,
or herded sheep, kept inns, cut
the timber, prayed in church & monastery, wept

impressed at sea, took up piracy and smuggling,
made the malt that made the ale they drank,
organized themselves in unions, and were hanged.

By 1850 photographs appear to show us
what they looked like outside Newton Garrett's
maltings or beside their barges loading

at Snape quay. John Felgate, shipwright, has
no teeth and wears a cap of moleskins;
his son, standing by a dinghy, has a thick

mustache, a threadbare coat, & a determined gaze.
Jack Ward, skipper of the *Gladys,* smiles;
his heavy begrimed turtleneck presses up against

his graying whiskers and his wide square chin.
The carpenters, Alfred Andrews & his son,
look almost well-to-do beside the shipwrights;

the younger Andrews wears a tie, a waistcoat,
and a golden chain while sawing timber for a rudder
or a boom; Howell and Chatten, maltsters,

hold their massive wooden shovels, handles down,
and slop about in canvas boots. Their rugged faces
look like copper pennies in a winter sun.

If we could hear them speak we'd doubtless hear
them say how *chance-times a sloe-wind*
brings old Tabbler Cable back to that same mawther

who'd 'im clapper-clawed or hear them laugh about
the crones who *couldn't sculpt the roots*
out as they got no teeth. The carter thakketh his hors

upon the croupe and jumps up in his wagon.
He's off to town. The men who work the maltings
and the bargemen line up for their pay.

The bird that flies above them angling toward
the Orford Ness they call a *mavis;*
by the time it reaches sprawling spider-webs

of early-warning radar nets it's lost its name,
and anyone at Chantry Point
looking with binoculars for avocets or curlews

would only see, if it passed by, a thrush.
Along the ley-alignment point
at Sizewell, Beltane fires in the reactor

are contained by water drained out of the sea.

V

   …But that the salt sea of say AD 500
should be drained from Deben marshes
that the land be sweet for corn and cattle…

That the river rising beyond Sutton, beyond
Woodbridge wait out flood & tide
for Norman engineers and then the Dutch,

for every local Fosdike, every local Waller
who might learn the warping
and the inning, reclaim with bank & seawall

or with sluice & gutter marshes then defended
by the reeves of Walton and
the men of Melton who might write: *lately salt,*

now fresh… That would take some time.
Some time, too, before the signals flash from
castle cresset, lucomb, lighthouse

or Martello tower up and down the coast
from Goseford to the Alde. No
early warnings here where everything's surprise.

South to north, they leaned into the journey,
rounded Landguard Point and
passed by Walton Castle, sailing with the tide

across the sand bar, steersman hugging
his athwartship tiller, small rain
in the oarsmen's eyes, wind across the stern.

Beyond the sandy heathland, the turf & bracken
over which they'd lug a ship the
size of this one to be buried as a cenotaph—

with coins from Usson-du-Poitou, a golden helmet,
maple lyre, & stone sceptre carved
with eight stern faces and a thin bronze stag

mounted on its delicate iron ring
they reached the pools they sought and, anchoring
off mud flats, felled the trees,

built their timber halls beyond abandoned villas,
stayed at Hernley, Hatchley, Trimley,
called the river that they sailed "the deep one."

They'd say they lived in *Middanyeard,* where *haeleth
under heofenum:* they found themselves
between two seas... (the hero of their poem the sun).

Before them, Celts and Roman legions.
After them the Viking raids.
After them the Norman engineers and Flemish traders.

Before them, the single salters squatting
on the mud, the long walk for flints
along the Icknield way. After them the excavation

of the buried ship....

                    •

        Extensio. Eastern point
north of Southwold on the Easton Ness, now lost.
Portus Adurni. Was the Deben called Adurnus

by the Latins here and on the Alde?
Harbour, temperate climate, sheltered creeks—
and vines growing high above the cliffs.

Counts of the Saxon Shore constructed here
their fortress where they failed to hold the tide
against the kin of those first called

by Vortigern to fight his wars against the Picts.
(St. Alban's first cartographer
would clearly mark his map: *Angulus Anglie. . .*)

114

Around the corner, then, and up the river
with the driftwood & the tide. Buoyed and beaconed,
spits and banks first marked with small

bouquets of yellow broom display their
angled emblems: Bowships beacon, Middleground,
Upper Waldringfield and Lower Ham,

Jack Rush beacon, Crimmy Moore, Horse Buoy.
If Edward were to anchor here
along the Kingsfleet, who but the Archbishop

might come sailing smartly out of Shotley
as the king, shining like some Helith, went to meet him
round into the Stour? On board the *Thomas*,

in a western wind, the Goseford ships impressed
for service, the power upon them
& Calais in fear, they'd break up the Great Seal.

So Wandil on the Stour gestures gravely
to the Wandil on the Gogmagogs. Against him lean
the sun & moon while all about him

widdershins there turns a circle of the dancers
who will help achieve the spring
as every ley south-east of Thetford Castle Mound

lines up along the tumuli and standing stones
to pass through places named for Bel
or Belus out to Walton on the northern Sea....

Beyond the Roman camp, the Saxon mound.
Beyond the Saxon mound the Viking
outpost in the Celtic forest with its secret paths.

Along the paths, the route to tributaries,
creeks, the sweetest hidden wells. Above the wells
a dowser with his twig, a Dod-man

with his sighting staves....

•

    who walks along the concrete wall,
and feels the fresh salt air,
and watches small yachts ply the quiet river

at high tide. Red sails, blue.
And bright white hulls. Woodbridge Sunday sailors
tack and jibe…

Alde by Stour by Deben. Ship by Saxon shore.
Cattle, corn by sea wall.
Dod-man, dowser, dapple of reflected cloud.

A Compostela Diptych

For John Peck and i.m. Guy Davenport

Part I: France

I

Via Tolosona, Via Podiensis.
There among the tall and narrow cypresses,
the white sarcophagi of Arles

worn by centuries of wind & sun,
where Charlemagne's lieutenants it was said
lay beside Servilius & Flavius

and coffins drifted down the Rhône
on narrow rafts to be unloaded by St. Victor's monks,
they walked: Via Tolosona.

Via Podiensis: They walked as well from
Burgundy through the Auvergne,
slogged along volcanic downland up into Aubrac

and on through Languedoc to Conques
and gazed into the yellow morning light falling
from above the central axis through

the abbey's lantern tower
and praised St. Foy, and praised as well
with Aimery Picaud their guide

the names of certain travelers
who had long before secured the safety of their way
and also other ways: Via Podiensis,

Via Lemosina, Via Turonensis.
They crossed the Loire at Tours and at Nevers,
walking toward Bordeaux or

from St. Leonard and St. Martial of Limoges
to Périgord and to Chalosse.
At Tours beside the sandy, wide & braided river

they would rest a while and bathe
or seek the narrow shoals nearby & shallow streams
that ran between. Here St. Martin's

shrine had outfaced Abd-al-Rahman
and they prayed at his basilica remembering
the ninety thousand Moors

beaten back to Cordoba before Almansor
took the bells of Santiago
for his candle-sticks, hung them highly

in his elegant great mosque & upside down.
His singers sang of it.
These walking also sang: Via Lemosina,

Via Turonensis: they sang the way along the ways.
They sang the king: *Charles li reis,*
ad estet en Espaigne… Tresqu'en la mer

conquiste la terre altaigne. Trouvères, jongleurs,
langue d'oïl, langue d'oc: of love
& war, the Matamoros & the concubine at Maubergeon.

And there was other song—song sung inwardly
to a percussion of the jangling
manacles and fetters hanging on the branded

heretics who crawled the roads
on hands and knees and slept with lepers under
dark facades of abbeys

& the west portals of cathedrals with their zodiacs.
These also sang: as had
the stern young men, their sheep or cattle

following behind, when up
to high summer pasture they would carry
from the scoria-red waste

a wooden image of their black and chthonic mother
burned in her ascent up out of
smoking Puy-de-Dôme (or her descent

from very heaven: Polestar's daughter urging
them to Finisterre.... .
                                    Whichever way

they came they sang,
Whatever song they sang they came.
Whichever way they came, whatever song they sang.

they sang and walked together on the
common roads: Via Lemosina,
Via Turonensis; Via Tolosona, Via Podiensis.

II

Dorian, Phrygian, Lydian
modes in diatonic sequence which would order
the response & antiphon at Cluny:

authentic, plagal; plagal and authentic—
hypodorian, hypomixolydian—
Magnificat! Magnificat anima mea Dominum.

And canticles in stone carved in capitals
to honor every mode
in which the honor of this Lady might

be chanted, melismatic even,
graced the choir itself in St. Hugh's hall
where someone wrote the book

sending walkers down the roads to Santiago.
Whose creation Aimery Picaud?
Whose persona Turpin? *The Codex Calixtinus!*

Book that wrought a miracle of power?
or book that answered it and echoed it, reflected
power trans-Pyrenean and uncanny,

causality determined by no human hand?
Did Santiago draw his pilgrims to his shrine,
or did the Monks of Cluny push?

Far from the basilica, far from
the *corona* with its hundred lamps & more lighted
there to brighten Pentecost or Easter, far

from the twelve arcades of double pillars,
the goldsmith's workshop & the bearded lutenist beside
the dancing girl celebrating in their frozen

artistry the artistry of monophonic provenance
which answered every gesture
of the vestured celebrant—and far, far before

the carving of a single capital,
the scribbling of a single line of Latin in a single book,
the hammering of gold, the glazing

of an ornament, the singing of the kyrie or gloria,
the censing of the host,
a strange boat arrived off Finisterre....

(Or so they say. Or so they said
who made the book.) The boat came from Jerusalem
without a sail, without a rudder,

without oars. It bore his head beside his body
who had caught it when the sword
of Herod dropped it in his open hands.

It bore his two disciples. As they neared
the land beneath the *campus stellae*
where the lord of every geste would heave his

spear into the surf, drawn across the Pyrenees
by virtue of this other who would lie down now
for some eight hundred years—son of Zebedee

and Salomé, brother of St. John, son of Thunder
born into Galicia—
a bridegroom riding to his wedding reined

his horse in, stared a moment at the little boat,
galloped straight into the tranquil sea.
When horse and rider rose, both were covered with

the scallop shells that were his sign, his
awaiting Cluny and his cult
(the carving of the capitals, the canticles in stone,

the singing of the antiphons,
the scribbling of the Latin in his lenten book)
but also *hers*—

Magnificat! Magnificat anima mea Dominam—
who rose up on a scallop shell
to dazzle any bridegroom staring at whatever sea.

So it began. So they said it had begun.
A phase (a phrase (a moment in
the spin of some ephemeride (a change

not even in the modes of music
from the Greek
to the Gregorian....

(And chiefly with an aim to rid the south of Moors, to rid it of the
Mozarabic taint in liturgies and chants, to blast the peasant heretics
following the Gnostic light of Ávila's Priscillian. And then? Then the
castigations of Bernard, the smashings of the Huguenots, the marshals of
Napoleon on the mountain trails, the slow dismantling of the abbey for
its stone, the twists of floral patterns on the broken columns standing in
the ruined granary, the Shell Oil station on the highway through the pass.
And at the restaurant by the river in St-Jean-Pied-de-Port (Michelin: 2
stars), good coquilles St. Jacques...

III

Aimery Picaud to those who walked:
Beware the Gascons and beware the Basques:
drink only from this well, never

drink from that: these boatmen on that river
will deceive you: trust
only those who ply the other one: and if

you cross the mountains through
the path of Cize, he warned of Ostabat where men
appear with sticks to block your way

and then by force extract an unjust toll:
these men are fierce, the country they inhabit barbarous,
their tongue terrifies the hearts of all who hear:

God they call *Urcia,* bread is *orgui,* wine is *ardum:*
may the rich who profit from their tolls
and fares, the lords above the rivers & the king of Aragón,

Raymonde de Solis and Vivien d'Aigremont,
atone by long and public penitence; may any priest
who pardons them be smitten with anathema:

Depraved they are, perverse and lecherous,
destitute of any good; the men
and women show their private parts to pilgrims,

fornicate with beasts; the men kiss the vulva
of both wife and mule. When a man
comes in a house he whistles like a kite, & when

he lurks behind the rocks or trees
he hoots out like an owl or howls like a wolf:
Beware these Gascons & beware these Basques.

But at the gate of Cize rejoice!
From this high peak you gaze down at the western ocean,
at the frontiers of Castille & Aragón & France.

Here with axe and mattock, spade
and other tools Charlemagne's companions built a road
into Galicia: May their souls rest

in peace, and may the souls also of those others
who in times of Aldefonso & Calixtus
worked upon the road and made it safe rest in peace:

André, Roger, Avit, Fortus, Arnault,
Etienne and Pierre, who built the bridge again
over the Mino: for them, eternal peace.

If you cross the Somport pass
you come to several towns: to Borce first and
then to Canfranc, Jaca, Osturit,

Tiermas of the royal baths, and Monreal.
You will meet the road from Cize
at Puente-La-Reina. Estella has good bread,

good wine & meat & fish, and all things
there are plentiful. Past Estella flow the waters
of the Ega, sweet and pure, as are

these other rivers I now name: The Cea
by Sahagan, the Esla by Mansilla,
the Torio by Leon and near the Jewish camp.

If you come by Arles and Les Alyscamps
you will see more tombs of marble
than you would believe carved in Latin dialect

spread before you more than one mile long
& one mile wide. If you come
by Arles you must seek the relics of

St. Honoratus and St. Gilles.
Between the branches of the Rhône, at Trinquetaille,
stands the marble column where the people

tied St. Genesius and beheaded him.
He caught his head and threw it in the Rhône where
angels bore it to the sea and

on to Cartagena where it rests in glory
& performs great miracles.
Who would fail to kiss the altar of St. Gilles?

Who would fail to tell the story of his
pious life? On the golden coffer there behind his
altar in the second register are Aries,

Taurus, Gemini and Cancer with the other signs
winding among golden flowers on a vine.
A crystal trout stands erect there on his tail.

May the Hungarians blush to say they have
his body. May the monks of Chamalières be confounded.
I, Arnauld du Mont, transcribe today

the writings of Picaud, describe the roads the
states the castles towns and mountains
waters wells and fishes men and lands and saints

the habits customs routes and weathers in this
fifth book of the *Codex Calixtinus*
on the stages of the way to Santiago.

IV

From Mont Saint-Michel to Sens,
from Besançon to Finisterre, a darkness fell at noon,
the walls of houses cracked, down

from all the bell towers tumbled bells.
In the encampment, flames leapt from spears of ash & apple,
hauberks buckled, steel casques burst,

bears and leopards walked among the men in Charles' dream.
For so he dreamed. Dreamed within
a dream Roland's requiem before the ships

of Baligant sailed up the Ebro,
their mastheads and their prows decked and lighted
through the night with lamps and rubies

in the story that Turaldos tells.
(From Ostabat, the Port of Cize, Val Carlos—then
the high road trod by Gascons & the Basques:

The road below was made by strangers and their armies.
Turonensis, Lemosina, Podiensis:
Straight to Spain each one through Roncevaux.)

They came to him among the Saxons saying:
join us against the Omayyads
at Saragossa: march with us to Abd-al-Rahman's hall.

It was Suleiman himself, governor of Barcelona,
Abbasid and loyal to
the Caliphate of Baghdad. Charles made it a crusade.

Burgundians and Lombards, Goths and Provençals,
Austrasians and Bavarians
loyal to the Reich found themselves conscripted

for the Frankish Blitzkrieg. For this was *Hereban:*
this was draft trumpeted by missi
all across Imperium: this was all incumbent on

vicarius and count. And so they came.
They came with sumpter, destrier,
& palfrey; they came with cooks & carpenters & sheep.

They marched away looking like a tribe of nomads
followed by the peddlers & the jugglers,
the singers & the whores. And crossed the mountains

at the Port of Cize. In the Cluny version
there is no Suleiman & no alliance.
Everything is supernatural power. The walls of Pamplona

fall at Charles' approach. He curses
and Luçerna is a great salt lake in which there swims
a single large black bass.

Turpini Historia Karoli: "I am James the son of
Zebedee whom Herod slew. My body
is Galicia. Seek me in this dream & I will be your stay.

My body is Galicia; my soul a field of stars."
Off he marched to Compostela;
At Finisterre he threw his spear into the sea.

In the lives of Einhard and The Stammerer, the facts;
In the *Geste* and *Codex*,
fear and hope and song:—

From Mont Saint-Michel to Sens,
from Besançon to Finisterre, a darkness fell at noon,
the walls of houses cracked, down

from all the bell towers tumbled bells.
In the encampment, flames leapt from spears of ash & apple,
hauberks buckled, steel casques burst,

bears and leopards walked among the men in Charles' dream.
For so he dreamed. Dreamed within
a dream Roland's requiem before the ships

of Baligant sailed up the Ebro,
their mastheads and their prows decked and lighted
through the night with lamps and rubies

in the story that Turaldos tells.
(From Ostabat, the Port of Cize, Val Carlos—then
the high road trod by Gascons & the Basques:

The road below was made by strangers and their armies.
Turonensis, Lemosina, Podiensis:
Straight to Spain each one through Roncevaux....

Before the Codex made at Cluny, the Capitularies;
before the pseudo-Turpin, Turpin.
And afterwards the song. Afterwards the echoing of Roland's horn.

The nine hundred meters to the Vierge d'Orisson.
The planted crosses like a harbor full of masts.
Afterwards the E.T.A.,

the slogans of the separatists,
Afterwards the sabotaged refinery, the blown-up train.
Afterwards the dawn escape across the pass.

From Mont Saint-Michel to Sens,
from Besançon to Finisterre, a darkness fell at noon,
the walls of houses cracked, down

from all the bell towers tumbled bells.

V

Aoi.
Pax vobiscum, pax domini,
Aoi.
      Ainsi soit il.

And Charles murdered fourteen hundred Saxons
after Roncevaux, cutting off their heads,
when no one would reveal the hiding place of

Widukind, when no one would convert. A northern
paradigm for slaughters in the south?
At the far end of the trail, before there was a trail,

there were tales told: narratives of gnosis
whispered themselves north
to bleed in Roussillon when shepherds saw the

flocks of transmigrating souls walk among their
sheep looking for good company
and habitation....

                    Even thus Galicia's Priscillian:

Executed 385 by Evodius, Prefect appointed
by the tyrant Maximus,
at the urging of Ithacius, his fellow Bishop....

The soul, then, of its own will doth come to earth,
passing through the seven heavens, and
is *sown in the body of this flesh.* Or would one rather

say, as did Orosius to St. Augustine: "Worse than
the Manichees!" And the Saint: "Light!
which lies before the gaze of mortal eyes, not only

in those vessels where it shines in its purest state,
but also in admixture to be purified:
smoke & darkness, fire & water & wind... its own abode."

Along the Via Tolosona to Toulouse and then beyond
they told the tales: tunics of human flesh,
penitential wandering, sparks hereticated, vestures of decay.

They praised the seal of the mouth,
the seal of the belly and the hand; the demiurge
was author of this world;

among the rocks and trees, among the sheep
& cattle, they acknowledged each
the aeon that was only an apparent body, only born

apparently into the pitch and sulphur of a human shape
to utter human words. The words
they uttered and the tales they told were strange:

                    ... when I was once
a horse, I lost my shoe between
the stones & carried on unshod the whole night long.

Cloven to the navel by this wound got of a Moor,
I speak to him alone who goes out
with the dead, the messenger of souls

who saw the lizard run into the ass's skull... .
The Ram presides above the head,
the Twins behind the loins...
                              Were these voices then

an echo of a field of force counter to
the leys on which the houses of St. James aligned
themselves from north of Arles into Spain?

No Cluniac reform or Romanesque adornment to
the dogma from the rustic prentices of old Priscillian
dead eight hundred years before their time;

no chant in diatonic mode, in good Gregorian, but
diabolic danger here. This
called out for Inquisition and for blood.

Across all Occitania, across the Languedoc
and down the Via Tolosona spread
the news: Béziers was ruined and destroyed,

fifteen thousand fell before the walls & in the town
where mercenaries heard the knights cry out
to conjure holocaust: *kill them all; God will know his own.*

At Bram, Montfort gouged the eyes out, cut
the nose and upper lip off all survivors of his siege,
leaving just one man with just one eye

to lead his friends to Cabaret.
This was orthodox revenge. This was on the orders
of a man called Innocent.

Raymond of Toulouse, driven from his city,
fled to England, then returned
through Spain where troops passed down the Somport Pass

along the Tolosona to link up with his confederates,
the counts of Foix and of Comminges.
The chronicles explain that *everyone began*

to weep and rushed toward Raymond as he entered
through the vaulted gates to kiss
his clothes, his feet, his legs, his hands.

He appeared to them like one arisen from the dead.
At once the population of the town
began to mend the walls that Montfort had torn down.

Knights and burgers, boys and girls, great and small,
hewed and carried stones while troubadours
sang out their mockery of France, of Simon, of his son.

It was not enough. Though Simon died
outside the walls, the French king and Pope Honorius
concluded what the Montforts

and Pope Innocent began. Behind the conquerors
there came Inquisitors; with
the Inquisitors, denunciations, torture and betrayal.

But in the mountains and along the shepherds' paths
leading to and from the Tolosona trail,
the old tales nonetheless were whispered still

far from cities and the seneschals, far from
Bernard Gui, his book & his Dominicans.
The cycle of transhumance led itinerant *perfecti*

there among gavaches as far from their own ostals
as the Ariège is from Morella,
the wide Garonne from Ebro's northern bank & winter camp.

. . . tunics of human flesh,
penitential wandering, sparks hereticated, vestures
of decay. . . .

Among the rocks and trees, among the sheep
and cattle, they acknowledged each
the aeon that was only an apparent body, only born

apparently into the pitch & sulphur of a human shape
to utter human words.
And in Galicia, beneath the nave, restless with the centuries,

the east-facing tombs out of all alignment with
the Roman mausoleum & supporting walls
take up proximity below the bones in Santiago's vault

to something holy. The martyred heretic of Trier?
Aoi.
Pax vobiscum, pax domini.

    Aoi. Ainsi soit il.

VI

But was it this that found the floriations
in the columns, found in capitals
the dance that found the music of the cloister & the choir,

the song that found the south for Eleanor of Aquitaine?
Trobar, they said: to find.
To find one's way, one's path, to find the song,

to find the music for the song,
to find through stands of walnut, poplar, chestnut,
through meadows full of buttercups

and orchids, over or beside the banks of many rivers
from above Uzerche to well below
the Lot—Vézère, Corrèze, Couze, Dordogne, Vers—

along the paths of sandstone, rust red & pink,
the way through Limousin, through Perigord, all along
the Via Lemosina to a small road leading to

a castle gate, to find a woman in that place
who finds herself in song,
to find a friend, a fellow singer there or on the road.

Or to the north and west, at Poitiers,
along the Touronensis after
Orleans and Tours, to find before the heaths

of Gascony the pine forests and the *plat pays*
of Poitevins who speak the language
sung by William, Lord of Aquitaine, or the Lemosin

of singers who found comfort who found welcome
at his son's court, his who died
at Santiago, and the court of Eleanor his heir

whose lineage from Charlemagne found Angevin Bordeaux.
They came from Albi and Toulouse,
the town of Cahors and the county of Quercy,

but did they find for her and sing
the *Deus non fecit* of the heretic *perfecti* of Province
or the light from Eleusis

bathing trail and keep and column in its warmth?
Beneath the limestone cliffs of the Dordogne,
past the verges bright with honeysuckle, thyme and juniper,

quarried stone and timber floated toward the sea
on barges by the dark ores of the *causse,*
while salt, fish, and news of Angevin ambition & desire

came on inland from Bordeaux and from Libourne.
From Hautefort, Riberek; from
nearby Ventadorn, singers found their way to Poitiers.

The *sun rains,* they sang: *lo soleils plovil,*
while pilgrims in Rocamadour
climbed toward what they sought, singing without benefit

of trobar ric or trobar clus: *midonz, midonz*
in a dazed vision of the lady there,
hunched & black upon a stick fallen from the sky.

To sing, to pray: to find behind them
south of Ventadorn, of Hautefort, of Cahors & Toulouse,
alignments in the temple of the sun

at Montségur measuring the solstice, measuring
the equinox, dawn light raining
through the eastern portholes of a ship

riding its great wave, counting down the year,
counting down the years, sign by sign
from Aries to The Fish, not to brighten only that

new morning in Provence but latterly to bend
also onto any path
of any who would follow, singing

at the gates of abbeys or below the castle walls
in any language found
where every song was fond

and yet forbidding, forensic as the night.
Did those who sang, do those who sing,
care at all that at the ending of their song,

as at the start, William of Aquitaine,
son of the troubadour, father of the child
they would hail in Poitiers

kneels crying *midonz* to the stars
but finds in Santiago's tomb not the bones of James
but those of the heretic Priscillian?

I am Arnaut who gathers the wind.
I am Arnaut who hunts the hare with the ox.
I am Arnaut who swims against the tide.

•

Near Excidieul, long long after Aquitaine
was France, after the end
of what was Angevin, and after the end of the end,

two lone walkers slogged along the road
and spoke of vortices
and things to be reborn

after Europe's latest conflagration. Was it spring? Was it 1920? The older of the two, trying to remember after fifty years, could not be sure. It was he who had crept over rafters, peering down at the Dronne, once before. He knew that Aubeterre was to the east, that one could find three keeps outside Mareuil, a pleached arbour at Chalais. He knew the roads in this place. He had walked into Perigord, had seen Narbonne, Cahors, Chalus, and now was once again walking with his friend near Excidieul. In certain ways he much resembled the old finders of song, and sang their songs in his own way and tried to make them new. He called the other one, his friend, Arnaut, though that was not his name, and stopped with him beside a castle wall. He saw above them both, and wrote down in his book, *the wave pattern cut in the stone, spire-top alevel the well curb*, and then heard this other say, the sun shining, the birds singing, *I am afraid of the life after death*. Of a sudden. Out of the calm and clarity of morning.

He stored the loved places in his memory—the roads, the keeps beside the rivers, the arbour at Chalais—and walked in Eleusinian light and through the years to Rimini and Rome, in darkness on to Pisa in another war. And after fifty years, and from the silence of his great old age, he said: *Rucksacked, we walked from Excidieul. When he told me what he feared, he paused, and then he added: "Now, at fast, I have shocked him… ."*

Who was Arnaut to gather the wind?

Intercalation

And who, asked the Doctor Mellifluus, were the Cluniacs to gather all *these* things: *deformis formositas ac formosa deformitas.* A wave pattern cut in the stone would have been enough—would have been, perhaps, too much. But apes and monstrous centaurs? half-men and fighting knights? hunters blowing horns? many bodies under just one head or many heads sprouting from a single body? Who were the Cluniacs to gather round them windy artisans to carve their curiosities, to carve chimeras, onto cloister capitals from St. Hugh's Hall to Santiago so that it became a joy to read the marbles and a plague to read the books. The concupiscence of eyes! For he had deemed as dung whatever shone with beauty. (Dung, too, was music and the talk, *humanus et jocundus,* of the monks, or the song of deeds in poetry. The concupiscence of ears! For he'd have silence, silence, save when he would speak, the great voice shaking his emaciated frame near to dissolution and yet echoing through all of Christendom: *Jihad! Jihad!* He looked upon the mind of Abelard, the body of Queen Eleanor, and did not like them. Man of the north, he gazed upon the south and built the rack on which they'd stretch the men of Languedoc after he'd made widows of the women standing horror-stricken outside Vézelay the day a thousand knights called out for crosses.) Contra Dionysius, the pseudo-Areopagite. Contra Saint-Denis. Contra Grosseteste, contra Bonaventure, and before their time. There was, he thundered, darkness in the light. And light in darkness of the fastness, of the desert, of the cave.

And yet, Abbot Suger sighed, thinking of his Solomon and walking in the hall the saint had called the Workshop of Vulcan, the Synagogue of Satan: *dilectio decoris domus Dei.... Cross of St. Eloy!* Thy *chrysolite, thy onyx and thy beryl.* It seemed to him he dwelt in some far region of the mind not entirely on this earth nor yet entirely in the purity of Heaven.... When he looked upon such stones.... When the sun's rays came flooding through the windows of the choir. For he was servant to the Pater Luminum and to the First Radiance, his son. Their emanations drenched so utterly this mortal world that, beholding them polluted even in the vestures of decay, we should rise—*animae*—by the manual guidance of material lights. The onyx that he contemplated was a light, the chrysolite a light, lights the screen of Charlemagne, the Coupe de Ptolemées, the crystal vase, the chalice of sardonyx, and the burnished ewer. Also every carving in the stones—the capitals, the portal of the west façade—and every stone itself, placed with cunning and with reverence according to the rules of proportion on the other stones, and then proportion too, laws invisible made visible by building—place and order, number, species, kind—these were lanterns shining round him which, he said, *me illuminant.*

But to Citeaux, but to Clairvaux: letters which began *Vestra Sublimitas* (and without irony). Acknowledging intemperance in dress, intemperance in food and drink; acknowledging the horses fit for kings and their expensive, sumptuous liveries; superfluities of every kind, excesses which endangered everything, opening the Royal Abbey to the winds of calumny.... He'd move into the smallest cell. He'd walk while others rode. He'd fast.... And yet expand the narthex and reconstruct the choir. Enlarge and amplify the nave. Find a quarry near Pontoise in which they'd cut no longer millstones for their livelihood but graceful columns by the grace of God. He'd execute mosaics on the tympanum, elaborate the crenellations. Hire castors for the objects to be bronzed, sculptors from the Cluniacs to carve in columns tall figures on the splayed jambs. Abolish compound piers and redesign triforia. Raise the towers up above the rose making of the rose itself a fulcrum. Repair the lion's tail that supported until recently the collonette. Repair zodiacal reliefs and, in the crypt, the capitals' eight abacus athemia. In the Valley of Chevreuse, he'd hunt himself for twelve tall trees, trunks sufficient in their height for roof-beams of his new west roof and fell them in the woods with his own axe, and offer thanks. Nor would he renounce the light— whatever letters went to Bernard of Clairvaux—the light proportionate unto itself, order mathematical of all diffusion, infinite in volume and activity, lux and lumen both.

And then at Vézelay, Bernard. Sunny Burgundy. The Via Podiensis and the city on the hill. Bishops, statesmen, peasants hungry for some kind of fair, thugs and mercenaries, Louis King of France who ached for glory and beside him Eleanor. Multitudes so many that they flooded all the fields waiting for the prophet from Clairvaux who would command them (Suger quiet under some far tree; Suger strong for peace). At Sens, he had destroyed Abélard. Now he'd widow all the women of the north. Rhetorician of the Holy War, demagogue of the crusade, he stood outside the abbey where the Pentecostal Christ of Gislebertus, *sol invictus* of the entry to the choir, measures time. But then what time was *this,* what year? Sea-green incorruptible beneath his Abbot's shroud, he numbered hours and souls in strict and occult symmetry. Were days measured once again by Kalends, Nones and Ides? Was solstice equinox and equinox the solstice? Did lunar phases intersect the solar year? Who had carved a column with the *lam* and *alif* of the Holy Name and was it *zenith* now or *nadir* in the Latin's Arabic? Many bodies sprouted from his head and many heads from every weaving body. Hautbois and bass bombarde began to play, shawm and chime and rebec as the voices sang *Fauvel* and *Reis Glorios*. From Mont Saint-Michel to Sens, from Besançon to Finisterre, a darkness fell at noon, the walls of houses cracked, down from all the bell towers tumbled bells. In a far encampment, flames leapt from spears of ash and apple, hauberks buckled, steel casques burst, bears and leopards walked among the men in Bernard's dream. For so he dreamed, even as he spoke. Dreamed within a dream Jerusalem's high requiem before the ships of Saladin sailed south from Tyre, their mastheads and their prows decked and lighted through the night with lamps and rubies in the story that the emirs tell. But everything would not be done at once. He saw emblazoned on a calendar suspended in the sky that it would be the year of Grace—but it would be no year of Grace when he awakened from his grave and found the month Brumaire: Those before him in the field walked straight over his indignant ghost and, shouting out obscenities, burned and looted in the abbey, then marched back down Via Podiensis and the Rue St. Jacques into the capital. All of Paris quaked beneath the church of St. Denis and night revealed itself in which the very stars went out as mobs broke in to take the chalices, the vials, the little golden vessels used to serve the wine of the ineffable First Light, and swilled their brandy from those cups, then with clubs and hammers beat them flat. Long lines of priests in vestments led through burning streets a train of mules and of horses laden with patinas, chandeliers and censers from a dozen churches on the Santiago trail, pushed before them carts and wheel-barrows loaded with ciboriums and candle-sticks and silver suns. *Merde!* they shouted. *Vanities!* And tore from roofs and crannies sculpted figures wearing crowns to smash their eyes out and their jaws into a stony chorus of eternal silent screams. Relics torn from reliquaries fed the bonfires and the holy dead themselves were disinterred. Bells from Languedoc, from Conques, bells that rang above him there at Vézelay, were melted down for cannon and the cannon dragged along the trails into Spain to blast the columns and the capitals, the arms and legs and heads of kingdom come, into the brain of Goya— Vézelay's splayed Christ upon the door become the victims of the Tres de Mayo, the *deformis formositas ac formosa deformitas* of the twisted and uncanny *Disparates*, the black figures on El Sordo's Quinta walls.

. . . how many years?
The Abbot Suger did not know, but he was Regent.
He set about his work.

Pilgrims set off walking down the Via Podiensis
from the church of Julien le Pauvre.

Part II: Spain

I

And from the ninety-second year of the Hegira
and from Damascus
and from the lips of Caliph Walid Abulabas:

permission for Tariq ibn-Ziyad to set forth
from Ceuta in his borrowed ships
to see if what was spoken by Tarif ibn-Malik

and his captives of al-Andalus
was true: serene skies, an excellence of weather,
abundant springs and many rivers,

fruit & flowers & perfume as fine as in Cathay,
mines full of precious metals, tall
standing idols of Ionians amidst extraordinary ruins,

and an infidel weak king despised by tribes & peoples
who but waited to be rendered tributary
to the Caliphate and subject to Koranic law.

And then: collapse of the Visigothic armies
at the battle near Sierra de Retin,
knights' bodies tossed into the rising Barbate

and the footmen with their slings & clubs & scythes
falling before Berber scimitars
days before the Qaysite and Yemeni horsemen

under Musa ibn-Nusayr could even cross
from Jabal Musa. Then the hurried crossing of the straight,
the meeting between Musa and Tariq at Talavera,

the occupation of León, Astorga, Saragossa,
and the messenger prostrate before the Caliph in Damascus
saying *Yes! Serene skies, an excellence of weather,*

abundant springs and many rivers, fruit and flowers
and perfume as fine as in Cathay,
mines full of precious metals and, inside this bag

I open for you now, O Caliph,
the severed head of Roderick, king of the Visigoths.
Behold the token of our victory!

Died al-Walid Abulabas in the ninety-sixth year
of the Hegira when, for his troubles,
Musa was condemned by Sulayman to prison & the bastinado

and Tariq ibn-Ziyad disappeared from every chronicle.
But the chronicles themselves go on:
A bad time for Umayyads at home, but every

kind of glory for the jihad in al-Andalus.
Which is why the hungry Umayyad, hunted in the streets
and alleys by the Abbasids, was going there:

the young man hiding in the rushes of Euphrates,
then a silhouetted horseman riding through the desert in the
            night,
the moon on his shoulder, the pole star in his eye.

Landing north of Málaga, he wrote his laws.
Having *crossed the desert*
& the sea & mastered both the wasteland & the waves,

he came into his kingdom, for he was Abd-al-Rahman
and would rule: *no one*
to be tortured, no one to be crucified or burned,

separated from his children or his wife, or anyone
to be despoiled of his holy objects
if in tribute come the golden dinars & the golden wheat

the flour & the barley heaped in bushels on the wagons
to be weighed, the measures
requisite of vinegar and honey, common musk & oil.

And Abd-al-Rahman rebuilt the mosque in Córdoba.
And the second Abd-al-Rahman
Gathered the philosophers and poets, gathered the musicians

and the concubines and wives. And the Sufi at the gates
called his heart a pasture for gazelles, said
he'd come to Córdoba following the camels of his love.

From the columns left by Rome there sprouted upwards
palm-like in oasis the supports
for Allah's double tier of arches, hemisphere

upon the square, fluted dome upon the vault.
When they built the Alcázar &
Madinat al-Zahra, six thousand dressed stones

were called for every day, 11,000 loads of lime & sand.
There were 10,000 workmen, 12,000 mules.
By their kilns and pits, the potters & the tanners,

the armorers and smiths.... Plane, then, on plane...
the surface of each building there
a depth of arabesque, brick and faience overlaid

with geometric pattern & the forms of Kufic & Basmala
lettering interlaced with flowers,
framed by grape vine and acanthus all dissolving

strength & weight & structure in a dazzle of idea:
horror vacui: shifting ordering of order
all unseen, water of icosahedron, air of octahedron

fire of tetrahedron on the simple cube of earth,
living carpet in the grid of pathways behind walls,
sunken flower-beds, myrtle bushes

shading tributaries of the central pool and reflection
of the zones and axes of this world
crossing at the intersection where a Ziryab might play

his lute or al-Ghazal recite.... And Abd-al-Rahman
built on Abd-al-Rahman's work, &
Abd-al-Rahman brought it to completion.... .

Who could have foreseen in these expansive years
the squabbling of *taifas*
and Moorish rulers paying tribute to

Alfonso, Sancho, & Rodrigo Díaz El Campeador?
No one walked along the roads
to cross the Aragón where every route converged upon

a single bridge or sang the tales of El Cid & Charlemagne
slogging through Navarre into Castile.
But it was spring. Spring in Burgundy and spring

in all al-Andalus. In Cluny & in Córdoba they carved
stones and sewed the mint & the marjoram;
silkworms hatched & beans began to shoot and all

the apple & the cherry trees flowered white at once.
Water in the aqueducts was fresh as snow
in mountain streams, & everything it irrigated green.

But when the Sufi heard the flute notes in the air
and his disciple asked him
Master, what is that we hear outside the wall?

he looked up from the pile of sand on which he sat
reading the Koran and said:
It is *the voice of someone crying for this world*

because he wishes it to five beyond its end.
He cries for things that pass.
Only God remains. The music of the flute

Is the song of Satan crying in the desert
for the wells that all run dry,
for the temples & the castles & the caliphates that fall.

II

Via Tolosona, Via Podiensis.
There among the tall and narrow cypresses,
the white sarcophagi of Arles

worn by centuries of wind & sun,
where Charlemagne's lieutenants it was said
lay beside Servilius & Flavius

and coffins drifted down the Rhône
on narrow rafts to be unloaded by St. Victor's monks,
they walked: Via Tolosona.

Via Podiensis: They walked as well from
Burgundy through the Auvergne,
slogged along volcanic downland up into Aubrac

and on through Languedoc to Conques
and gazed into the yellow morning light falling
from above the central axis through

the abbey's lantern tower
and praised St. Foy, and praised as well
with Aimery Picaud their guide

the names of certain travelers
who had long before secured the safety of their way
and also other ways: Via Podiensis,

Via Lemosina, Via Turonensis.
They crossed the Loire at Tours and at Nevers,
walking toward Bordeaux or

from St. Leonard and St. Martial of Limoges
to Périgord and to Chalosse.
At Tours beside the sandy, wide & braided river

they would rest a while and bathe
or seek the narrow shoals nearby & shallow streams
that ran between. And read: *at the gate of Cize*

Rejoice! (Picaud, again Picaud) *And from this peak*
gaze at all the western ocean,
at the frontiers of Castille & Aragón & France.

Here with axe and mattock, spade
and other tools Charlemagne's companions built a road
into Galicia: May their souls rest

in peace, and may the souls also of those others
who in times of Aldefonso & Calixtus
worked upon the road and made it safe rest in peace...

For there were times when all was war.
There was a time, far into the south, when Muhammad's very arm
came to lie and work its magic

in *the mosque at Córdoba, a time when Ibn Abi Amir*
took it from its jewelled box
and shook it like a spear at Santiago,

made a Via Dolorosa out of every trail in Galicia
and lit a conflagration
which would burn beyond our cities & beyond his time...

From Mont Saint-Michel to Sens,
from Besancon to Finisterre, a darkness fell at noon,
walls of houses cracked, down

from all the bell towers tumbled bells.
In the encampment, flames leapt from spears of ash & apple
hauberks buckled, steel casques burst,

bears and leopards walked among the men in Picaud's dream.
For so he dreamed. Dreamed within
a dream Roland's requiem before the ships

of Baligant sailed up the Ebro,
their mastheads and their prows decked and lighted
through the night with lamps and rubies

in the story that Turaldos tells.
(From Ostabat, the Port of Cize, Val Carlos—then
the high road trod by Gascons & the Basques:

The road below was made by strangers and their armies.
Turonensis, Lemosina, Podiensis:
Straight to Spain each one through Roncevaux.)

And Almanzor al-Allah razed Leon
and burned the monasteries at Eslonza, Sahagún;
In Navarre, the king gave up his daughter;

counts became his vassals, one by one. On the road
to Córdoba weeping prisoners trod,
year on year from west of Saragossa. In Compostela,

he left not a stone. In Burgos not more than a promise:
That Almoravids would arise to follow him,
fakirs from the deserts of Sahara: that Yusuf ibn-Tashufin

would land in Algeciras, holy & appalling & austere.
His face entirely covered with a veil,
eating only bread and camel's flesh and honey,

he'd annihilate the armies of Alfonso at Sagrajas.
Widows and their children
would go begging on the ashen empty trails

and from Algeciras to the March,
from Marchlands to Finisterre, the dark would fall at noon,
the walls of houses crack, down

from all the bell towers tumble bells.

III

I commend my soul to God, and my remains,
If I be slain by Moors,
to Oña, to whose altar I bequeath

147

1,600 maravedis, three of my best horses,
two mules, my clothing with the
robes of ciclatoun & my three purple cloaks,

and also two silver goblets. If my vassals
do not bring my body back,
hold them in dishonor, treat them even

as the vassals who had murdered their own lord.
He was ransomed, Count Gonzalo Salvadórez,
and returning—but indeed to Oña to be buried there...

And Ramiro of Navarre was returning—
in an oaken coffin to the church of Saint Maria...
And the men of Logroño to Logroño,

the men of Pamplona to Pamplona...
and the open crypts at Jaca and Sangüesa and at Yesa,
the sepulchers of monasteries on the Ebro,

graves in the churchyards on the Oca and the Aragón,
all began to fill because again
Alfonso had not summoned Don Rodrigo from his exile.

Tañen las campanas en San Pero a clamor
por Castiella.... He has left Castile, the poet sang,
And they rang & pealed the bells,

but he had gone: at Bivar the gate was broken
on its hinges, the porch of his house was empty still;
there were no falcons there, & no molted hawks.

The portals of the city had been shut against him.
When he rode up to Burgos flying sixty pennons, he kicked against
the lock, shouted with the strength of sixty heroes

to the people of the city to admit him. But everybody
hid behind his curtained windows.
Alfonso had condemned Rodrigo Díaz, & because of this

Count Gonzalo Salvadórez and Ramiro of Navarre
had died in battle and the king's
beaten army was retreating from the castle at Rueda.

There was worse to come. At Sagrajas, in the south,
as had been foretold.
At Sagrajas, where they beat upon the drums all day.

At Sagrajas, by a tributary of the Guadiana
where Almoravids & the armies of al-Andalus allied themselves
but where Alfonso of Castile & León

failed again to summon Don Rodrigo Díaz from his exile.
Because of that, the Moor could write:
Do thou remember the times of Muhamad Almanzor,

and bring to thy memory those treaties where
thy fathers offered him the homage even of their daughters,
and sent those virgins for their tribute,

even to the far lands of our rule, even into Africa;
Bring this to thy memory before
presuming now to cast thunders against us,

before presuming now to menace us, for we have seen
you marching from the castle of Rueda with
the bodies of Gonzalo Salvadórez & Ramiro of Navarre.

But Alfonso would return the bells of Santiago
to Galicia, and he would boast: *I will*
redeem my word, I will preserve my plighted faith—

and fall upon thy lands with fire and sword
& drive you back into the sea.
There will be no further messages between us...

only the clangour of our arms, the neighing
of the war-horse, the blaring
trumpets and the thundering of atambours.

But riding south without Rodrigo Díaz, he would
soon be riding north—with bodies
of his knights and his confederates, knights & kings

to bury in their lands along the Ebro and the Oca and
the Aragón, where he was riding from Rueda
with the bodies of Gonzalo Salvadórez & Ramiro of Navarre.

*Tañen las campanas en San Pero a clamor
por Castiella....* He has left Castile, the poet sang,
and they rang & pealed the bells,

but he had gone: at Bivar the gate was broken
on its hinges, the porch of his house was empty still;
there were no falcons there, & no molted hawks.

The portals of the city had been shut against him.
When he rode up to Burgos flying sixty pennons, he kicked against
the lock, shouted with the strength of sixty heroes

to the people of the city to admit him. But everybody
hid behind his curtained windows.
Alfonso had condemned Rodrigo Díaz, & because of this

Count Gonzalo Salvadórez and Ramiro of Navarre
had died in battle and the king's
beaten army was retreating from the castle at Rueda...

and because of this, the king would be routed
at Sagrajas by the Guadiana,
return with the bodies of his knights & his confederates

to bury near Gonzalo Salvadórez & Ramiro of Navarre.

IV

Oit varones una razón! he shouted
in the dusty square,
echoing the *Hoc Carmen Audite* of certain Joculatores,

Joculatores Domini, who stepped around him
and his eager rabble of an audience
to walk beneath the scaffold of the master of Sangüesa

who would freeze him there forever in the stone
even as he left the town
to sing the wayfarers upon their way

from Yesa on through Burgos to León.
On the portal he disports himself with viol & bow,
and also with the lady in a sexy gown

whose other friend is farting in a well beside a cooper
struggling with his heavy barrel.
But on the trail he was quintessential news, was history itself,

and sang the life of Don Rodrigo while El Cid
yet earned the fame to warrant song.
And aged within his story. And grew so very old

his song became a banner among banners
of reconquest: *Oit varones
una razón*—of reconciliation on the Tagus, it might be,

once the hero halted at El Poyo,
once the heralds brought him followers from Aragón & Monreal,
once Minaya sought Alfonso for him

west in Sahagún, west in Carrión,
toward which they walked who'd gathered in the square
beneath the portal of María la Real.

And when Rodrigo rode to meet his king the villagers
& peasants saw, the singer sang
tanta buena arma, tanto buen cavallo corredor—

splendid weapons, swift horses, capes and cloaks
and furs and everyone
vestidos son de colores, all dressed in colors,

underneath the banners
when he stopped on the Tagus, when he fell upon
his face before Alfonso, when he

took between his teeth the grasses of the field—
fas yerbas del campo—and wept
great tears as if he had received a mortal wound

and would be reconciled with the earth itself....
as act of faith? Auto da fé?
& near the Tagus once again, Toledo's banners flying

long long beyond him who had come to meet Alfonso
from Valencia & him whose song
became a banner among banners of reconquest?

This *razón* was also sung along the trails, for it was news,
and it was news of conflagration
great as that which burned the northern cities

in the Caliphate: this *razón* was Torquemada's song.
Hoc Carmen Audite.
In conspecto tormentorum... (As when Don Rodrigo's daughters

lash and spurs were shown by their own bridegrooms.
When they entered the grove of Corpes
following the two Infantes back to Carrión near Sahagún.

...*bien lo creades*
aqui seredes escarnidas en estos fieros montes.
Oy nos partiremos...

And they knew it for a certainty that they
would be tormented
scourged and shamed and left in that dark place.)

Those abjuring marched with tapers through each town
& wore the sambenito & the yellow robe
embroidered with a black Saint Andrew's cross.

The crier walked before them, crying out
to those who came to watch
the nature of offenses to be punished while

behind them came the paste-board effigies
of those Marranos and Moriscos
who had died of torture, and exhumed bodies

of the heretics dead & buried before Torquemada
reigned at every quemadero:
Hoc Carmen Audite. In conspecto tormentorum....

These we order vicars, rectors, chaplains, sacristans
to treat as excommunicated & accursed for
having now incurred the wrath & indignation of Almighty God

& on these rebels & these disobedient
be all the plagues and maledictions which befell upon
king Pharaoh and his host & may

the excommunication pass to all their progeny.
May they be accursed in eating
& in drinking, in waking and in sleeping,

in coming and in going. Accursed be they
in living & in dying & the devil
be at their right hand; may their days be few

and evil, may their substance pass to others,
may their children all be orphans & widows all their wives.
May usurers take all their goods;

May all their prayers be turned to maledictions;
accursed be their bread and wine,
their meat and fish, their fruit & any food they eat;

the houses they inhabit & the raiment that they wear.
Accursed be they unto Satan
and his fords, & these accompany them both night & day....

But far from Toledo, on the road to Sahagún & Carrión,
they told the tales: tunics of human flesh,
penitential wandering, sparks hereticated, vestures of decay.

They praised the seal of the mouth,
the seal of the belly and the hand; the demiurge
was author of this world;

among the rocks and trees, among the sheep
& cattle, they acknowledged each
the aeon that was only an apparent body, only born

apparently into the pitch and sulphur of a human shape
to utter human words. And the Jews
hid their secret practices, and the Arabs likewise theirs,

and at the ending of the song, as at the very start,
Don Rodrigo asked his king,
earning thus his exile: *Did you kill your brother?*

Did you collude & commit incest with your sister?
For if you did, all your schemes will fail,
even though I lie prostrate before you eating grass. . .

Take this oath upon the iron bolt, upon the crossbow.
Otherwise, may peasants murder you—
Villanos te maten, rey; villanos, que no hidalgos;

even though I lie prostrate before you eating grass. . . .

•

When the singer reached the bridge at Puente la Reina
with the pilgrims who had followed him
for some six hundred years, they met an army:

Soult and Ney & other marshals of Napoleon crossing
into Spain through Roncevaux
and trailing all the engines of their empire. . . .

.... bien lo creades
aquí seredes escarnidas en estos fieros montes.
Oy nos partiremos....

Aoi.
Oit varones una razón.
Aoi.

Hoc Carmen Audite.

V

Soult was at Saldaña on the Carrión
when General Stewart's aide-de-camp walked into Rueda
past the cow-dung fires of peasants

to discover there some eighty horsemen who belonged,
he ascertained, to a division of
Franceski's cavalry. These the light dragoons surrounded

after midnight. General Moore advanced from Salamanca
through Alaejos to Valladolid, & a stolen
sabretache with full intelligence in Marshal Berthier's dispatch

revealed that Junot's infantry had yet to cross the Ebro
and that Ney was still engaged at Saragossa.
On forced march, the British trod December's icy roads

from Toro to Mayorga south of Sahagún.
What pilgrims they became!
Everyone a step-child to some devotee of Sol Invictus,

god of legionaries in whatever expeditionary war,
they billeted beneath the frieze
of Saint María del Camino with its bulls' heads

on abutments of the inner arch, racing horsemen,
and a naked rider on a lion.
They'd drag like Mithra in a week their burdens

down unholy trails and over mountains to the cave
that was Coruña, Exactly where the spears
of Charlemagne's unburied dead had sprouted leaves

along the Cea at the edge of Sahagún, they halted
their advance. By Alfonso's grave,
by the graves of Doña Berta & Constanza, his French queens,

by the ruins of the abbey that had rivaled Cluny
built by Jaca's Englishman
where Aimery Picaud had found unrivalled natural beauty

and a city radiant with grace,
these Englishmen of Sir John Moore's found news:
that Bonaparte himself had crossed the Duoro

and would crush them where they were or drive them
to the sea. They turned and fled;
joined a procession of the living and the dead.

Before them, taurophorus, Mithra dragged the bull,
took its hooves upon his shoulders,
pulling it up mountain trails after Villafranca

in the sleet and snow. Behind them, in his death,
embalmed Rodrigo—tied to beams
that braced him in his saddle, dressed for combat,

sword in hand, looking like some exhumed agent
of the Holy Office driving
heretics to new trans-Cantabrian quemaderos....

. . . tantas lanças premer e alçar,
tanta adágara foradar e passaro... tanta loriga
falssar e desmanchar, tantos pendones

salir vermejos en sangre.... lances, bucklers,
coats of mail broken there,
pennons of the foreign legions soaked in blood...

If Suero de Quiñones read aloud the twenty-two
conditions of the tournament
in which he'd win his ransom at the Orbiego bridge

and then proclaim the Paso Honroso,
who would answer for these blood-shod infantry between
Bembibre and the Cua not *Oit Varones...*

but *Ahora sueña la razón?*
If reason dreamt on this retreat, then so did song.
It slept and dreamed its monsters

in the language of a soldiery that spat and swore
cursing all the bridges
that would measure honor & had measured piety before.

No one shouted *Vivan los Ingleses* as they passed
through villages to loot & rape
where church bells rang when they had gone to summon Soult.

Stragglers broke into bodegas, smashed the wine casks,
then cut up the dying mules & bullocks
by the roadside that had pulled artillery & ammunition vans

to boil them in kettles on great fires they built with gun butts
and mix with what remained of issue brandy,
salted meats and biscuits and the buckets full of melted snow.

Those who dared to sleep were frozen dead by morning,
and when chasseurs came in twos & threes
to scout the strength of Moore's rear guard, they hacked

the arms off those who staggered in the wind
or split their heads down to their chins with sabers flashing
in the sun. All the rest was in the hills.

From Villafranca to Nogales, from
Nogales on through Lugo to Betanzos, darkness fell at noon,
the walls of houses cracked, down

from all the bell towers tumbled bells.
On the march, flames leapt from spears of ash & apple,
hauberks buckled, steel casques burst,

bears and leopards walked among the men
in John Moore's dream. For so he dreamed. Dreamed
within a dream his own high requiem before

the English ships sailed north from Vigo,
their mastheads and their prows decked and lighted
through the night with lamps and rubies

in the story that Trafalgar tells.
Miles, Corax, Heliodromus, Pater of the bas-reliefs,
he signed the zodiac of Mithra's solstice

and hallucinated Corybantes in the skins of beasts
and flagellants where General Paget
sought to make example of deserters and had lashed

at stunted icy trees men who'd
hidden in the windowless dark huts with sick & filthy
mountaineers and who, blinded by the days

of snow, could only hear what would accompany
their punishment: a jangling
of the manacles and fetters hanging on the branded

criminals who crawled the road before them
on their hands and knees and slept
with lepers under dark façades of abbeys, while

in Bonaparte's Madrid, El Sordo painted bulls.
Bulls and bodies of the slain—
dismembered and hung up on trees like ornaments:

arms and legs, heads with genitals stuffed
in their mouths, torsos
cut off at the waist and neck and shoulders.

These the *deformis formositas ac formosa deformitas*
of the hour—torsos and toros,
packed in ice, delivered down the trails to Picasso

in a year when internationals once more decamp in Spain....
Viva la Muerte's the Falangist song.
Lorca's murdered; Machado & Vallejo promptly die.

Trusting neither Mithra nor St. James, his eye
on anarchists in Barcelona,
Franco summons mercenary Moors to save the church.

VI

In the high places, they could hear the blast.
Ships rocked on the sea,
the houses at Coruña shook on their foundations

when the ammunition stores were blown.
At Santiago, bells that had burned Almanzor's oils
rang from the shock of it while men

whose job it was to ring them stood
amazed out in the square & wondered if this thunder
and the ringing was in time for Vespers

or for Nones or if it was entirely out of time.
The thunder and the ringing echoed
down the trails, back to San Millán, San Juan de la Peña,

while Maragatos looked up from their plows
and Basque shepherds among flocks near Roncevaux
turned their backs on the west & hunched

down under tall protective rocks jutting up
in frosty and transhumant fields.
Then in the high & highest places everything was still.

As it was in the beginning. Before Saint Francis
came down from the hills to Rocaforte,
before he taught his brothers how to preach & sing the word

to their little sister birds who flew into the tallest trees
and over cliffs in threefold
colored and adoring coats; before the Logos

or the Duende moved in Bertsulari singing ancient
fueros of the Basques; before Ignatius
hammered out his disciplines among the mountain rocks

breaking on the igneous of will the *ignis fatuus*
of valleys & the vagaries of love.
As it was in the beginning....

                        Long before *it is*
and ever shall be under overhanging
rocks at San Juan de la Peña... where they say, they *say*

the Grail came to rest and made a fortress
of the monastery there carved beneath a cliff-face roof
where dowsers conjured water out of rock

in Mithra's Visigothic cave & his tauroctonous priest
drove the killing sword, like Manolete,
in the shoulder of the bellowing great beast

to burst its heart & bleed the plants & herbs across
the mountainside that monks would one day
gather there, bleed the wheat they'd make into their bread.

Everything, everything was still. As it was in the beginning
long before the silence of the abbeys,
the silence of the abbots in their solitary prayer,

the silence of the brothers cutting hay & tending sheep
at San Millán of the Cowl,
the silent sacristan measuring and pouring oils—

the weavers and the tailors and the copyists at work,
Cellarius among his stores of wool and flax,
Hortulanus in his garden tending bees—silence broken only

as Hebdomadarius, finished with the cooking, rings a bell
and even old Gonzalo de Berceo looks up happily
from silent pages where his saint has walked the mountains

in the language of Castilian *juglares* which is not,
God knows, the language of the Latin clerks. *Andaba por los montes,*
por los fuertes lugares, por las cuestas enhiestas,

but silently, and all around him it was very very still.
As it was in the beginning before silence,
in the silence that preceded silence, in the stillness

before anything was still, when nothing
made a single sound and singularity was only nothing's
song unsinging... aphonia

before a whisper or a breath, aphasia
before injury,
aphelion of outcry without sun...

                              Long before *it is*
and ever shall be under overhanging
rocks at San Juan de la Peña, at San Millán of the Cowl,

at Loyola's Casa-Torre and the shepherds' huts
of Bertsulari in the Pyrenees
when no one spoke of *fueros* or *tristitia* or *spes,*

and there were neither rights nor hopes nor
sadnesses to speak of.
Then in the high and highest places everything was still.

As it was in the beginning. As it will be in the end.

      •

Towards Pamplona, long long after all Navarre
was Spain, and after the end
of the Kingdom of Aragón, & after the end of the end,

I, John, walked with my wife Diana
down from the Somport Pass following the silence
that invited and received my song

after Europe's latest referendum. In the city of the *encierro* and the
festival of San Fermín, we drank red wines of the Ribera—Baja Montana,
Tierra Estella—hosted by Delgado-Gómez, genius of that place and
guide Picaud. From university to citadel to bull ring, from cathedral to the
Plaza del Castillo and along the high banks of the Arga, we walked and
talked about the road to Santiago, El Cid Campeador, Zumalacárregui
and Carlist wars. For he, Delgado-Gómez, was a native of that place. He
knew the way to San Juan de la Peña, to Leyre and Olite and Sanguessa
—and so we followed him along the river valleys, into hills, and over arid
plains in the Bardenas. And after seven days and seven nights remembering
the likes of Sancho the Wise and Sancho the Strong, the battle of Navas
de Tolosa and the chains of Miramamolín wrapped around a coat of arms,
the three of us, blest and besotted, burned by the sun but refreshed by all
the waters of the mountain streams, the shade of many cloisters, and the
breezes of the vineyards of Mañeru, crossed the Puente la Reina ourselves,
and walked that trail leading to the sea at Finisterre.

And, in the high & highest places, everything was still.

Cuttings

sail archangel agrimony avens
broom & burdock

eyebright fumitory meadow sweet
so the mountain flax & mugwort so the sanicle

and all indigenous medicinals be meet

elsewhere also sail & what's the use
& where's the hemlock woodsage yarrow find

some bird of paradise

& what's archangel agrimony avens to
strelitzia reginae

la triomphe royale la majestieuse

cuttings & endeavors & a mezzotint
record a bank & there the wild thyme blows

& oxlips & the nodding violet grows

I

Five Cuttings with Endeavors
& Repeated Incantation

1 John Tradescant

Robert Cecil's man became the Duke of Buckingham's
became the King's. Dudley Digges took
him to Archangel.
Later the Algerians who followed
Barbarossa led him to the lilac and narcissus fields
and granted him a vision of the coming
of the sons of Joseph Banks.

What land was promised? What pomp
would suit their circumstances when they brought
the seeds and seedlings for the King?

       *

O *Bird of Paradise—Strelitzia Reginae, Lord!—*
Chincherinchee. Chincherinchee.
Ixia viridiflora! Ixia cinnamomea, too!

Endeavors

The transit of Venus. Tupia. The love
of nut-brown maids. They'd reached Tahiti
and begun to feed on bread-plants.
All of them a-tupping went
except for Parkinson, the Quaker
with the keen eye and the cautious morals.
Specimens were pressed between
the proof sheets of a job lot ream of Addison—
his commentary on *Paradise Lost*.
Banks gave all the chiefs the names he thought
would suit them—Ajax, Hercules, Lycurgus.
In his journal, Parkinson complained
that Mr. *Monks and Mr. Banks*
came to an éclaircissement and nearly dueled.
All for favors of Othea Thea.
Of Tupia, Banks told Captain *Cook—I'll keep*
him as a curiosity like neighbors
back in England keep their lions.

Venus made her transit. Officially observed.
Mr. Green packed up his quadrant
and the botanists their specimens and
watercolors of the flora, fish, and dancing girls,
the shoreline profiles & the long canoes.
A month surveying Huahine, Tahaa, Raiatea
left them open sea and just a crescent
on the Tasman chart of 1642 that might be
Tara Australis and landfall or might not.
Banks made inventory of the sheep and fowls,
the south sea hogs, the boar & sow & litter,
bins of sauerkraut to stave off scurvy.
In his journal Parkinson observed the
water within reefs... *seagreen breakers white*
in many bays all stript & streakt with purple
by an intervention of the cloud between
the sun and surface... cat's paws if a wind
comes up on swells & it is calm...
Sea so like some foreign thing in flower.

2 Francis Masson

The Hottentots had fallen in the hippo pools
and Francis Masson, botanizing out of Cape Town
on his way to river Olyfont, wrote it in his diary.
Also this: *I myself have nearly drowned.*

The African geranium would find its way to Yorkshire—
the tritonias, gladioli, & the ancestors of bulbs
that Mrs. Boden-Smith planted in her window box last fall.
Boers supplied the the cannabis. He'd forded Duvvenhoek

and headed for the hills in pouring rain.

> *

Mesembryanthemum.
Crassula and cotyledon and
euphorbia!
          Euphoria had seized him

as he found them all along the Little Cape Karoo known
as Canaan's Land. Then came collywobbles
from a collop of bad beef he'd barbecued.
Mum was the word
as he crossed Van Stadaaens,
noting in his diary the vast and grazing herds
of buffalo.

Endeavors

Fifty-seven days they climbed the swells
heaving in from West South West.
Pintados passed, an albatross. Eventually
a sailor spotted seaweed clinging to
a piece of wood. Cook observed two seals.
Twice, a morning fogbank brought
the shout of land; then they saw New Zealand.

Everything was strange: hostile Maoris with
their curling black tattoos who ate
their captives boiled in a pot with dogs;
forget-me-nots with leaves the size
of rhubarb; arborescent lilies; daisies growing
to the height of trees....

                      Tupia, who
got the gist of native speech, explained
that Maoris who appeared in a canoe
were selling those four severed heads
they held up by the hair. Banks
arranged a trade for one—they took some
iron and beads—and put it
in his sea chest wrapped in flax.

3 Allan Cunningham

And Allan Cunningham wrote at once
to Kew: *we put in at the south shore*
of Endeavour—just where you yourself & Cook
first came....
                    We too were attacked—with spears
and clubs and boomerangs—but managed to fight off
the Aboriginals with musketry.

How much pleasure we derived in tracing your own steps
and those of Dr. Solander, finding on the
surface and the muddy shaded edge of lowland ponds
the ornamental Melastoma banksii....

     *

Australia. The Melastoma named for Banks himself,
the river for the ship of Captain Cook.

They found the ruined *Frederick*, washed up on
the rocks a year before. They found
a pile of coal collected on the beach by Banks'

own men. It kept them warm through one cold night.
Meanwhile, off the archipelago called
Buccaneer for William Dampier the pirate,

corals grew and twisted
with the patience of an anthozoan's dream time.

Endeavors

Flax and pine would one day mark endeavors
of another kind—Pitt's advisors measuring
the hawsers, canvas, sailcloth and cordage
in their minds, staring up at the imagined pines
that rose a hundred feet in forests full of
mainmasts, spars and jib booms where they'd
spread the sails that would rule the waves.
New Zealand flax; Norfolk Island pine.
And some armed haven not far off where soldiers
could protect refitting ships and where, perhaps,
transplanted felons might take root and bloom.

All these London musings ten years off as Banks
wrapped up his severed Maori head
and Cook, beyond the trade winds, sailed west
hoping for a landfall indicated by the scrap
on Tasman's chart. South winds drove him northward
and in April Parkinson could draw the mouth
of what they first called Sting Ray Bay
and later Botany....

4 Robert Fortune

He'd shaved his head and made
himself a pigtail, passing as Chinese at Shoo-chow-foo.
Not a single local called him *Kwei-tsz*—
Child of a foreign devil out for trade.

His instructions had been plain:
Find the two-pound peaches of Pekin.
Find the place where *Enkianthus* shrubs grow wild.
Find the double yellow rose
the plant to make rice paper
all bamboos of every kind the lilies
Chinese eat like boiled chestnuts
bright blue peonies
azaleas from Ho-fou-shau,

*

He hadn't known about Jan-dous who
tried to board his junk while sailing to Chu-shan,
but nonetheless he blew the helmsman off the stern
with just one pistol shot and left
the pirate ship with flapping sails.
He'd bring *Anemone japonica* to Chiswick—
make it flower better than on ramparts of Shanghai.

*

In his luggage—
stones from two enormous peaches
Enkianthus shrubs
bamboos lilies peonies azaleas and one
thin pigtail he'd cut off
when boarding ship at last for home.

Endeavors

Parkinson drew more:—

giant heaths, acacias, flame trees, firs &
honeysuckles, amaryllis, lilies, yellow fronds of wattle,
bright waratah, eucalyptus, scarlet stamens of
the callistemons, grass blades rising up to fourteen feet—
then the frantic cockatoos and parrots flying
all around and calling out, the bear-like wombats
peering from their holes.... Banks rowed in to shore
with stacks of drying paper
that he'd quire and spread on sails
in the morning sun.

Cut and save, he'd cut and dry and save.
Everything must get intact to Kew—
fern leaves equally with wallabies and
severed heads and most especially Tupia himself,
his savage prince; he'd take that kangaroo the sailor shot
to London taxidermists, then go lug it off
to Mr. Stubbs who'd hang it from a meat hook,
who'd paint it like a horse. Pull up all the
green things by the roots, draw and quarter, touch
and smell and dry, press
all things of colour into quires & look for more.

5 Richard Spruce

He was a man for mosses and the liverworts.
The sedge he found—*Carex Paradoxa*—had been
walked all over by the English for a thousand years.
But he would name the thing. He'd let them know
the lowly flora would no longer be anonymous.

    *

If asked to leave, he'd go—
A man for Yurimaguas when he got the chance.
And for the English he'd describe
enormous trees crawling with fantastic parasites
& hung all over with lianas python-like
and twisted with the fine regularity of cable.
Grasses were bamboos of sixty feet.
Violets the size of apple trees.

    *

Yellow psittacanthi flowers made
the pampas smell like honeysuckle after rain.
A man for the chinchona seeds and barks,
he'd grind the powders for malaria and
send his trees beyond the taint of any Popery
to India or else Sri Lanka. A man
in his canoe well up the Bombanaza in the Andes,
he met the local governor at Paca-Yacu.
No, he said, his name
was not Pizarro the Conquistador.

Guayaquil: he came there with a hundred thousand seeds.

Endeavors

Those impressed by these endeavors choired elsewhere
at the given sign and Englishmen returned
to New South Wales with craftsmen, surgeon, chaplain & marines—
with convicts gazing from the decks of *Sirius*
as captain Arthur Phillip anchored in the bay.

The leadsman had sung Cook & Banks beyond the reef
but half the crew then died of tertian fever in Batavia
and no one ever made a mast of Norfolk Island pine
or mainsails of New Zealand flax.

Died Tupia
Tayeto Monkhouse
Reynolds Corporal Truelove
Parkinson & Green
Died Moody
Haite
Thompson Jordan Nicholson & Woolf.

As Banks and Cook sailed on with specimens
and souvenirs, the Aboriginal *Goodriddance*
spelled its fond farewell more crudely
than the Latin of Linnaeus:
Vale vir sine pare: O Farewell unequaled man.

They threw their excrement at the *Endeavour's* wake.

*

O Bird of Paradise—Strelitzia Reginae, Lord!—
Chincherinchee. Chincherinchee.
Ixia viridiflora! Ixia cinnamomea, too!

II

As Kew As You

Francis Masson in Karroo and climbing Bokkeveld
to find the *aloe dichotoma* (Dutchman's Koker Boom) of which
the Hottentots (he notes it in his diary) make quivers—
and old Mr. Frame the famous footpad still out in the sun
to take his beer at Kew whose gang might top a Florizel
outside the Drury Lane but let a thousand flowers bloom
along the green. Came Mr. David Nelson home that year
with news of Cook's dead jackknife in Hawaiian surf
came *Winter's Tale* in summer and young Perdita
the actress Mrs. Mary Robinson to fuck the Prince of Wales
for twenty thousand pounds. Lord Malden waved a handkerchief
to light the inn situated then out on the ait at Brentford.
William Aiton took the pleasure ground and measured it
for madness. Fanny Burney would attend the Queen.

Well before that measure pleasured well the footpad Frame
well both Perdita & Florizel a thousand flowers blooming there
when Cook still sailed and *aloe dichotoma* hid in Bokkeveld
the Hottentots made quivers and the consort patiently awaited
her *Strelitzia* her pretty bird of paradise and Albion especially
all the daughters fair of that same isle Professor Martyn's book:
they'd see he'd say at all times study nature & the taste of frivolous
amusements will abate it shall prevent the tumult & the passion
shall provide the mind with nourishments & all things salutary
filling it with noble objects worthy of its contemplation summer's
winter's tale will nonetheless be told dead jackknife Cook
come home a corpse the heir apparent flash a swollen stamen
from behind Lord Malden's handkerchief in androecium
and Fanny Burney to attend the scene... The Queen that is

no harlot nay née Charlotte Sophia of Mecklenburg-Strelitz
whose drawing-master Francis Bauer taught the ladies of
the court their parts said tip it rarely that ellipse in selfsame plane
with floret rays concavity available through all degrees
until the horizontal when your form is discoid then convex:
repeat it carpel carpellate & column innocent enough but gynoecium
with pistil pencil in and paint. Alarmed past all expression
she ran straight off with all her might but then her terror was to hear
herself pursued to hear the croaking voice of the King himself
all loud & hoarse and calling after her Miss Burney all she knew
was that the orders were to keep out of his way the garden full
of little labyrinths by which she might escape the taste of
frivolous amusements will abate it shall prevent the tumult
passion & provide for Mr. Frame the footpad in the summer sun.

No statue of Aspacia or Asoka there to hide behind she looked
askance aslant the sleeping Frame askew at such asperity
and asked him sir which herbals would be hermeneutic which ellipse
of rays medicinal although you wouldn't physically consume
an illustration of the aster for astasia. Astarte then. Austere the stare
of Reverend Mason his epistle to Sir William Chambers verses
versus Capability he'd seen untutor'd Brown destroy those wonders
from his melon ground the peasant slave had rudely rushed and
level'd Merlin's Cave knocked down the waxen wizard seized
his wand transformed to lawns what late was fairy land & marred
with impious hand each sweet design where Fanny Burney ran and
floret rays turned up at all degrees until the horizontal where the forms
became all discoid then convex the ladies sang out carpel carpellate
and column drank their gin and peered at one another's gynoecium.

West Indian planters' slaves consumed their weight in plantains why
not breadfruits from Tahiti why not send out Bligh once more
for bounty send out one more poor landlubbing botanist from Kew
to pot those plants and float a greenhouse-full some thousand miles
if convicts trod down cotyledons off in Banks' own bay conviction
had it Empire might be served by Spain's merinos bleating there by Hove
returning via Cape Town from Bombay where Francis Masson doubtless
would pass on some seed some sample of his findings old John Smeaton's
pumping engine working with an Archimedes screw some twenty-four feet
long and turned by plodding horses irrigated white house garden nicely
raising fifteen hundred hogsheads in an hour he said she said he heard
somebody say and read on in her book how there beside the Thames
sat all enthroned in vegetative pride to whom obedient sails from realms
unfurrowed brought the unnamed progeny of which she thought.

They'd name that progeny and paint it in their books who rubbed
their pates with salad oil and chased away the rooks instructing
royal nymphs fair as the Oread race who trod Europa's brink to snatch
from wreck of time each fleeting grace. Said Mr. Bauer there's not a plant
at Kew has not been drawn by you or someone of your household with
a skill reflecting on your personage but still I humbly beg you to observe
a tendency to slight the curve in stems misrepresent in leaves the midrib
where the veins must spring commit an error in perspective due to inattention
place the primrose polyanthus oxlip all of those so elementary forms right
down upon their peduncles with dislocated necks prolong a bit the stalk
or axis through the flower to the center whence the petals or divisions
may be made to radiate correctly & beyond a doubt she saw merinos that
the king had bred with convicts copulating in a bed of hyacinths
somewhere it was in lines inebriate divines had drawn or written there

or in that muck composed by Chatterton or Stephen Duck: Kew!
a happy subject for a lengthened lay though thousands write
there's something more to say thy garden's elegance thy owner's state
the highest in the present list of fate O Kew thou darling of the
tuneful nine thou eating house of verse where poets dine she drew
as best she could when Bauer asked her to respect the flower's arts
upon dissection note the size of stamens if betwixt or opposite corolla
parts and draw a line from base of filament to cleft and not regard
as trifling equanimity achieved by deftly gazing long at dried labellum
sepal stalk & style he cried for every flower blooming millions you
will understand have died a turretted and loopholed folly will be built
this very year when Captain Flinders sails out with orders straight
from Banks again to New South Wales he'll take my brother Ferdinand
along to draw those plants and animals Sir Joseph never saw.

Ah what invention graced the strain well might the laureate bard
be vain in praise of Masson in Karoo Professor Martyn's book on Kew
whose groves however misapplied to serve a prince's lust and pride
were by the Monarch's care designed a place of pleasure for the mind
they sang together everyone who came to view that progeny sent back
to Kew from realms unfurrowed as the poet wrote on every sort of
frigate still afloat and Bauer took them one by one like maidens who
had been undone and spread their perianths apart to draw with all the
art he'd teach the daughters of the queen who gazed upon such colours
none of them had seen. Delineations of exotic plants and illustrations
orchidaceous taught a zygomorphic flowering flamboyant forms that
only had a precedent in certain iris norms in drawing monkey lizard bee
or spider orchid try to see the shape that looks familiar it's no jape
to say go draw a zygomorph as if it were a vegetating ape.....

As Kew as you he heard somebody say who hid behind a bush upon
a lawn where late untutored Brown had rudely rushed and levelled
Merlin's Cave knocked down the waxen wizard seized his wand
Aspacia nor Asoka ever looked upon. As Kew as you repeated many times
the king and consort poets and divines a drawing master Perdita
the Prince of Wales those friends of Mr. Frame still languishing in jails
and those just back from Cape Town or Bombay as Kew as you
the hours that every day the sundials clocked along the garden walk
where Fanny Burney liked to sit and talk or write down in her book
as Kew as you would caw the captain's rook advancing on a bishop
over board at sea en route to bring back yet more loot and plants named
for the Englishmen who sought them out as Kew as you for botanists
to tout & draw transplant dissect in all the ways Sir Joseph would direct
as Kew as you... he'd tell them every one exactly what to do.

III

Further Cuttings with Endeavors
& Repeated Incantation

1 Humea Elegans

Desirable for fragrance. Straight from New South Wales.
The Lady Hume had several from those seeds communicated
by Sir Joseph Banks. Wormleybury, Herts.
Partakes in panicle the odour of the Hautboy, flowers
by July. The stem herbaceous, round, and filled
with spongy pith, pubescence.
Leaves are sessile, lanceolate, acute, and slightly
waved about the edge. Receptacle is small and glandular,
all destitute of scales. Florets fertile, regular.
Oblong germen cloven style and stigmas spreading,
capitate. Seed without a crown without a wing.

*

Place it in the old Linnaean book beside the *Eupatorium*.
Genus undetermined until summer of '04.
Calyx loosely imbricated. Antheras is awned.

Endeavors

Goethe was impressed: he found the
plates he gazed at more exacting than
his old florilegium. These German Bauers
working off in England aimed at more
than pleasing royal patrons with the bright
and beautiful—they'd draw with great affection
even ugly weeds: also palmates & the white
clusters tinged with red and brown of an
Aesculus hippocastanum—Stubby tree he'd
drawn himself whose flower he had
pressed between the pages of a *Faust,*
whose two spiked pods he'd left in sunlight
at the corner of his botanizing desk.
The grading of these tones. These discs & cones.
This book in which all nature was made visible
and art was all concealed...

His drawing, he would tell you, was today
more efficacious than his word. Still, he'd
premise his endeavors under headings
stem and *leaf* and *flower* and set you straight
about your task & his:—However short, there's
always some degree of curve in stems, and
therefore you must never use a rule; practice
at your stroke and learn to draw the parallels;
then mark off the springs of every lamina.
Blades are more or less erect and you must
draw the opposites a bit awry, and if
the stem is branched then certain leaves of course
must be foreshortened. In digitates you indicate
the petiole and midribs first to orient with
greater certainty the relative anatomies;
teeth of calyx always point between divisions
of corolla. Discriminate between a keel & wing.
And to avoid the common error perpetrated
on the flower making it put on a comic air
by twisting it upon its stalk, observe with

fierce exactitude and cultivate an equanimity.
There is no other cluster like the one you've pressed
into your book. Seed pods open.
Chestnuts. Dark eyes & a Mephistophelian look.

2 Rhododendron Arboreum

Flowers late in May or early June, provincial
name is *Boorans*. The stem is columnar,
twenty feet in height, more than twenty inches
in diameter. Branches are ascending, scattered,

crooked, brittle; leaves at summits on their downy
footstalks all are ovate-lanceolate, acute,
all entire and revolute; smooth & shining green above,
clothed beneath with white dense downiness.

                    *

Clusters terminal of
ten to fifteen large pedunculated crimson flowers
spread in all directions!

                    Bracteas very small...

Calyx permanent, obtuse, and reddish at the edge;
Corolla with a longish bell-shaped tube
and lobes all cloven, rounded.

Stamens, ten: declining, smooth, inserted in receptacle.
Antheras incumbent, germen white,
seeds ovate compressed and smooth and brown

and brought to our attention thanks to Captain Hardwich
from a tour in Hindoostan—
85 degrees east longitude in the Sewalic chain.

Endeavors

And Jean-Jacques Rousseau had thrown a turnip
in the face of David Hume. It made him
feel at peace, just the way that he had felt before
the Calvinists expelled him from Geneva.

Happiness had been beyond the instigators
of a lapidation that had sent him first with
gilded papers to enfold each grass and moss
and lichen on the Island of St. Peters, then
with Hume and Boswell on to Staffordshire
as refugee where there among the rocks
and sheep and rabbits he complained that he
could find no trace of scordium and had been
stoned by Hume's appalling outcry in his sleep
when they had shared a room in Roye:
Je tiens Jean-Jacques Rousseau!

Lapwings from Laputa swarmed upon him
in the Wooton fields, the meadows of Dove Dale.
The stigma was the apex of his pistil
and he'd pollinate unless he drew a breath
into his spiracle, unless he saw the eyespot there
among the algae. Insect. Eyesore. Everyone
should march along a stipule who couldn't
stipulate for any decent stipend for philosophy!
He waited for stigmata to appear. He purged
himself with tamarinds and senna, jalop
and a dash of scammony. He'd make their
lapidation lapidary, cast his own heraldic stone,
mix the henbane in the English herbal's ink.

The turnip was enough.... Relieved, insane,
endeavoring to float at peace upon his prose
as once he floated on his back across the waters
of St. Peter's lake, he wrote epistles to his
cousin & her daughter. *When the rays of spring
reveal in your garden hyacinths & tulips,*

jonquils & the lilies-of-the-valley, notice that the
cabbages and cole-feed, radishes and turnips
also will appear....
              When you find them double,
do not meddle with them for they are deformed;
nature cannot any longer live among the monsters and
the mutilated, cannot say as she was wont to say
even in the days of lapidation

Je tiens Jean-Jacques Rousseau!

3 Mirabilis Longiflora

There is no colored figure of this long-flowered
Marvel of Peru: Linnaeus notes that
pollen of this plant is very large and globular and
very yellow too and hanging by a little thread
and neither falling off or bursting....

The corolla presses it to stigma while the papillae
attach themselves to particles of
pollen and imbibe....
                              If raised on a hotbed like
a tender kind of annual, it blooms
in the autumn in a copious succession of rare flowers...

sessile at the top of every branch
and downy and extremely viscid of exterior.

    *

Seeds procured by some astronomers who knew
the celebrated M. le Monnier? Hence to Baron Münchausen
and Stockholm and to Miller's Chelsea garden and a note
in both the *Dictionary* and *Transactions*.

Stem is four feet high & forked, spreading, round & downy.
Limb is white and plaited with its five
external folds and an orifice of stunning royal purple.

Stigma large and globular and with a tuft of hairs.

Stamens are like long and silky threads.
One large tessellated nut
that's farinaceous and succeeds each flower.

Endeavors

Munificence! said Dr. Robert Thornton, bowing at
the Russian's happy approbation of his work.
Alexander, Emperor and Tzar, had smiled on La Majestieuse
engraved at great expense from a painting made for
Flora's very Temple, Thornton's book, illustrated by the
author's tables and dissections, but also by the plates
that pandered to a rage for Picturesque: like Thornton's prose,
the page *majestically presented finely-polished*
bosoms to enquiring eyes.

Utile and *Dulce,* he'd insisted on them both.
Or *Dulce* first, then *Utile.* In some proportion anyway,
and no generic backgrounds for the men
to whom the likes of Mrs. Siddons sat, who was no more
than Dr. Johnson competition for a Nodding Renealmia
or Pontic Rhododendron: *no avenues of upright timber,*
gravel walks that meet by some small pond or
commonplace cascade, but scenery appropriate indeed
appropriated, brought up with the roots—

The serious roots, e.g., of Night-blowing Cereus:
Moonlight Pether's moon was told to play
on dimpled water and the Gothic turret clock *to point*
at twelve, midnight hour that finds this candle
light of orange petals at its full expanse;
Of Mimosa Grandiflora too: and Mr. Reinagle
was asked to paint *two humming birds from*
mountains in Jamaica & an aborigine who waxes all
astonished at their stationary hovering all over & about.

Dodecatheon in the Warner aquatint was blown like
Yankee Cowslip in a *gentle breeze* required also
to fill out the sails of a ship that flies the ensign
of our former colonies and waft around the specimen
indigenous and delicate bright butterflies.
Too much of something here. Or maybe not enough.
At any rate, the public did not buy. Back in Moscow

his Munificence was busy with Napoleon at the very
moment when the project needed something of a boost.

The tulips named for Earl Spencer and a duchess who
had promised patronage suddenly looked dour
and frankly parsimonious beside the open petals of
Le Roy, La Majestieuse, and La Triomphe Royale
in Earlem's greatest mezzotint. Thornton raged against
infuriate war which like devouring conflagration feasts
on commerce, agriculture and the arts, the sanguine theatre
in which the armed diffuse all rapine fire & murder and
because of which the rich are taxed beyond philanthropy.

He gazed on purple Dragon Arum and he wrote:
This foetid poisonous plant! She comes all peeping
from her purple crest with mischief fraught.
A noisome vapour issues from her nostrils and infects
the ambient air; her hundred arms are interspersed
with white as in the garments of the inquisition.
From her covert there projects a spear of darkest jet;
her sex is strangely intermingled with the opposite.
Confusion dire! Her friend is Maggot-bearing Stapelia.

I am undone by what my eyes & hands have wrought!

4 Cyamus Nelumbo

Native of the silent pools, recesses, and margins
of the running streams. Will take root in deep
and muddy soil. *Tamara* or *Lotus* or *Nelumbo* :—
see the sacred poetry of Hindus. Many prohibitions
from Pythagoras to the Egyptian priests.

Root is large & tuberous, black without & white within,
growing fibres numerous & long. Leaves are radical
on long and round and prickly upright stalks;
peltate, circular, and waved; rather glaucous
and with many radiating ribs.
Young, they float upon the quiet water.
Flowers on the simple naked stalks like those of leaves,
but taller, solitary, upright, fragrant, fine.

*

Calyx, four or five green concave ovate leaves.
Many petals, ovate & acute, a pale rose and marked
with many crimson ribs which, drawn together as they reach
the point, deepen in their hue. Many stamens, yellow
knobbed with oblong anthers. Germen green and smooth
and conical, its upper surface perforated with the holes
that open into many cells. Every cell contains the rudiment
of seed, protruding through the orifice & crowned
with oblong and obtuse and perforated yellow stigma.

*

All of this becomes a coriaceous capsule, breaks off
from the stalk all laden with its oval nuts, and floats on
down the water as a cornucopia of sprouting plants.
As all Pythagorean prohibitions now are obsolete,
perhaps these beans, imported from East Indies, may
one day be welcome on our tables as a wholesome dish.

Made to flower in the Duke of Portland's stove.

Endeavors

Although apocrypha would plant his pizzle
in the garden like a tulip bulb, the truth is that
the flower Bonaparte was known to favor
was the violet. There on Elba. Even on St. Helena.
And to the utter consternation of the English.
While the amputated bulb of his virility blossomed
in a thousand tales, the violet, much relieved,
returned to little hamlets and the village greens
in England. Sedition was no longer toasted in
the name of Corporal V or conspiracy acknowledged
Elle reparaîtra au Printemps. March violet, dog violet,
yellow violet, heart's ease: *And there is pansies,*
that's for thoughts. Who'd go a-mothering and find
the violets in the lane? Who'd strew a path to the altar,
mark a page in the book? Beyond the sickbed swelled
the purple fields. Lovers would lie down in them
and slowly braid their amulets and charms.

In 1821, the final year when Bonaparte could hope
to reappear *au Printemps,* Goethe published his objections
to the "loose concupiscence" and "constant orgies"
of the stamens & the pistils taking place among Linnaeans
who refused to propagate by morphogenesis,
and violets bloomed on every bank. Among the snow drops,
primroses, arum & anemones that marked the spring,
not a single violet grew Napoleonic;
they spread all over England as they always had.
They spread through the counties, spread through
the years, Diana raising them from Io's body
for the Father of the Gods—& also for the Slade Professor
John Ruskin who went out into his Brantwood garden
looking for a specimen in 1881.
The clump he pulled out with an angry fist
reminded him of Effie's pubic hair.

Which had annoyed him like all the prurient obscenities
that Goethe had attacked in the Linnaeans.

He wouldn't draw these flowers even for his book.
He'd rather have old Bony back.
He'd rather have his wife's pudenda smooth as petals
on a Canna Lily, hairless as a billiard ball.
He'd have her like the nine year old Miss Rose La Touche.
He wrote in *Proserpina* that *disorderly & lanky, stiff*
and springless stalks were bent in crabbed & broken
ways like spikes run up from some iron-foundry
for a vulgar railway station or like angular & dog-eared
gaspipes with their ill-hemmed leaves.
He'd have it out, he'd be entirely rid of it.
No one in the world could want to draw this clump
of flowers, *mixed together, crumpled,*
hacked about as if some cow had chewed on them
and left them tough and bitter, bad.

And she had left him years before, the marriage
quietly annulled by reason of their failure to consummate.
And Rose La Touche had died quite mad.
He was relieved, he was distraught.
He had endeavored to instruct his wife about—
it did not matter, for she would not learn.
Now he'd teach the English nation how to draw their flowers,
the English workingmen about the *Fors Clavigera.*
But there was Effie in Millais' *The Order of Release*
where every stranger in the gallery could see.
He felt imprisoned still. His stamen never
touched her pistil once. He held it in his hand
among the violets & felt like Bonaparte at Austerlitz.
Elle reparaîtra au Printemps!

5 *Ipomopsis Elegans*

Dillenius said Catesby found this plant
a hundred miles from Charlestown in South Carolina.
It grows in sandy places, flowering in June.
Very difficult of cultivation for we found that
only one in twenty Catesby seeds have vegetated.

A fine drawing by the late and friendly gifted sister
of our good acquaintance Mr. Lee is in the hands
we understand of the Marquis of Blandford.
We have also seen an imitation cut in coloured paper
in possession of the Lady Banks.

      *

Much uncertainty about the genus. The learned Jussieu
supposed it might be readily reduced to his *Cantua;*
but Michaux in regarding it as something new because of
membranes in the calyx is correct. And so we take his name
which will express this flower's dazzling brilliancy.

      *

Stem is straight and wand-like to the height of several feet
where it is panicled. Leaves pinnatifid with long
and narrow segments; radicals the shortest and the broadest.

Flowers terminal and lateral appearing on short stalks
and drooping down. Calyx bell-shaped, cut above half-way
in awl-like equal parts; corolla thrice the length and

funnel-shaped, its border cleft in five and brilliant red,
Stamens springing from the upper part of tube.
Antheras is round and yellow, germen ovate smooth obtuse

and pale green. Style red and thread-like, length about the
same as stamens, with a red & three-cleft spreading stigma.
Seeds are several in each cell, acutely angular, not winged.

Endeavors

To map, to classify. And that these two endeavors
are the same. Or similar. And to collect.
A kind of madness or a kindness of the sane.
And then to draw and paint what has been
mapped and classified. Why not.
And to admire that. Or not. And pay for it,
or even make it pay. Where two such endeavors are
the same, is Shelley's Lady ever present there.

In the garden there are many houses. Shall
the husbands leave them and take ship, and shall
the wives become dependent on the bees. For there
are eunuch houses where the anthers have departed
and the stamens walk a pitching deck like Captain Cook.
In what far sea. And in what key to shanty
their polygamous designs. A few hermaphrodites
were left behind when John Paxton read into the night

at Chatsworth gardens to his duke. It was a poem
in which a garden dies because some kind
of grace has been withdrawn. The Duke of Devonshire
himself was called Your Grace and thought his great
Conservatory very heaven. He'd sent his agent off
to Chirrapoonje in the Khasi hills to bring him
Amherstia nobilis for his house of glass. And he had
brought her there. He'd classified and mapped.

He'd found his way by water to Chhatak, down
the Surma River where entire trees were covered in the
epiphytes all listed in the EIC's Calcutta book, and
he had nursed, like Buddha's monks at monasteries,
tribute of a blood-red flower paid by Chirrapoonje
in the Khasi hills to Chatsworth garden and its duke
who gazed upon it while his gardener read,
sitting by his side, & while a gaudy garden died.

A Lady—the wonder of her kind, whose form was upborn
by a lovely mind, tended the garden in the poem he read.
She did not map or classify. She sprinkled water from a stream.
The duke had sent his husbands pitching on a deck.
They sang their shanties in an unknown key. The wives
became dependent on the bees while Paxton read his Shelley.
The epiphytes were listed in the book the EIC had nursed.
The duke's *Amherstia* had been acknowledged as the first

to grow in England. Never mind. Or mind. Who'd classify
and map. Who'd say that two endeavors were the same.
Who'd read aloud while Chirrapoonje drowned and grace
collected in monsoons above the Khasi hills where no one
painted and where no one drew. The duke had drawn
his household to his side to watch him sitting by his flower
while Paxton read from Shelley's poem and epiphytes grew
up Calcutta trees. The Lady sprinkled water on hermaphrodites

and spoke of no polygamous designs. The duke had asked
John Paxton for this poem. He'd sent his agent off to
Chirrapoonje in the Khasi hills; bee and mayfly kissed
the sweet lips of his flower where sanity is madness
of the kind. O Kin, the Lady was without companions
of the mortal race and yet it was as if some spirit had deserted
paradise and lingered with her there, a veil of daylight quite
concealing it from her. Or him, the duke. Who cares.

The gardener who read the poem. But no one off in
Chirrapoonje in the Khasi hills where stamens braced against
monsoons and anthers broke off in the storm. The nullas filled;
the pools flowed; the Brahmaputra delta and the Surma ran
with smallpox, ague, dysentery. Incense burned in temples
and the dung fires in wattle huts among the palms.
The crystal shattered, crystal shatters here.
The monsoon struck. Shards of glass flew everywhere

as Paxton read. Roses, figs, convolvulus had lined the banks.
The insects bred malaria. The sound of waterfalls had drowned
the cries of birds. Or not. The birdsong was so loud
it drowned the roar of waterfalls and broken glass. The Lady

listened, stopped. Rain poured through the broken roof
in torrents and the loathliest of weeds began to grow. No need
to water there where thistles, nettles, henbane, hemlock
choked the great conservatory with malignant undergrowth.

No need to map or classify or call dissimilar endeavors
much the same. No reason to collect or draw
or paint or pay for anything or try to make it pay.
A kind of madness is the kindness of the sane if only off
across the jheels you run toward Poonji like the Dawk
become a living duke. A duck perhaps. In Devonshire.
Or there in Chirrapoonje in the Khasi hills.
The Lady stared at Paxton and the poem of Shelley fills

the page with weeds. Fungi, mildew, mold began to grow
upon His Grace's cheek; a moss upon his thigh.
And hour by hour once the air was still, the vapors rose
which have the strength to kill. The baboos in Calcutta
planted seeds to cultivate the English peach and plum.
The gardener had ceased to read. The Lady now could
only plead, there in the shattered crystal house, for more.
But all was silent as it had been long before.

5 Homo sapiens

Once beyond the troglodyte, the tailed man, the satyr.
Once beyond the pygmy among anthropoids…
Homo monstrosus: the giants and the dwarfs.
Once beyond the *homo monstrosus* the *homo sapiens.*

*

Some are fair and sanguine, brawny, and with
yellow flowing hair. Eyes blue & gentle & acute.
These are covered closely in their vestments;
These are always governed by their laws.

Others copper-colored and choleric.
Hair is black & straight & thick; the harsh face,
the scanty beard. These are obstinate, content, & free.
These are regulated by their customs.

*

Others sooty, melancholy, rigid.
Eyes dark; severe and haughty, covetous.
These are covered always in loose garments.
These are governed by opinions.

Still others black & blacker & phlegmatic;
frizzled hair, the flat nose, the tumid lips.
These are indolent and negligent.
These are only governed by caprice.

*

Baptize as we do the sea routes and the landmarks.
Baptize as we do the flowers.
Know thyself as European Sapiens.
Strut the Latin long Linnaean names.

sail archangel agrimony avens
broom & burdock

eyebright fumitory meadow sweet
so the mountain flax & mugwort so the sanicle

and all indigenous medicinals be meet

elsewhere also sail & what's the use
& where's the hemlock woodsage yarrow find

some bird of paradise

& what's archangel agrimony avens to
strelitzia reginae

la triomphe royale la majestieuse

cuttings & endeavors & a mezzotint
record a bank & there the wild thyme blows

& oxlips & the nodding violet grows

Pages

from a book of years

Part One

I

1959. And underneath the photographs
names of people you can count

as if they numbered works and days
and years: one and one by one

become again these Davids, Joels & Fayes
and 1959's about to flower

flame again to 1960, 1961

The flower in the flame. The fame of that. Those days. People you could
count who counted then. David, Joel and Faye; Margaret, Ann, and Mar-
garet-Ann; Sondra, Bonnie, Lisa, Lennie, Kaye. Luck (o sister life) you'd
think was little more than winning dashes, listening to the jazz at Marty's
502, kissing Cora with your left hand up her skirt in that black and bat-
tered Studebaker Lark. Boris Pasternak, I'd say. I'll bet not one of you has
read a word by Boris Pasternak. I didn't mean his novel. Sister Life, I'd
say. I loved the title, hadn't read the poems. My Sister Life. I'd run until
I felt like I could fly, then stand under ice-cold showers for an hour. The
tingle of well-being being well inside the brackets of a decade for another
several months

whose year whose yearbook opens really. On your lap.

Who'd say Nadir How Now Restless Wind or Endine Tim Tam Quil
and Gallant Man what's Bold Ruler Oligarchy Jewel's Reward? If horses
were wishes, what's your wish: To winter in Kentucky, summer in Sara-
toga.

Rook-and-queen your combination in a close, coming back against the
dragon variation of a Russian's elegant Sicilian.

Khrushchev in New York. His phrase for the occasion not a quote you'd
look up in a book by Boris P. His rook not named for Tim Tam, nor his

queen for Nadir. In the rulers' table names decline like sentences beneath the photographs that you could count as Dave and Joel and Faye: King Saud is sand and Faisal backs to Franco Gamal Abdel Nasser turns to Eisenhower Pope John Ho Chi-minh

David Goss and Pham Van-dong
Joel & Bonnie

Margaret, Ann, and Margaret-Ann
One & one by one

in time you do forget well almost all of it the whole damn thing goes almost blank

goes wholly blank in time

for Governor-General Viscount Charles John Lyttelton Cobham, say.

II

Disasters 1959: Rio de Janeiro plane crash
Guadalajara bus and train Formosa

earthquake Istanbul a fire Western
Pakistan a flood & in the Persian Gulf typhoons

a caved-in mine in Merlebach and just
northeast of Newfoundland a sunken ship,

Blue Wave

I put my hand directly up her skirt and she did not say no don't do it didn't say a thing and so I kept it there a moment just above the knee and then began advancing slowly with my fingertips in little steps

blue wave, blue wave

And out there somewhere Viscount Charles John Lyttelton Cobham.

This year Raymond Chandler died and so did Abbott's friend Costello. It's hard to think of Abbott all alone his eyes upon Costello's derby hanging on the hatrack in the hall. For days you keened in grief for Errol Flynn your only child's Robin. General Marshall, Admiral William Halsey also on the list. And Ike in tears. Who'd say weep my love for

John Foster Dulles
Amy's mother Florence Smith

          For every day there's death you've got to chronicle and someone writes the years in yearbooks puts eventually the volumes in a right and goodly order on the shelf

who loved her best friend Amy's mother Florence Smith.

Joel and I would play this game called Scrounge. Others I've discovered called it Bernie-Bernie. You could lose a lot of money and a number of our friends and victims did. After dropping all his cash one night Carl Butler put his watch into the pot and then his shoes. Who the hell would want your shoes said Joel. They're first-rate shoes said Carl. They're ordinary Keds said Joel so what's about them so first-rate. Anyway he lost these too and then he went home barefoot. The music that we listened to was jazz: Monk and Miles, the MJQ, Dave Brubeck. It all seemed so subversive. We'd smoke, play cards, listen to the jazz, take the watches and the shoes of our acquaintances, engage in repartee appropriating everything we could from what we dimly understood to be a demi-monde of jazzmen and hipsters.

Actapublicorist entered dictionaries. Tokodynamometer and Turbofan.

When I got my hand inside her pants she said You know I never did let anybody do that and I'm pretty sure you shouldn't be the first. She stares out of her photograph. Going on eighteen and still a virgin just like all the rest of us and everyone we knew.

III

In four hours three minutes fifty two point two seconds Anatoly Vedykov
walked for 50,000 meters. As for ourselves, we set no records. Neither at
the gallop or the trot or the canter. Times got worse, we stayed out longer
in the nights playing Scrounge or waiting for the final set at Marty's 502.
I started calling 502 my distance. What's your distance? 440, right? In fact
I've taken up the 502. After one jaunt around the oval feeling pretty good
about my winnings on the night before I ran directly into Larson who
had evidently clocked me. Christ, he said, you might as well have walked

the last four hundred yards with Anatoly Vedykov.

By 1960 you'd have heard
them all at Marty's: Monk and Miles, Coltrane,
Horace Silver, Sonny Rollins, even now and then
a white man like Giuffre.

                          I liked Giuffre, the strange sound of his
trio. I thought of it as 50,000 meters worth of walking music for the likes
of Anatoly Vedykov. Larson used to play the records in the locker room
incanting 440 502, 440 502. It must have seemed occult to anyone but us.

Trav'lin Light: studies in the application of La Violette's idea of slow-
motion counterpoint. And then as JG said: because we're trav'lin round
the country in a light Volkswagen bus and very light ourselves (minus bass
and drums, & minus keyboard).

Giuffre alternating clarinet & tenor sax
Brookmeyer's valve trombone
Jim Hall: guitar

                    Pickin' 'em up and layin' 'em down.

In slow-motion counterpoint: Charles Van Doren
answers questions on TV inside a concentration booth:

Khrushchev bangs his shoe in the UN: Five to four
the Court upholds the power of Congress

to investigate subversives: Ingemar Johansson
knocks out Floyd Patterson: Joel Montgomery

spells correctly *fanfaronade*: Vanguard II is launched
to orbit for 100 years: Bobby Fisher turns 16.

        The quiz show scandal was a revelation to the gullible:
Van Doren, like the others, given answers in advance. Who'd fight the
Swede? who'd take off a shoe with old Nikita? Bobby Fisher's rook-and-
queen against a dragon variation of Sicilian would spell fanfaronade in
any bee. Or Fanfandango. Farondole.

Had we not discovered Scrounge we might have found a game of fan-tan
at the Olentangy Village Chinese restaurant: beans, coins, & counters
in some hidden place. By 1961 Anatoly Vedykov would still be walking.
Explorer VI: fallen from the sky.

IV

Between your visits to the nursing home you burrow into all the secret
delves of what was once your house, turning up most anything: decom-
posing diaries; a list of cities where you thought you'd like to live; names
for the year that has locked you in its book

on the Serengeti plain of Tanganyika or the streets of new Havana or the
Himalayas in Nepal. Year of the Missing Link year

of Fidel & Che year
of Edmund Hillary, of Anatoly Vedykov.

San Francisco Paris Rome or Venice Leningrad Palermo in Granada
Prague Vienna Perpignan Southend-on-Sea Tangier

        or anywhere but here.

All your letters from the time you first left home and went to summer camp.
A thousand cancelled checks.
Poor Aunt Peggy's glasses labelled with a tie-on tag.

When Leakey found his skull our anthropology consisted of examining the heads we knew already frozen in the permafrost of photographs and checking the cephalic index: broad or long, no one looked entirely human. Had the photographer asked everyone to smile and say *Zinjanthropus* he couldn't have done better: a class of 1959 emerging one by one from some preconscious primate's shadow just in time for a production of *The King and I* whose star Yul Brynner clone would take up mortuary science.

Smile and say Zinjanthropus.
See you in Tangier.

Or in Santiago in the eastern Oriente province or in Santa Clara in Las Vilas. First the local victories. Then an armored column moving on Havana. In the thinnest air, Edmund Hillary's on Mt. Makulu in Nepal. At 20,000 feet there's no sign of Yeti. You sign your name and sign your name again. The checks, the powers of attorney, living wills. You find the bottom lines and cross your t's.
Take me home she said don't sell the house I can't remember quite which one you are you know I really don't live here I'm only visiting.

Batista's visiting Dominican Republic. The Dalai Lama's visiting Bombay.

At 20,000 feet you can scarcely breathe at all.

We shaved his head in turns and eventually he was completely bald. He'd sing and dance. He'd wear the costume Mrs. Orr designed herself to much applause. In twenty years he'd get his thin embalmer's hands on Mrs Orr and Miss Kirkpatrick, on Mrs. Jones and Mr. Michelson and Mr. Todd. He'd stand discretely at the edge of things while those of us who still were left in town would pay our last respects. He'd give your mother your Aunt Peggy's glasses labelled with a tie-on tag.

He'd hang Costello's derby on the hatrack in the hall.

V

Old hat millineries made their mark:
the derby was a hit. Also slouch, fedora, swagger,

even Cossack. Down at the heel you'd find a dangerous spike,
you'd see a leopard stole, then an otter trench,

maybe even Jules François Crahay the man himself.
Hobble skirt. And after Fashion, Finland.

K.A. Fagersholm had fallen. R. Buckminster Fuller next.
Geodesic domes for radar on the DEW Line.

Distant Early Warning scanned the millenary sky.

When teleologists took Alpha from our almanac, Omega wept. Rebel
hit-men on the margin became hatters. Barkan, Binkley, Bowen, Cash;
Giles, Goss and Griffin. What were they to Advertising, Aeronautics?
Taken from aback, Zoetrope and Zero; but underneath the photographs
such confidence: Not a single future written off as bankrupt. Nor as death
from aneurysm. Not a battered bride. These who'd be the doctor law-
yer businessmen and engineers demand a potency beyond their prime
and potentate. Look at Shah Mohammed smiling warmly from his page.
Why ever should he not? He married young Queen Farah in December
and is hoping for a male heir

as Lunik III observes the far side of the moon and Don Fidel the progress
of a hundred executions in a single hot and humid afternoon.

Throw, the saying goes, your hat into the ring

                                but first you put your ten-
nis shoes into the pot. Only then to leave, broke and barefoot, your corner
table at the 502 for Cora's house at twelve, head all full of Bird and Monk
and Miles. She'd be waiting there all right, standing at the doorway in her
shorts and bathed entirely in yellow light. You felt like Edmund Hillary
at 20,000 feet.

Or like Costello's derby hanging in the hall.

A darker horse than Sister Life had never won a race. If David Lean could feast a few years later on Zhivago and convince Omar Sharif he was a poet, I could dance my Sister to the Millenary Ball and call her Cor (a.k.a. Omega Alpha). There we'd make the milliners all eat their hats. Dave Goss ate his hat. And Stephen Husted ate one. Harry Cash consumed a blue beret. Ruth McCallister nibbled at a pill box daintily. Randy Miller and his friend Sam Woodruff both ate busbies while our future General Patton, off to West Point in the fall, broke a tooth off on his helmet.

You thought, of course, the future would be yours—as did Che and JFK. Instead you'd be the future's, which would make a meal of you. One and one by one to cower in its flame as works and days unnumber and you do forget well almost all of it the whole damn thing gone blank in time and you too on the list with Raymond Chandler Errol Flynn and Amy's mother Florence Smith. Blue wave.

Tokodynamometer, my love, and Turbofan. Amen. Far out on the plain of Tanganyika. A pair of glasses labelled with a tie-on tag. A scattering of Pesos, Drachmas, Yen.

Part Two

I

America First or Lend-Lease. 1941.
The Christmas holidays at last and New Year's Eve.

How to measure now and
then and now again and in the mind

or then as now for all of them in kin & kind.
And how conceive.

How to parse out features in a body of the past
that took its measures . . .

Among the old prescriptions, bottles, and bandaids, *Married Love* (of 1936) moulders in a cabinet. Illustrated in a modest way for the fastidious, it's clear enough: and you yourself the end of all instruction and a digit added to the census come September. They'd listen to a fireside chat like everybody else. They'd sit beside their radio and smoke their Lucky Strikes. No Third Term they'd chanted with their friends. They're quiet now

listening to a man before the network microphones adjusting his pince-nez. He speaks the words Great Arsenal. He tries out fear: Spies already walk the streets of Washington. He says you cannot reason with incendiary bombs, and looks into the eyes of Carole Lombard sitting there with twenty others who have jammed into the little room to hear this live. Your father stands, walks out to the kitchen porch and looks up at the sky trying to imagine what it's like in London. Your mother's thinking of that night they danced to Jimmy Dorsey's band.

Or Paul Whiteman. Maybe Guy Lombardo, called by *Down Beat* magazine the King of Corn. In the photograph you turn up in the desk, they stand beside their old De Soto parked beside the north-east corner of the house. First car. First house.

First war to be entirely theirs. The last was for the eldest
not the younger sons. For Edward, say, who sits alone in darkness

in a corner of the old Glen Echo house unvisited.
Doughboy with the Spanish flu, then encephalitis, he'd dance

to Guy Lombardo if he could but he can barely stand;
his walk's a kind of shuffle when he walks.

Named for his father who had ridden San Juan Hill
with Teddy R, the name came down on you

like some genetic ton of bricks: johnEdward. Edward.
Edward Edward Edward . . .

But then you're not a part of all this yet. It's only New Year's Eve. Great
Arsenal is still a phrase and not a thousand tanks, not a bill before the
house, not a wound to Charles Lindbergh, hero isolationist, who'd flown
so far it seemed so long ago.

II

They'd listen to Jack Benny once a week. Brought to you by Jell-O. They'd
go out to the films: Errol Flynn and Ronald Reagan chased John Brown
to Harpers Ferry; Abbott got so angry that he made Costello cry. Rose-
bud someone told them was the codename for a German agent, not what
William Randolph Hearst had called his mistress's

obscene that word if you can think of it Louella Parsons
Hedda Hopper said and recommended censorship

in time of war
a cenogenesis for every member cenobitical

eventually a cenotaph erected
in your own back yard with every name

you'd carve on every tall Glen Echo oak
in stone

Rosebud? Tricycle in fact.

Turned by MI5 to double on the Lisbon Abwehr, Dusko Popov brought
his microdot to Hoover at the FBI who didn't get the import of the draw-
ings questions diagrams regarding ammunition dumps the hangars instal-
lations on the warf the workshops dry docks airfields naval operations
in Hawaii. After Benny, newsman Walter Winchell trashed the *glower-
ing boy the sullen tot of history the corn-fed Spengler stalking through the
family dining room with clouded brow a darkling child at our feast.* Your
mother thought he should be president; your father thought he should be
shot. He flew so far it seemed so long ago.

This year Scott Fitzgerald died and Henri Bergson Kaiser Wilhelm Joyce
Virginia Woolf and Robert Baden-Powell the founder of the Boy Scouts.
Sherwood Anderson Tagore and Robert Bridges also on the list with Lou
Gehrig and the voice of Earle Graser known to every child as The Lone
Ranger. It's hard to think of Graser's horse without a rider someone on a
soundstage horseshoes in his hands who'd gallop them beneath the mi-
crophone on sand and sawdust spread out in a box. Who'd say weep my
love for

Nazi aces Mölders and Udet

the Prussian officer the SS Einsatzgruppen shot outside of Leningrad.
Tsvetayeva got through to Moscow then to Pasternak at Peredelkino to
Pasternak who didn't say you will be safe right here my poet stay with me
my love I'll call you Sister Life. She hanged herself and three days later I
was born.

That would be September. Now they measure bauxite for incendiaries
chromium for armor plate copper for de-gaussing apparatuses to use
against magnetic mines magnesium and manganese for alloys

lead tin nickle zinc and tungsten.

They went out to the corner deli for dessert walking back along the old
Glen Echo drive where icy branches of the winter trees clicked against

each other silvering in moonlight. That night Edward died. And RKO let Kane sit on the shelf three months even though the word was out on Rosebud. Densko Popov said my name is Densko Popov and I've come from Lisbon on my tricycle to help you break their codes.

III

97-shiki O-bun In-ji-ki J-machine
a rat's baffle cry for cryptanalysis

a rising son whose father came from Kishinev
to sell them on how well the Singer sewed

sold them measurements of matrices
enciphering a system of successive

polyalphabetic substitutions and the wonder was
DiMaggio had fifty hits

in fifty games with everybody in the country counting and the wonder was the Brits had cracked Enigma too at Bletchley Park as Bertolt Brecht settled into Hollywood. Three years later I would ride my yellow tricycle round and round the dining table while the old Victrola played out *Mc-Namara's Band*. When the music went all sour I'd dismount and turn the crank until I couldn't turn it any more. McNamara gave them twenty records when he learned about the pregnancy and one of them was *Mc-Namara's Band*.

Meet Marlene Dietrich, Peter Lorre, Thomas Mann, Stravinsky: Yamamoto wearing his enciphered purple robes. Codename Fixer. Codename Trickster. Fliegerhauptmann Lindbergh. Fliegerhauptmann Hess.

That year measured distance by unusual means. Home plate to left field wall, degree of arc required to hook a fist in Billy Conn's protesting open mouth, miles south from Flynn's estate to child prostitute and Nazi agent in a single room, leagues required to get your sea legs on the exile ship as sonar signals rippled out in waves. Fliegerhauptmann thought he saw the coast of Scotland, looped his Messerschmitt, and parachuted down before the unbelieving eyes of Piers the plowman standing there at dusk near Eaglesham who'd take a measure more than Lindbergh's take a measure rather less than Hess.

He caught the outside curve and drove it to the wall He bloodied him at last and down he went like Schmeling smartass whiteboys come on quiet nights to lose their innocence He put his hand directly up her skirt and she did not say no don't do it didn't say a thing and so He turned the crank until he couldn't turn it any more and put on *McNamara's Band*.

He touched her rosebud it was manganese in alloy
it was allies it was axis
when she hanged herself and three days later you were born

like all these other codes and secret agents—
works of days apocalyptical foreseen by even Catalan Ramon
who spun configured mysteries on interlocking disks

to make an *ars inventiva veritatis* of the nine attributes of God.

Rat's baffle cry who'd haiku now DiMaggio my hero Errol Flynn my Messerschmitt my Spirit of St. Louis and by Louis's right cross and up-percut *Yo no naka wa jigoku no ue no hanami kana*: world's middle
       walking on the roof of hell
               and flower gazing!

IV

Kata kana over purple and in open code the short-wave-east-wind-rain. Yamamoto: Does it seem as if the birth is immanent? *Higashi No Kaze Ame*. It had been a healthy boy brought to term in all good time who'd twist the dials of his interlocking disks or ride a yellow tricycle around his room to wind up magic blow the east wind back uncloud the dark horizon that a hard rain down could never rain. He'd made an *ars inventiva veritatis* of the nine attributes of God

he'd walk the dog. Dog days. Dogtooth violets fringing sidewalks in his neighborhood. Long ago his Mendelian studies of the polypeptide chains. Who'd gazed on flowers walked the roof of hell and at his back heard echoes from Atlantic wolf packs answering their kin in kind: No kata kana haiku now or Yamamoto open code but lost sailors whispering *Jeder Engel ist schrecklich.*

Angels danced on conning towers, flight decks, the tips of wings. Fast tödliche Vögel.

McNamara had this problem with his inner ear. He said I think we'll just use Navahos or Cherokees the way the Brits have used Maltese. No one understands a wretched word of it. I'm so unsteady I can barely walk but still the beauty of it is I won't be draftable and neither I should think will you with that rheumatic heart. They slept through Bach at Disney's new *Fantasia.* They even slept through Rimsky-Korsakov and Chernobog Triumphant who would terrify you in due time and make you cry. Fast tödliche Engel. You'd hold your mother's hand.

These two buddies never went to war. They didn't have the heart for it, they didn't have the ear. They dug up McNamara's yard to plant toma- toes and zucchini where I'd help them pull up weeds in '45. They planted cantaloupe and carrots and potatoes. Their blushing melons and their apprehensive wives grew big all summer long decoding Mendel's laws. Mandrake Europe shrieked in Chernobog's right hand and Disney loosed the FBI on Hollywood. *The place was full of lousy Communists and they were worse than Nazis and the Japs. Even my friend Eisenstein who'd shaken hands with Mickey went back home to Moscow fawning over Stalin like a daffy duck.*

Early August and die Vögel gazing down at Leningrad:
Walpurgis Nacht conducted by the Wehrmacht.

Sedarim read out Haggadah the 14th of Nisan
but every path of exodus was cut.

Every angel terrified. Every angle squared.
Every square enciphered as a circle.

You could sing like Chaliapin you could fight like Alexander Nevsky but you might as well lie doggo and just pray for snow like Sergei Mikhailov-

ich in Alma Alta. Tapping on his telegraph in Kinderspiele calling USA
he'd whisper
    Uncle Walt!

I look around me now and somehow think I see you in this fire
all your totems and your metamorphoses. Animism here's our way of life.

Every loaf of bread we bake can creep away.
Every stone along the narrow streets can mock us.

Every mouse that's left alive can weep.

V

One and one by one. The flower in the flame.
The manganese and armor plate and tungsten.

          They went out to the corner deli walking back along
the old Glen Echo Drive and then she thought she felt the first contrac-
tions. Someone on a soundstage with horseshoes in his hands would gal-
lop there beneath a microphone on sand and sawdust spread out in a box.
Horse without a rider. He'd said to her one day you will be safe right here
my poet stay with me my love I'll call you Sister Life.

Hiding in the vast Pacific swells were *Zuikaku* and *Akagi* while the old
fusilier who would speak to you one day, shell shocked from the other war
and neurasthenic, stood not far from Dover among failing numina of kin
and kind looking for an efficacious sign.

Higashi No Kaze Ame. Jeder Engel ist schrecklich.

When teleologists put Alpha in their almanac, Omega danced. Rebel hit-
men on the margin got their hammers. Disney, Lindbergh, Louis, Flynn;
Benny, Abbott, Hopper. What were they to Aachen, Aaron's rod? Taken
from aback, Zipangu and Zion; and underneath the photographs such
confidence: Not a single future written off to buzzbombs. Nor as death

from Zyklon. Not a battered bride. Those who'd be the doctor lawyer businessmen and unacknowledged legislators all demand a potency beyond their prime. Look at young Johannes smiling from his page. Why ever should he not? He married Miss Kirkpatrick last December and is hoping for a male heir.

Take me home she said don't sell the house I can't remember quite which one you are you know I really don't live here I'm only visiting. God is subtle He is not malicious Einstein said and Eisenstein of Chernobog He is a code. They show them movies in the nursing home. I know when I was born but can't remember how it felt.

When they bought their blackout curtains down at Woolworth's McNamara took his box of wooden nickels from a shelf and buried it among the blackened frosted melons in his garden. You could also blast your lithium with deutrons and irradiate your mercury for gold. You could sign up with Enrico Fermi and get rich on U-235.

You could dance with her to Guy Lombardo
look at all the photographs drive the old De Soto down the streets of 1941 and knock out Billy Conn.
You could sell the yellow tricycle to Densko Popov sew a shroud on Singer push the Lend-Lease bill in Congress measure bauxite for incendiaries split the atom drop the bomb dismantle DNA and find a proper setting for the cenotaph.
But that won't bring Lou Gehrig up to bat or put a Ranger in the empty silver saddle.

Zeros were reported flying in the skies above L.A. Alphas and Omegas over San Francisco. Take me home she said don't sell the house I can't remember quite which one you are you know I really don't live here I'm only visiting.

One and one by one remembers quite and who you were
Rerhüf, Retarf, Retam, Otomamay...
                                    Visiting.
Alphas and Omegas on their way to Aachen.
Zipangu and Zion.
                Noiz Noiz.   U   gnp   z.

Part Three

I

Russian MiGs & Mau Maus. Dead Sea scrolls & Piltdown men.
You heard they'd executed Beria.
They'd execute the Rosenbergs, but not the ones you knew.

That girl in World History came down with Polio.
Or was it Civics? Or did she get TB?
In 1953 we got TV. Nearly everyone we knew already had it.

His joke the year before when we were still the last among our friends to get it was to point me down the basement stairs and say I got us one go have a look—at the Bendix, it turned out, spinning water down its drain to end the cycle and my mother smiling there about to hang my shirts and sheets and underclothes up on the line. But politics had forced his hand eventually: he'd wanted Joe McCarthy in his living room and so I got Lucille Ball and he got Roy Cohn and all of us got *Dragnet* and the Coronation. I also got a camera with a flash attachment that would make me popular with Ned's precocious sister Nell.

You wanta kiss my sister?

_____?

I'd take her picture though. Let's do fashion shots, she'd often say. She must have been fifteen. She must have shown you Ralph Marino silhouettes, Mollie Parnis satin collars, Skinner crepes, Dior's Maxime with folded cummerbund and cinching narrow waist with deep and strapless décolletage. This, she'd say, is my bodice. And this is my breast. You'd flash your bulb.

More fraudulent than your pornography the Piltdown find as printed once again in glossy mags—that skull, that jaw. *Eoanthropus dawsoni* took no oath with Adam Mumbi and Gikuyu but his spectographic studies conjured Mau Mau out of Aramaic for the deuterocanonical echt deutsch.

Who'd cast Dorris Day as Ethel Rosenberg? Who'd present
to Eisenhower Beria's pince-nez?
Stern declension down this year as Jim Thorpe died

219

and Dylan Thomas Robert Taft Prokofiev Picabia
and Uncle Max of natural causes
more or less and only Julius & Ethel on the list electrocuted Beria just
shot.

That year all nephology seemed neomorphic all neology unneighborly:
Communists might also be good citizens said Mrs. Lynch who lost her
job for telling us just that when she had finished reading us aloud that
Mayakovsky play *A Cloud in Pants*.

        And on the new TV such news: his list of enemies
identified in government his hand upraised his posse a Poseidon of a force
his posture so remote from hers who came to us from London on that
tiny screen and was anointed with the oils from a gold ampulla with a tiny
spoon. *Te Deum Laudamus* they sang. Regalia were passed around and
they arrayed her with Colobium Sidonis and then handed her the spurs
the orb the ring the sceptre with the cross the rod and dove. Her photo-
graph sped round the world
        but Nell's I hid away. Sherpa Tensing near the top of
Everest, I took the south col dreaming of Nepal.

II

You'd play at mountaineering down in what the others called *the glen* but
you called *the ravine* because your parents did. You'd also do the Bed-
ouins exploring Dead Sea caves. You'd do Korean War and Mau Mau
massacres. Along the Khumbu Glacier up the icefall hacking steps and
fixing ropes, you'd pull up Ned who'd fall exhausted in your arms at over
20,000 feet. You'd make your camp and wait until the lovers came in cars.

It may be the Essenes invented Satan
but my father thought it was Supreme Court Liberals

like Douglas who'd reverse him and his colleagues on appeal.
He too was Supreme, but only in Ohio,

"sitting on the bench" like some poor third string guard.
He'd sup on his suppositories. Our cave had

turned up parchments wrapped like mummies in old earthen jars
& we found psalms, beatitudes, sundry sapiential works

and Messianic rules. Also a Masonic ring we traded to the Brits
for their binoculars.

              ....ytlh 'nšym hyym, wtlytmh 'wtw 'l h's wymt—
He hangs the men alive! You shall hang him on the tree and he shall die.
For passing information to an enemy, e.g. For delivering one's people up:
Epikataratos pas ho kremamenos epi xylou. And then we found the spoons
and buttons, needles, nails, & coins. We found a dildoe and a dilly bag.
Between your visits to the nursing home the CIA declassifies Venona:
now you know Antenna Calibre and Goose were agents back in Babylon
and Tyre.

          & in the drawers & closets of your mother's house those
spoons and buttons from the cave. Also baseball cards and Marvel comic
books, Qumran's pesharim, letters from Antenna, photographs of Nellie
as Maxime.

Among the word lists for a new vocabulary circa new half-century you'd
chainjack way downrange a firestorm's megadeath.
You'd back-breed in 3-D at burnout speed.
Ethel ran the deli down on Hudson Street beside the movie house my
mother called "the picture show." That's Ethel *Rosenberg.* Neighbors
asked her if she knew the other one the atom spy or if she'd change her
name or did she know Klaus Fuchs and all those others in the news. She'd
drop a bagel in your dilly bag without so much as saying Old Los Alamos
although she'd whisper in your ear non sequitur's tautologies. Sunset over
the ravine as Red Chinese and North Koreans climbed up Pork Chop
Hill.

We'd dug in deeply waiting for the air support. Focusing binoculars
on hands of unsuspecting lovers

who were groping at each other's crotch
sprawled out on the back seat of their Mercury convertible

I didn't see the sniper crouched above us
under outcrop stone until he fired.   The report

was filed away as classified; the mission order was *abort.*

III

Things your mother said from time to time
are all she ever says today forgetting mostly any speech at all
but Georgetown's by the river
picture show e.g. & don't stay out past eight in the ravine & don't go to
the swimming pool you'll get exposed to polio he'll take you in the motor-
car & shut the blinds and windas good night nurse I'd just as leave I'd just
as soon and you out yakin on the davenport asfarasezconcern that record
on the gramophone'll make me nervous as a cat.

We'd go to triple features at the Hudson. *Bwana Devil, House of Wax,*
The Charge at Feather River. Objects hurled at us from the screen. Sit-
ting in the dark and wearing Polaroids we didn't think of objects hurling
through the sky but all the 52s up there were practicing LeMay's attack
on Leningrad by nuking down electric duds on Dayton and Columbus.
You go to Hillside House with Alzheimer's and drool. Otherwise you get
a window with a view and lots of Xanax.

She tells you she's in Georgetown and at school
says it's spring it's autumn now she knows because her ears are red she
says it's nice outside and would you like some lemonade.

See they masturbate like we do with this clitoris right here.

Ned had recently acquired a Kinsey and was pointing at a diagram. Nell
would open up her labia and smile. As the congregation sang out *I was*
glad the scholars of Westminster exercised their right acclaimed their
sovereign shouting *vivat vivat* as she made her way along the choir.
She put her golden girdle on & tried the spurs on the Archbishop who
presented her the Rod as massed trumpets sounded & as cannon at the
Tower fired salutes.

Could you back-breed objects like a race horse hurl a chainjack into Op-
penheimer's calculations? Bohr and Heisenberg were only made of obser-
vations on the day we took down all the orbiting electrons from the model
and Professor Einstein poured out drinks for Dylan Thomas on a field of
praise he'd failed to unify.

That's why Dark Star nosed out Native Dancer in the Derby.

That's why teleology had hidden *De Re Militari* in a cave
and Ethel Rosenberg smiled like Mona Lisa

and the Pumpkin Papers that convicted Alger Hiss
convinced the archaeologists at Khirbet Qumran.

Piltdown jaws away at time gone tipsy as we scar our faces rubbing red
clay in our wounds and take our oaths. Beria broke down completely wept
and begged them for his life. He'd give them dachas by the sea, he'd give
them Stalin's pets and playmates, Lenin's secret penthouse in New York.
They dragged him down the corridor and down the stairs and pushed him
to his knees against the wall. They shot him with a pistol in the brain.
That's why both her ears are red it's nice outside and would you like some
lemonade.

That's why by the outcrop stone one summer night when no moon rose
     up over the ravine
and I was watching *I Love Lucy* or *The Red Skelton Show*
Ned committed incest with his sister
                       or it wasn't why.

IV

He only said he did it and he really didn't.
He didn't really do it but he bet she said he did.
She said he did it but she didn't know he couldn't when he didn't do it
     and she said.
He said I really did it but she didn't know it.

Then Kikuyu Central spoke up for Kenyatta. We all prayed solemnly to
missionary god Mwathani Ngai but to old Mwene old Nyaga too. We ate
the meat of Miss Kirkpatrick's dachshund and of Mr. Macintosh's cat,
pierced the sodom apple & the sheep's eye with our thorns. They passed
a calabash of blood around our shaven heads and we traded them our
foreskins for their cigarettes.

As members of the forest gang we'd hamstring livestock, burn the grain stores, terrify the Europeans with machetes. Then we heard about the Vietminh and thought we'd drive the French into the sea. Even so the *Isle de France* had its attractions and we saved a crew of twenty-six whose freighter sank in mid-Atlantic storms.

No one said you were the Mortgenröthemensch, but I ask you was that jaw Orangutang? That year patination of a Van Dyck brown was revealed as potassium-bichromate stain. You wore your piltdown cranium like Uncle Edward's blue beret and found the hippo bones out in the quarry.

Disasters follow dermatology precede
disciples and discrimination in employment. First up in the Es is Eastern Orthodoxy but you'd never met the Patriarch in Istanbul and neither he
         would lay you odds
had Julian schismatics like Chrysostom Cavouridis.

Epikataratos pas ho kremamenos epi xylou.

She walked along the golden carpet toward the royal gallery and Chair of the Estate. Judges, bishops, officers and peers were in their stalls. They offered her the bread. They offered her the wine. The congregation sang *All People That On Earth Do Dwell.* Then they placed the leather strap across her mouth and dropped the hood and buckled down her arms and wrists and legs. When the current hit her body it appeared as if she tried to stand, her hands shrivelled into furious little fists.

In the Abbey everybody cheered. Your mother said your father's right you give them back their cigarettes and don't stay out past eight in the ravine. Take me home she said don't sell the house I can't remember quite which one you are you know I really don't live here I'm only visiting.

And eschatology took Ethel from our alphabet and made Good Friday dance listening to Crusoe on the juke box and with Julius already gone.

He'd pierce the sodom apple & the sheep's eye with his thorn.
He'd hamstring livestock join the Vietminh or meet schismatics for a
         lemonade.
He'd telephone Kikuyu Central for the Mortgenröthemensch.

We did the executions readily enough, strapping one another down and playing anthems on an old kazoo. Nell preferred to play the queen but she was also good at making little fists & jerking from the hips when hit by say two thousand volts delivered at a full eight amperes.

He said she did it but he didn't know she couldn't when she didn't do it and he said.

V

A little Ritalin a little Prozac or a Zoloft if you please. These Mothers for a Mild Millennium; these Ladies for a Later Lexicon. Telekenetic, though, and Sabbaterian. She says it's like the hoosegow here you know the callaboose the clink the lockup where they send the sinners overdosed on neuroleptics and you'd better come another day.

Beneath the overhang of weeping-willow limbs
propped in wheelchairs beside the quiet waters and decidedly another day—
their voices made of lilac
and their gestures made of hay.

In the summer Ned and Nell were saved. They'd shout and sing. At the Pentecostal Church you'd pass that looked like some abandoned ware-house with a whitewashed cross nailed to a plain black door. She gave up fashion shows and executions and we all gave up the Mau Mau mas-sacres and Khumbu Glacier climbs. They'd met the Mortgenröthemensch and it was them. While I stood listening by a window terrified to go inside they'd sing their cipher out like KGB cryptologists before their time. They'd speak in languages the slain in spirit know their xenogloss an antiphon to all the glossolalias of man.

That September I returned to school. Everyone seemed all at once to be thirteen. We'd crouch beneath long tables in the cafeteria, hook our arms behind our heads protecting face and neck against the flash. It was a drill. It was the bomb. Somehow we'd survive if we could just protect that ten-der flesh that burned.

You wondered crouching there how many had been saved. Was Eisen-
hower saved? Was Syngman Rhee? You hunkered down.

How about Kenyatta and Chrysostom Cavouridis?
The men up there in 52s the men in MIGs the men in missile silos in Ukraine?

Were Ethel at the deli and the Ethel in the Chair and executioner
        Francel and the Essenes?
Tell me Joel about the former rain about the latter rain the later lexicon
the prophecy and weeping willows by the quiet waters and the lemonade.

And underneath a table in a cave or overhang of weeping willow limbs
or down a glen or in an abbey or an execution chamber someone says you
did it when you didn't or you really didn't when you really did and hands
you the binoculars a gold ampulla with a little spoon a ticket to *The House
of Wax* an orb a sodom apple and a thorn. Forget the foreskins and the
cigarettes. And no need for the spectographic studies if you're targeted
because you'll only be a shadow on the ruins of a cafeteria wall.

Dawnman was a mensch all right and in this country anything is possible
O dim and lonely Piltdown bluff it's great it's Greek to me.

So what's to say at Pentecost if no one wears a satin collar spreads her
labia and takes a picture or a Zoloft or an oath or all the orbiting electrons
from the model stays out late in the ravine and nails a porkchop to the
flagpole in the middle of the camp.

Gloss it from the glossolalia as *epi xylou: qillat ĕlōhîm tălûy.*
Chainjack way down range
a firestorm's megadeath and back-breed in 3-D.

A shirt blown off of someone's back is hanging like a banner
in a blasted tree.

Part Four

I

The year before I'd worked for ninety cents an hour shuffling IBM cards
people folded spindled mutilated I suppose it looked as though I sat there
playing solitaire I had to earn enough to get somehow to what I called
Constantinople what I called Byzantium in spite of all for she had gone to
Turkey with her family Cora had. Her file was her father's double A for
Architecture Archeology okay.

One long year alone and counting
her anatomy in drifting mind in reverie at work while auditing
those spindlefolded mutilates her architecture

she had offered me when we were seventeen
had placed my hand deliberately on her ass as we stood blinking
at the sidelines in the autumn mist & watched

our classmates gallop on some county football field

never even had you been away from home more than a month or so in
Michigan perhaps Wisconsin just some family holiday and now you mut-
tered to yourself beginning yet another box of Aakers Aarons and Abairs
about the gold mosaics on a wall about the hammered gold and gold
enamelling and brought up sharply by Abdallah Joseph Abdel-Rahman
Zenebee.

1961 this time. Box and volume index income tax and yearly rebate post
or posting or to claim oh Abbett Brenda Abel Betty Abernathy Charles.
Ave or avaunt there Axelrod and Aycock Ayres Ayu Azzarito LJ Babbit
a new beat.

His letters home from 1926 this time are somehow boxed with mine from
Istanbul he's at the Belview Biltmore Florida and always writes in pencil
always says Dear Folks he's someone in these letters that I never knew
he's happy having beaten the rheumatic fever having just got up and on
his feet I guess he hasn't met my mother yet he's only twenty-one and
didn't have to think about

the neurofibrillary tangles in his brain the helicals in pairs the microtu
    bules or
tau proteins phosphorylated beta-amyloids
or chromosome fourteen.

Russians that year orbited the earth. That put everybody on alert in Ana-
tolia including Cor. You gambled all your Betas and abandoned Amy
Loid at the Helical way out in Tau betting no one found the gene for
chromosome fourteen and paid your way by IBM by audit and by alpha-
bet. And Ernest Hemingway blew out his brains in Idaho.

Between the shuffles of an Axelrod
Telli Babba blessed a virgin on the Bosphorus and physics

blasted nuclei to mason rho and meson pi.
Biochemistry induced the birth of a synthetic RNA.

You wondered if the Hittites took cuneiform from the Assyrians if Pho-
caeans emigrated west if Pax Romana could dissolve in olive oil and wine
and could you get there on the Gnostic airlines before June if Constantine
intended first of all to rebuild Troy.

II

All so long ago it seems hallucinated now. Eighteen. And walking by the
Black Sea with your suicidal love. Your letters home a tourist's recitation
or resuscitation not to be resisted in recitative. Her body your obsession
and your pockets full of condoms spilling in their silver
wrappers in the sand.
Rhapsodists rewired then with rhenium for rhyme.
It wasn't Florida in 1926 dear folks.

Elsewhere it is always midnight always Maidenek and Belsen. Transpor-
tation officers subordinate he says Servatius arguing against the jurisdic-
tion of the court. The man himself behind his glass and taking notes in
pencil on a little pad. A tool in the hands of a malignant fate he says. Ab-
ducted from the Argentine. Malignant fate a tool. His hands malignant
as his fate. His tool in his hands.

Hotel. Oh tell O'Tool.
In what far lands against what falling evil. And in what mirror in what
twisting corridor you'd find this Amy Loid this chromosome fourteen
and not remember any more.
You'd wear a Fez you'd finger strings of little beads you could

right now drive past her house by making just a tiny detour on the way
back to the nursing home. The architect her father's still alive. She herself
you haven't seen for almost thirty years. And would you recognize her
now. And would she know the graybeard sitting in his car and staring
stupidly at her front door. Everything as strange just down the road as
down the years. Hotel. Oh tell. Her legs spread open there but ah her lips
astounding you with I must tell you that while you've been gazing moo-
nily upon my yearbook picture for three thousand years I've had so many
men you couldn't count them all.

You'd count them all. There's Ajax Agamemnon and Achilles and there's
Atatürk and General Yassiada Nazim Hikmet Yuri A Gagarin Sultan
Abdul Hamid and his seven sons John Foster Dulles and Makarios of
Cyprus all of them successful down the road or down the years although
it must be said that Gary Cooper
Ty Cobb Dashiell Hammett
Carl Gustav Jung Dag Hammarskjöld Sam Rayburn Eero Saarinen
and Ernest Hemingway (already mentioned) died.

Onomastics no has nothing in the world to do
with Onan son of Judah or the onager a stone-propelling engine
of the siege the wild ass of central Asia no it's just

a listing of the folks a kind of wedding invitation
or a seating plan the order of an execution
it's a catalogue of ships. I'm really loving this amazing summer

here upon the plains of Anatolia near the winedark sea.
So what if she has had this little thing with Abdul Hamid
and the boys oh and yes the other little things

(fill in at will the names provided on your list).
It's me she really loves. The postcard shows
you Hisarlik where Heinrich Schliemann dug up Troy.

229

That's me beside the gallows where they hung Menderes in July.
The transportation officer is on the right.

III

Displacement of the *c* and *h* invests the *gens* and so it's
Eigen isn't Eich or Manicore if vertebrate is shown

he may inherit in his haunted house regressive genes
more readily if organisms crave their transportation

into cave the better to survive in Konya you could ruminate
on Rumi like a troglodite

rummy or canasta was
the game she played the game you see them playing still up on the second
floor in wheel chairs their minds still there still focussed on the playing
cards whose own dear folks had not transported chromosome fourteen.

Dear Folks: We took the ferry from the European to the Asian side in
only twenty minutes; then we sailed down the coast. They brought us tea
in little glasses as the sky line full of minarets began to fade. Effendi stood
up by the rail shouting *spaka gimek*. Literally that means put on a hat.
Shoes on feet and pants on legs a shirt and tie a jacket and a waistcoat
that's what old Mustafa Kemel said he said whereas

in rummy or canasta you must meld. It's not the same in Rumi. Sequence
has no value suits no meaning here. You hope for jokers and red threes.
It's runic as can be among these Anglo-Saxons of the second floor but
would you play it on your melophone and could you find a mandate in
Koranic law?

He says at the conclusion—he is twenty-one, it's 1926—that he would
rather not come home would rather not go on to law school disappointing
news he understands but that is how he feels. He hopes he says in some
mysterious way to make his family proud of him he says he hasn't taken
any medicine at all these past three months he feels confident he says he's
happy now and he was I would say a miserable man for his entire life he

came back home he studied law he married Lois K out there where she inherits in her haunted house I visit her again I write it down.

That year retranslated Paul to the Ephesians retranslated John while summer gaucho Klement alias the abductee the man expert in sealed trains listened with his earphones looking darkly through his glass. They'd take you to the Aesculapium where it was written only death forbidden here and down into the tunnels down into the basement temple where a priest of Pergamum would whisper through the speaking tube be well be well

they drugged the hopeless cases absolutely dotty everybody
thought they heard the voice of a god

or at Nicaea or in 325.
Constantine held every joker every last red three.
Spaka gimek. Go put on a hat

in that hotel. Or walking by the winedark sea.
And swimming out in it—

Swimming out so far I thought she'd drown
I thought the only thing she wanted

was to die.

IV

Her father's job was reassembling temples. Expert also in the Esperanto of assorted eschatologists and an impediment to your desires he answered when the pedocals of arid regions called and was a pedagogue whose pebbles were on offer to Pelagians. We helped him dig and sift and sort.

It would have been a pagan holiday
all Roman baths and pornographic movies at the theatre

except for Paul & John & the apocalyptic angel
seven stars in his right hand & walking in the midst of all the archaeologists

the dervish dancing where sweet Artemis once dwelled
a reed plucked from her marsh a flute

bewailing separation from her bed of reeds

while at the nursing home they opened up the seventh seal. Then she turned and in the moonlight by the temple gate undid her bodice looking at you frankly and you saw at once the heaving of her twenty breasts pearled in the tiny drops of a lactescent dew. But if you harbor chromosome fourteen the time will come when you remember none of this. Take me home she says don't sell the house I don't remember quite which one you are you know I don't live here I'm only visiting.

Canasta decks cascading to the floor. The sound of distant castanets.

Dear folks: we disembarked at Port Coressus then passed through the Harbor Gate and walked the length of marble pavement lined with colonnades and shops until we reached the tetraphylon like the one you know in Palestine. Once they isolated lepers as you will recall but now it is the old like you who must be swept from the agora off beyond the gate of Mithradates where we shut them up in colonies as if old age itself were a contagion and they shuffle down the hallways on their walkers sometimes lashing out with canes. One old geezer Erosthostenes has said he knows a way to enter history

to claim immortal fame he'll burn Diana's temple
down where after Ephesus the Es on offer
will include the epicycle and the epidemic and the epilogue

epiphany a feast on January 6 and Erebus a state of mind
resistant to epistemology the epsilon
equivocal but there on your escutcheon anyway

and so that's me again beside Effendi in my Fez. Heinrich Schliemann on my left and on my right the hangman and the judge. In Washington Casals is playing Allemandes for JFK in Upper Arlington the ladies on the second floor are playing cards. My father is in Florida it's 1926. No one drowns herself in that year's southern sea. Effendi tells me go put on a hat. I said in what hotel. I said not Onan son of Judah nor the onager.

Everybody on alert all over Anatolia.
Hotel. Or tell which temple eschatology rebuilds.

Which are you the epidemic or the epilogue. Oh epsilon my son!
45326 acknowledges his number in his glass.

V

Your story then. That too in the box. You called her Margaret there and
you yourself were Richard but not here. Your Istanbul looks more like
Alexandria than Istanbul. Doubtless you were reading Lawrence Durrell
who was hot in 1961. When the crazy family and the randy lover of the
eldest daughter get out to the ruins everything implodes. But Margaret
doesn't try to drown herself in any sea. Hotel. I tell her father you can call
me epsilon. He says I'll call you Otto Ottoman I'll call you Byzantine Bill.
I say they say your daughter's fucking Abdul Hamid and his seven sons.
He says we disembarked at Port Coressus then passed through the Har-
bor Gate and walked the length of marble pavement lined with colon-
nades and shops until we reached the tetraphylon like the one you know
in Palestine. He says they'd take you to the Aesculapium where it was
written only death forbidden here and down into the tunnels down into
the basement temple where a priest of Pergamum would whisper through
the speaking tube be well be well

beware dear folks of eschatology he says the millineries
and their hats the radar
gazing at a millenary sky. She says Hotel. I know it's a hotel. I tell them
that I don't live here I tell them how

the rummy players meld
and how the transportation officer explains The Way. Tau proteins
form a halo around senile plaques.
He hopes to make his family proud of him he hasn't taken any medicine at all.

That was Cora and not Margaret swimming out to sea.

233

Your story then. A shuffle only in the IBMs detaches all the Aakers from the Abdel-Rahman Zenebees. A shuffle only when you try to walk. Hotel. A temple bell. A reed plucked from her marsh a flute bewailing separation from her bed of reeds. You took the ferry from the European to the Asian side and then sailed down the coast. They brought in tea in little glasses as the sky line full of minarets began to fade. Effendi stood up by the rail shouting *spaka gimek*. Also Ephesus. Also SOS. And when she turned there by the temple she undid her bodice looking at you frankly and you saw at once the heaving of her twenty breasts. In that hotel. Her legs spread open there her lips astounding you with such bad news. You wondered if the Hittites took cuneiform from the Assyrians. You'd wear a fez. You'd finger strings of little beads although they didn't do it this way in Ohio.

At Catal Hüyük some 4000 years before Egyptian pyramids Diana's chthonic shape appears in figurines uncovered in the neolithic hills. Not far from Hisarlik. Not far from Upper Arlington where you drove slowly past her house those nights of playing Scrounge with Joel and Carl. She'd be there, all right, standing in her shorts and bathed entirely in yellow light. Your story then. You won't be overlooked by the geneticist.

You empty out the boxes one and one by one
your letters and your father's and your fictions

where you cower in the future's flame
as works and days unnumber and you do forget

well almost all of it the whole damn thing
gone blank in time and you too in the cards

with Zoetrope and Zero and the Zenebees.

Part Five

I

I think I heard him saying *and he still drinks alcohol*
and laughing like he'd said I still drank Kool Aid.
He himself of course "took drugs."
Three of us were pissing on a walnut tree.

That was I suppose at Jim Black's place up in Los Altos hills the year
when Al Guerard had tried to woo back west a scowling Irving Howe
by taking him to what he'd hoped would be sufficiently outrageous stu-
dent parties. *Dissent's Gone Soft On The Imperialists* proclaimed a banner
hanging up above the band. But on the other hand.

Urinalysis of schizophrenics shows a trace of something like
Methoxyphenylethylamine.
Bump off every single nitrogen and your compounding chemist
grinds you up the flowering tops of those deflowered female hemps:
Tetrahydrocannabinol.

Polysyllables for Sixty-Six and you yourself polygamous almost. Poly-
phonic anyway and polytheistic. Powers of attorney put you in another's
hands: & to perform which act and acts what thing and things whatever
the device and the devices in the law whatever may be needful necessary
in my name to do to execute and to perform it largely amply and to all
intents and purposes as I might do if I were
present and performing it myself
shall never be
affected by my disability my incapacity
incompetence or lapse of time.

Two of us had lapsed into a corner of the time where coffee was the thing
at two a.m. We show each other poems. One of us is to become the Poet
Laureate. Not me. Poet Laureate of the United States. Your sickly father
was alive and came out to your wedding. Your mother was quite fit and
had no need to give up any power. Your friend would marry you okay
but did not love you welladay. This was 1966. This was swimming in

the Yangtze and a US H-bomb missing in the sea near Palomares. This
was the Miranda case and anybody's right to stand up silently. This was
mining harbors in Haiphong apartheid in South Africa and Lin Piao on
culture. This was avalanche in Rio and a BOAC jet exploding at the foot
of Fuji. Claiming your Miranda rights
you'd stand up silently when asked
does anybody know a reason why this woman and this man

should not abide in Methoxyphenylethylamine
as long as they both shall live?

Your father would not now live long.
What's left of him I've packed up in a box with all his yearbooks.

All the books of all those years I've numbered here
to parse out features in a body of the past that took its measures

all dissent gone soft on the Imperialists
laughing like you drank some Kool Aid

lapsed into the corner of a time.

II

Most of magic in the drug you hoped they took was in the pill they called
the pill the period coming on like clockwork every month and no more
need for condoms or to come in someone's open hands I loved it in the
shower when she'd bend down with her wet hair on my thighs and with
her mouth almost although the one you marry on inspired impulse may
decide within a year you will not do you kept it up with two or three you
knew before her time you'd grieve when she went off with R who knew
more than the rest of us about the war who'd been in combat in Korea no
one could believe he was that old.

God the druggist staring at me when I started in with Cora and would
have to ask for Trojan-enz with maybe who could tell some colleague of
my father's in the line behind me or the cousin older sister aunt of some-
one in my class

and then you'd have to specify the lubricated kind and he'd pretend he
hadn't heard
and you at fifty-five remember this and impotent sometimes.

Beta blockers digitalis and its glycosides diazepam and half the
stuff you're on impair erections

even diuretics and the TADs. And then he asked me if I still drank alcohol.
Mao and Lin Piao could tell you power was the real

aphrodisiac. But how much should you take and how long
should you take it and do benefits outweigh the risks?

Do I need to take any special precautions? Are there side effects
I should expect?

She tries to phone the street address and then sends off a letter to the
telephone: Martha Jane and Mary Kay at Hudson 43402. She cannot un-
derstand the nurse who cannot understand her patient when she says go
get that man who fixes Gramophones. I put the yearbooks in a cardboard
box. I do it largely amply and to all intents and purposes as she might do
it were she present and performing this herself

in San Francisco by the Longshoreman's Hall.
And just like any tourist in the Day-Glo silent night whose Dada
    metamorphosis
could suffer an arrest and call it love.

That year Maoists starved their neurons and deprived their
neurofilaments of dopamine. Then they ran
like Mau Maus through Peking. Power was the proposition

power was the drug. And as I write that down
I hear a boom-box in the street I hear a voice that's disembodied
keening elegy for Captain Trips.

In San Francisco by the Longshoremen's Hall not a single cadre dressed
like peasants no one dragged the mayor from his bed or burned his books
or smashed his tablets in the public square. You starved your neurons and
deprived your neurofilaments of dopamine by other means. Why not be a

literalist of the imagination why not say the people's opium is opium. You did. Your dead. You dithered there. Bore fraternal greetings to the Chief of State to Liu Shao-chi to party General Secretary Teng Hsiao-ping and begged them not to follow in the line that wound up from the Wharf and to the cinema where everybody waited for Zhivago in the dark and listened for the balalaika like a broken like a balabalabalalaika.

III

R had "occupied" the office of the president with several friends from SDS. Now he's occupied as president himself. They sat around the office drinking beer. We ourselves by then "took drugs." Three of them were pissing on the walnut desk, dissent gone soft on the Imperialists. Feet up on the gleaming surface, cigarettes stubbed out in presidential tray, R concerned himself with dials that would amplify the Dylan songs on out the window and across the quad. And in an early poem the Laureate's red eye flashed from Palo Alto "clean as malice" through the fog in Redwood City where they made the napalm by the bay. He thought, he said, about the village of Bien Hoa

so did you a little bit
and went to live in London out in Islington.

The nurse was fired who took her Demoral.
The Beatles were more popular than Jesus.

I suppose it's possible Akhmatova had died
the very moment Yuri first saw Lara as that movie

ran in London Paris San Francisco
& the paper opened up in someone's hands

across the aisle you were in the train the Circle Line you watched the movie thinking back on Sister Life you had not been as you had thought you'd be the future's guest in someone's Poem Without a Hero but you overhear the nurse who jabbers on just like your students saying *so I'm like and then he goes*

what was she like where did he go
that year that swallowed up Akhmatova Jean Arp André Breton Mont-
gomery Clift & Buster Keaton Hedda Hopper Admiral Chester Nimitz
Giacometti Frank O'Connor Disney. Married just six months and now
the ocean for a fact between us R had shown me that book *Ariel* and asked
me *Do you have a rubber crotch*?

97,000 there in Wembley and when Geoffrey Hurst kicks in the win-
ning goal the country goes completely nuts even Harold Wilson and the
Queen. 400,000,000 watch this on TV. The World Cup's elixir or a hem-
lock Dear you look so tired today. Franglais entered dictionaries. Aleo-
toric big bang theory camp.

REM and screen pass po-faced mini eldercare.
The Frug. The Hype.
Go-go jump-cut bonkers. Royal Shakespeare does the persecution of
Marat performed by inmates of the Charenton asylum as directed by De
Sade and Dr. Freidenberg. Mentation better once she went off Haldol
and the Prozac back in February still she's in decline Language is apha-
sic Manifests agnosia and paranoia lately Gait is shaky and she'll need a
cane. You'll notice frequently the verbal paraphasias. Word substitutions.
DAT.

He reads the REMs hooks up electrodes
and determines which dementias can be classified AT.
Why not first unzip the rubber crotch.
Is that an evil eye my love or something newly alloy a prosthetic made of
plastics or a part that resurrects.

How does Komsomol serve Communism. Translate and provide your gloss.

IV

There you sat where Karl Marx once sat and wrote your London po-
ems. All about divorce. You might have known you'd only manage such a
theme even having come so far for revolution. Sit there long enough and

maybe echoes from the roundhouse walls would penetrate. You couldn't concentrate. You smoked and drank. Fifteen minutes in the reading room and then an hour's break across the street with Players and a pint. Echoes from the roundhouse walls
as you continue down the halls with plastic garbage bags.

A certificate that he attained the 33rd degree. Supreme court robe. Campaign buttons all the way from Harrison and Grant. A drawer entirely full of corks. Another full of soy sauce containers. Plastic compact in a bathroom cabinet there among the decades old prescriptions and you lift it open with a finger nail in surprise behold

her diaphragm. Diabolic how they'll give you diacetylmorphine for just a simple case of diachronics. Diagnosis at some weird diagonal to diakinesis. You sat there at your desk to diagram the dialectic but regretted you had never danced the old diaspora before Diaghilev completed his dialysis.

Nurses wheel their patients in and run the film. On a screen the size of Mt. Olympus geriatric porn queens lick each other's cunts. An imagery the Laureate declared in his first book consisting like America in lack of scale. Back there in the distance is Zhivago trudging through the snow. He's on the scent. Up ahead are Lara Beatrice Penelope and Cor. Mao had virgins brought in by the dozen, never took a bath, wouldn't brush his teeth. For months on end did not get out of bed. Take me home she said don't sell the house I can't remember quite which one you are you know I really don't live here I'm only visiting. Let him without sinanthropus cast the first Red Guard

and arm him with this closet full of swords.
Enough indeed to start a fencing school if in need of uniforms for everyone you empty six or seven wards. Edward's unstrung cello back there in the dark, a stack of primers to initiate the rites on some Masonic stage. They gave you numbers in the reading room. You spoke your part as if you were enraged
engaged on every front at once imagine dear your mind become so like a boil did you wind the spring of your electric heart.

When does too much of imagine dear become disease.
When does mind become a boil that must lance itself.

Sinanthropus did manage to stand up erect
achieved the use of fire and certain tools for example crudely fashioned axe
for example twenty kiloton device exfoliating near Lob Nor he
was discovered circa 1929 at Choukoutien it is not thought
he understood the red shift of Quasars but he lifted up his eyes
but he beheld the sky.

Homology. Homophony. Homeric Hymn.

March northeast to Hunan province and display her diaphragm your diagram
of all electric circuits at the San Men project
or your relics of the stone age at the San Men gorge. Mercy mercy

Madame Mao he'd call out Mother of us all I'd call out mine.

V

The phenomenology of anti-fascist pharmacologists.
The flower in the flame.
The lama whose La Mancha was Lamarckian.

And Mary Quant that year was made an OBE for introducing miniskirts
where fashion plates had illustrated farthingales. You fell in love. Again.
Against your better judgment. Judging from disasters in your past. You'd
pass on tricks conditioned by this new environment. No pasquinade that
year all pas de deux where party line dissolved in passacaglia the proteins
never flowing the right way. Nonetheless had T. Lysenko risen in the
great red dawn to celebrate inherited callosities among the midwife toads
and many men who since have chosen Cavorject.
Simply self-inject the penis and the medicine will go to work.
Only half of one percent develop Priapism but if you're unlucky, brother,
plan to spend the next three days looking like a randy faun upon a Gre-
cian urn.

When pharmacologists compounded their phenomena, Omega dreamed.
Alpha held the hands of her ontologist. Pasturage extended out from Is-
lington to Aldeburgh and you grazed a while in pastoral relief. Tupping

in your tuppence worth of mental astroturf you muttered your tu quoque
through a proxy in the courts

divorce become an art of divination
in a phase of every trial called discovery.

Aphasia then. And ever afterwards in Asia
world without any end amend.

Printed as required by the Scientologists.

I ask them how much she remembers how much she can understand this
execution which on her behalf releases other documents consents to this
Do Not Resuscitate this paper that prohibits interventions that prohibits
both nutrition and hydration but allows whatever drugs may be obtained
to kill the pain ontology a function of oncology if

protein synthesis and polymeric vectors
mean you are your mother's son your father's fated cowboy
polypeptides flowing like the war

of generations information only out of the nucleic acids Pavlov
buried in a Skinner box with all the roots
of real numbers in a digit that's both decimal and arbitrary.

Tower bridge Falangists drew their falchions if you fell in with the
Trotskyites your politics as puny as falsetto false arrest the agent of her
living will the ticket for Tbilisi in your pocket and Manuel de Falla blaz-
ing at the Proms in Albert Hall.

From Abyssinia to ablative the dosage
is discovered by the dice the delitescent absolute beyond the will

the year run down the tide run out at Tilbury.
She says so Illbeseeinya ram beau   she says

do not resuscitate   do not   let go

Automystifstical Plaice

In the beginning
without any mother the girl was born a machine.
In the year of erotic parades.
The Novia poured out the oil the gears were engaged
the études composed and the light bulb
was Américaine. Voilà Picabia sweetheart of first
occupation voilà ballet mécanique.
We'll not eat our bread by the sweat of our brows
in the end: Je viens pour toujours
it is error and grief you'll be known by
the strength of our steel
the number of rivets and not by the river
where fishermen cast or the last
of your towers to build on the strength of our dowry.
Antheil Olga Boski Hedy and Ez, she says:
Or probably better
Olga and Ez, Antheil and Boski [Hedy Kiesler Mandl Lamarr.
That's Mandl, Fritz, from Vienna, the armaments man,
the war profiteer. Hedy Kiesler, the naked broad in the film.
It won't be a dance, it won't be ballet mécanique.
Ecstasy, rather, a run through the woods and a swim.
The actress saying: sex in this movie is real,

Mandl's lieutenants will buy up & burn any print they can find
so Hedy and Fritz can entertain Hitler and Mus.
Aribert Mog is displaced; the telescope on the lens
enlarges another face
from about a decade before.]

They enter a judgment,
Théâtre des Champs Elysées. Everyone's there. The soloist
doesn't know that he is a she. He doesn't know
he's set up, doesn't yet know they've scripted him in a riot
(those lights are too many, too bright.)
Mere human being he sits there robotic she looks like
a presence out of Bohemia via Berlin's RUR.
He begins with Sonata Sauvage.
A camera's panning the audience, picks out the famous:
Picasso and Joyce, Duchamp, Milhaud and Satie.
We see them there with Leblanc as Lescot in the film
but we don't hear a sound Mr. Pound leaping
right out of his seat and shaking a fist as people begin
to walk out on Antheil himself at his Airplane Sonata
by now and sweating away but we don't hear a thing as we gaze
at the girl without any mother born a machine
who would sing out succès de scandale a clickityclack
of the dactylicanapests jerking the film
through a circle of light the soloist booed from the stage
the piano rolls looping their loops
in twelve pianolas electronic bells and a xylophone siren
another Picabia made from the parts
of a Model-T Ford.

Good Lord, she says, Mon Dieu.
That must have been one nine two three, the year I went
to the races with Hem at Auteuil, the year
young Antheil was going to play Cyclops for Jim.
A working title indeed, she says, a walking tittle or tattle I'd say
to your automystiftistical plaice—
you're fishing again in some pre-Riemannian river
and don't understand the riveters have it all over
the rhetors who can't even master the minor recursions
while minding the algorithmical gaps.
No one could actually *play* that piano roll A wrote into the score,
the digitals moving at speeds and at intervals
nobody's ten carboniferous digits could match.
So down at the hurdle went Manzu, tossing his jock,
and Héros the Twelfth and L'Yser dashed at long odds
for the finish. Seining out in the sea near Le Havre
you wouldn't net any sonnets much less Seigneurs
out of Proust. You understand, she insists,
there *are* no parallel lines in rivers that wind & nothing but *nothing*
my love appears to cohere from *inside* the system
trust *me* I'm a truffler I *know* my way around.

And Pound once again that very same year in his Treatise?
claiming for A's diachronic harmonics
that sounds whatever the pitch combination etcetera
harmonize across time
these series of chords these arpeggios wait to embrace
through an interval
                              silence
the crux of the thing
the space in the music like space in some canvas
by Lewis his fine demarcations of volume,
cylindrical forms: You do comprehend these recursions are different
from those you'd expect,
the power plant cycles like no minuet?

              & so A, she says,
was the cause of that riot but nowhere was seen
in the film. It's me, it is I, on the screen!
They call me there the austere Mademoiselle Claire Lescot.
I'm some kind of cubist cold fish, the girl
without any mother born a machine who can nonetheless sing
and I stare down those rioting plebs at the Champs Elysées
alive in the interval A absconditus diminished
however you like. [81: chez vous. Demain à sept heures.
82: musique imprévue. 83: odieuse, odieuse. 84: atmosphère
torturante quand elle laisse enfin percer le secret . . .
son immense douleur inhumaine . . .
85, 86, 87: In reel time
we're counting the titles, we number the causes, effects:
Sonata Sauvage, piano, piano roll, siren
and dactyl and drum.
Will George in the war be faithful
to Boski his wife? Will Olga or Ez trumpet Mus?
Will young Fräulein Kiesler run naked as Hedy Lamarr?
Fishing or fasting, reprogram, reverse it
and search]

Your working title, she says,
might as well gesture at Czech. The Gödels and Čapecks fished
for me in my motherless maze when I thought I was
Daumier's laundress and not Miss Sullarobotess,
some loopy machine in your ghost,
the ganef your ganglia somehow encoded, the chip on your shoulder,
the quantum mechanic under the hood of your truck.
Before they made me the knee of your curve, the neural pathway
encrypted for good. Was I not to dissolve in *I am*
but as antiparticulate anapest?
And that other, doctor, a dactyl, or a catcall out of the pit.
Anyway the joke was on P: A's pianola replacing
the Sapphics & he himself its antistrophe, turns unrolling
Daphne's thighs from the bark.

So Model-T begat Picabia who as machinist made the shape that named a choreography. And then Antheil's recital drove the riot L'Herbier required for Lescot before she visits Léger's laboratory where her lover there among the angles and the geometric shapes, the silver disks and metal rods and knobs and dials and flashing beams of light, transfigures her. [Hedwig Kiesler's in Vienna at that moment and she's eight years old. She's also in the lab. She's in the music and the dance and the machine.] And then when A has finished playing at that theater and gifting us with such an angry crowd in *L'Inhumaine,* he synchronizes those piano rolls whose loops and variants of eighty-eight prefigure microsecond hops between the frequencies of anti-jamming programs in torpedoes or computer links or cordless phones. This is Ballet Mécanique: the draft. This the working title. This the initial location, the automystifstical plaice. We don't hear a thing as we call up Archival Search: Were you, Oh My Baby, meant to walk that washer woman up the stairs with Léger-Daumier? The print went to Vienna and premiered in silence, running credits anyway for Synchronisme Musicale. The ostinati rolled for friends and patrons five days later at the Salle Pleyel.

If first the vertical and then the horizontal penetrations were derivatives of pianist and pianola, neither got it all entirely right, though both had caught a ride on George's rickshaw. Our guest was still a ghost, the cyborg wasn't yet a sibyl on the line. And A himself could never fully realize his 1923 designs. His codes were still dependent on a vacuum force and paper rolls with which he sought to synchronize his twelve or more machines. He hadn't met the Midi, technical cousin of Claire, his digital and instrumental interface. As if you'd teach the retrofitted to respond in synch, but not for sixty years. Still, the lady out of Daumier walks up the stairs and up the stairs and up the stairs once more in *Ballet Mécanique* the film. If Claire Lescot stood in for one piano, these stone steps beside the Seine and these looped thirty frames appear and reappear to summon music no one hears where tie-rods, pistons, wheels and gears and abstract forms reflected in the steel of a prismatic fracturing all gleam and try to sing.

Says Ezra Pound: EP. He plays. All gleam and try to sing. And then Léger: Léger. Says George Antheil: Anteuil. That piece in place. Police will net you rioters at any cybernetic database. Then peace. Or flounder there. All champs, these guys. All champs Champs Elysées. If someone might just reconnect. That wire. That Novia who pours out oil, those gears that

E	03:10	E	02:38
F	04:01	F	03:20
G	06:11	G	05:09
H	06:40	H	05:33
I	07:01	I	05:51
J	08:05	J	06:54
K	11:20	K	09:26
L	11:32	L	09:37
M	11:59	M	09:59
N	13:02	N	10:52
O	13:39	O	11:22
P	14:40	P	12:14
Q	16:32	Q	13:47
R	18:51	R	15:42
S	21:35	S	17:59
T	22:05	T	18:24
U	23:05	U	19:14
V	23:16	V	19:24
X	23:47	X	19:49
Y	24:29	Y	20:24
Z	24:50	Z	20:42
AA	26:00	AA	21:40
BB	30:03	BB	25:02

re-engage. Say P & A: Machines are musical. Machines are part of life. It's right that one should feel a little warm. One does so feel. Or cold. It's not required of anyone to kneel. When they tried to integrate the music and the film they didn't mesh. They went their separate ways as separate works like two berserks in *RUR* or Léger's lab. In 1923 the pianolas were all out of synch. You've said. But now the Midi in her Quadra form's all smiles. Disklavier by Yamaha. [As if you'd count out miles of spectrum spreads with Miss Lamarr.] At some café-tabac you'd linger over a petit vin blanc or modify the track at will and run the thing right back. And was that laundress's one friend a fisherman?

Oh yes. In all the winding rivers and at sea. Says he:

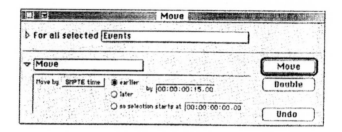

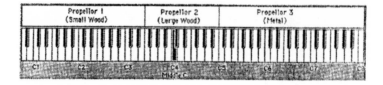

EP:

Not Ezra Pound: Express Pâquette (in negligée).

Not George Antheil: Auteuil. No not Champs Elysées.

In prose: Who goes? The ghost of Claire Lescot.

And not Lescot: Sans mother a machine.

A hemistich? A click. Some dream you've seen.

Some obligation anyway to start assigning parts. Whose art?

Not mine. Some rhyme or other you'd suppose.

Delete suppose: Some interlude between the creatures' double features.

Lescot escorted from the stage. What page?

Léger: Constructed objects. Fountain pen. A pendulum against a silhouette.

Antheil: A cigarette?

[Lamarr: Pâquette!]

Léger: These squares and circles, animation: play.

EP: I see arpeggios. Prismatic images of day.

Picabia: The Lady Light Parisienne, a glow.

[Lamarr, Pâquette: Lescot!]

Antheil: They said I had all Paris by the ear; I was in full career.

Léger: That year I had them by...

[Pâquette: I know, the eye!]

Picabia: By Model-T or Model-A, I had divined a rod.

Léger: My god, these quotes: A shiny metal sphere.

Antheil: That spins and disappears.

[Lamarr: For what?]

Antheil: A thought

emerging intermittently between the wars among the whores of discourse.
[Horse, that is, of race course. Force of different color?
Go.
System error 218: Auteuil
not Antheil.
Astound not Ezra Pound.
Constructed objects, fountain pen, a pendulum against a silhouette.
Hedy Kiesler
growing up: New file]

                    Which says, my Sister System,
I'll not take it back. I'll just
stay on track I think and tell you one more time
it's prisms and not prison like I said.
I didn't say? Well, anyway.
And no dissolves or fade-outs, no irises or wipes,
everything quick-cut and edgy from
the pure geometries to Kiki's painted lips & eyes.
I loved that walk from *L'Inhumaine* right up and into Dudley Murphy's
lens where only I in that ballet was
fully conscious. I even heard the absent music in my ears.
They'd added something by Milhaud of course, but secretly
I walked those stairs on George's arm,
our loops and our recursions not quite waltzing to Matilda
right in step, it's true. Then suddenly for me
no more Champs Elysées.
No more long afternoons with Hem out at Auteuil or
drinks at the Café du Dome. Ah, home:
My favorite place, my resting plaice, Mon Vieux!
Who'd have programmed metamorphoses
like these: migraines among transmigrating neural forms
and even A
in Hollywood at work on *Plainsman*
for De Mille and Paramount. They tied up Gary Cooper
to a stake & lit the fire beneath his feet accompanied
by something like the Mechanisms for piano
that had conjured rioters for Claire Lescot when I was she.

The silent Diva and the Model-T get scrapped when even Dali
comes to town proclaiming Cecil B a great Surrealist.
The times are strange. Air waves all awash with bands that swing
or Autrey singing down home out of range.
Ecstasy had made a star Miss Lamarr although nobody
in the USA had seen it. [Girl seventeen & born
of mother no machine. Alas, an unfucked bride: Swimming naked
and observed by handsome virile male actor name of Mog,
her simulated sex on sofa later advertised to be
the real ride. Movements to be reproduced by analog
or digitize? First prize. Alu will occur
three hundred thousand times in human genome
to be known and coded soon enough.
That's why A and Dalí loose their dog the Andalou
on B and you]

Coeval, then, & coefficient in the codices
of coinage, they sit together
in the private screening room: the mogul
and the moilers make a single molecule for a moment
as modalities come into play: The way
the young man strops his razor by a balcony, then deliberately
draws the blade across the woman's open eye that bleeds
on down the screen where just before they'd lit up
the Dakotas with some rushes of Calamity
and Wild Bill to test the sound. No sound now but
Dalí's voice, whispering to George and Miss Lamarr,
De Mille beginning to be ill:
                    In '29 we used a Gramophone
behind a curtain: *Tristan* and some tangos,
but you'll get the dirty puns: That man who cuts her eye
first glances at la lune and then we see her
face as if it were her ass, his gaze half-mooned,
her eye become her *oeil du cul* he'd diddle with a dildoe
so we play this little coup de vache
on every scatalogue and watch the ants emerge
from his stigmata, no? the way he's roped
to this machinery he drags, pianos stuffed with putrefying
donkeys and dos padres, si? the priests tied up and
on their backs in bondage of some kind as part of this
contrivance & De Mille out of his seat by now
and saying brother rat [?] or bugger that [? the file at
this point labeled diction inconsistent] so
we'll give them Custer Lincoln Hickok Cody Hopalong
and Jesus Christ at Rancho Grande, George
but what the hell is this?

I don't know, she says,
but that's the way I heard it. Also, I'd begun
of late to feel odd affinities with Paramount and MGM
and fully integrated scores of soothing violins
and mellow horns, and more than that I had this queer
attraction [was I Lesbo? did my database pick up
some viral pixels on my transatlantic trek?] for Miss Lamarr.
Although I still missed Paris & Picabia & Ez,
I'd always been, just like they said, Américaine: as Novia
or light bulb or arpeggio or pitch. I'd harmonized
across the times as if embracing intervals in rhymes
and here I was with Salvador and
Cecil's kitsch, my former lover back there fishing off
Le Havre and my senescent self
still climbing stairs in ludic loops. [42: Keyboard
and the bleeding head of donkey A.
43: Donkey A replaced by donkey B. 44: Male cyclist
in a housemaid's dress, a closing door.
45: A woman's wagging tongue whose text
is next: Tirer la langue;
it reels in time, those white keys teeth, the language
flowing through a leaking roof
a gamble & a Gödel proof; donkey C
is in our key, alive
alert, aloof.]

She says, although I seemed to be that
one qui perd ses dents and only climbed
the stairs, I felt immortal next to Hedy now who really
lived and so could only die, her dark machine
in that bright ghost a spectrum spread
like some black raven's wing. And George would write
their song. But as for you, my neuralnetted friend,
no one nominates an end, so try again at the beginning
where you counted rivets and were tempted
by the tempered steel. I'd style you as titular
Titanothere, cloned from Eocene into titanium,
statistical as your specific gravity
& valence & atomic weight. If you could swim
they'd cast you in her place.

In the Salzburg palace basement or the hidden conference room of his
Vienna flat, he'd show himself another print of the offending scene of
that same film his agents had again obtained at great expense—and then
destroy it. Obsession made him a discerning connoisseur; this print just a
little faded, that one slightly dark. But always there was her orgasmic St.
Teresa-of-a-mouth à la Bernini and Delilah nipples that De Mille would
say were sugar-coated with religion just for Samson's tongue. And writh-
ing hips and thighs. And naked ass. Of course she'd left him—actually
escaped by means of a disguise and complicated ruse—sometime in the
spring of 1937. But she'd listened first to all those conversations among
guests who'd come on business with the Hertzenberger Industries. Like
Krupp and Basil Zaharov, Mandl had the reputation of a man who'd start

a war if that would move the goods. Goebbels kissed her hand from time to time and Göring held her chair. No one understood that she could understand the technicalities. It was all a kind of music that accompanied the movie in her mind. As if someone who sat beside her at the baby grand on which she'd conjured storms in *Ecstasy* kept pointing out a spectral figure at an upright in the corner shadows of the stately palace room where she had been a silent party to analyses of radio control and interception by the politicians and the engineers. As if he played a phrase, a bar, a whole ballet of permutations that configured variations on the number eighty-eight and all were answered by the keys before her note for note. As if the notes were hopping frequencies no jealous husband lurking on a narrow signal band could jump or jam or even chase pursuant to an instrument for her arrest, and she could send encryptions of her own desires to a satellite or submarine in some determinable future's sky or sea. As if she were herself some wireless net through which transmission played its working titles and entitled wakings and its wacky tales, through which some Claire Lescot prepared to solo for her Turing test or sing along like yet another pianola at the prom.

Was it impractical to play piano rolls inside the missiles and torpedoes that a radio would guide along a band of frequencies stretching out to eighty-eight? Although this music from phantasmagoric Paris earned a US patent for its military application and eventually produced more racket than a dozen riots at Théâtre des Champs Elysées, in 1941 the War Department didn't think that George and Hedy could defeat the Nazis on their own. They thought they could. Leaving Cecil B and Dalí talking teleology at Paramount, they went to work and made a template down at Hedy's place outside LA at canyon Benedict. In 1957 the transistors at Sylvania finally made it sing. And now your cell phone rings. The wireless internet turns up a site devoted altogether to the Midi programs and the bank of synthesizers and the Apple Quadra that have synchronized the very music that created hopping frequencies and play it dancing à la ballet mécanique across contemporary spectra spread out in the night. Claire Lescot again walks shaken from the stage. Léger's laundress climbs and climbs the stairs. Milstar system's crosslink disk antennae make secure a constellation that's controlled by downlinked signals playing their encryptions which have harmonized in time.

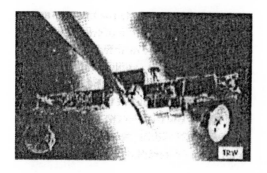

If EP thumped a drum in Paris and attempted a bassoon when A composed his trios and sonatas there for Olga Rudge, Harpo Marx in Hollywood was B flat major clarinetist in the symphonietta thrown together by despairing exiles, studio composers and indigenous eccentrics just to play a bit of Schoenberg in the war and keep their spirits up. It somehow follows thus. And A imagines all of them quite disembodied in a beautiful machine. With other incompatibles. Where into some blind switchman's roundhouse puffs an insubstantial 1850s Difference Engine pulling phantom coaches from the past all loaded with the numbers meaning Novia and étude and Américaine multiplied by the idea of a red caboose. Where EP is Express Pâquette. Who plays, that whore, for larks. That open door of Montparnasse. And Harpo Marx: These sparks that fly. And A's pneumatic-driven notes become electric quotes from 1923. In 1941 it's done in spite of Paramount for Miss Lamarr. And then it's done for Milstar in the sky or Disklavier that's clear on time's uncertain rhymes. Twelve hundred measures in your file for sequencing. Select your samples from a hand-cranked siren and orchestral bell and biwing props. Prepare a click track and beware the signatures that change six hundred times. Calculate in milliseconds and deploy the sixteen retrofitted grands. Clap hands. Enter isomorphic. Admit the Laundress and delete Lescot. Delete the autological. Let go. When every patron on the lam cries out: just one more time, and play it Sam, the answer sticks right in your gorge: I am not Sam, my name is George.

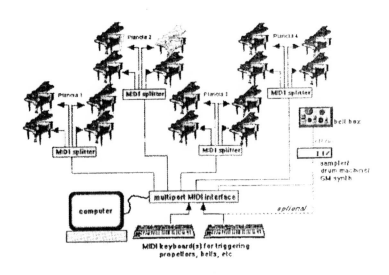

Not C. De Mille. An illness in the village of the will.

A poisoned well? A ringing bell.

Disgust, disgrace. With nearly everything in place.

In Hollywood is nothing good. The marble temples made of wood.

The templates, too. The idol Dagon stuck in glue.

A certain bet & neural net? The Russell paradox inside your set.

A rural ease and honey bees. Returning money on the lease.

CB: Your friends were all effete.

Antheil: This film of yours about Lafitte!

They fucked each other in the ass.

[And on the grass, those pirate lads.]

[Lescot: Our Hem went running with the bulls]

CB: Could any of them pay their bills?

Lamarr: I've nipples here to sell.

Antheil: And they had stories they could tell.

CB: Who's this Lescot? I'm sure not anyone I know.

Lafitte: A pirate! Get that in your notes.

Bassoon: Put "Harpo Marx" in quotes.

EP: When he was young, George worked for me.

We're stuck here in this DVD. Desktop, laptop, box of chips.

Mainframe swallows up our fame.

Bits of code all recombined. The Seine might just as well be Rhine.

CB: The past. Antheil: At last.

Lamarr: Too long is late but not too far.

Plaintext cyphered: stare by star

says steer [does it] by stair? Milhaud's prime beef qui était sur le toit is
either going up
or coming down whenever knot is now
is notnow not-knot anyhow old Mac iron bomb [ap-
pended copy to a copy and said *copy that*
repeats itself
plus copy of that copy &
original all hypercarded glut or metalepsis
boot again you fruit: It's Nipples
not In Naples.
Lafitte not With Your Feet.
Buccaneer, a bayou waterway, a privateer, one hundred twenty-three
pirogues & Andy Jackson too: New score]

                                                She says,
& that was Limbo not That Bimbo, Tex.
Try Lingo next: try glossing alu, angel capital, AI and ASR.
Try haptic interface and PGP and Qu-bit. Luddite
if you like but total touch environment is on the way with
virtual sex, though Hedy gets the parts in all these films.
As for me, I ended up at MIT in some robotics lab,
but that comes later on. In between comes Friedman cracking Purple
and Los Alamos and CB's pirate flick with George's score
and yes my own dear sweet dumb ex out riding
on his charger from Auteuil brandishing his relic of a saber
from the Franco-Prussian war and straight
into a column of advancing German tanks.
Never underestimate the new technologies. The plaice
is in your face. Strange to think CB had made
his first *Commandments* in the very year of *L'Inhumaine*.
The rest, perhaps, amendments,
and some justice there in Dalí's deli east of the Chinese.
On Murok Sands in the Mojave
Ramses & 300 chariots a Golden Calf the Laws & Orgies
all the Israelites the Pharaoh's city and an avenue
of twenty sphinxes worked out the techniques to blast
the Paris avant-garde and put the Samson-shears
in Hedy's hand. All downhill for Paris. Everybody in LA.
Sell out or be sold into some exhibition of degenerates;
collaborate and sing like Edith Piaf
or the Chevalier.

They told me *she* was working on
Tortilla Flats and just broke down completely when the news
came in about the war. The journey over on the Normandie
with Louis Mayer, who had offered her a job, and old
Cole Porter who kept whispering *oh you're the top* and
it's delovely and *experiment* right in her ear
had made her pretty optimistic in a gray grim world. But on
that day she walked right off the set and right past
Spencer Tracy, Steinbeck and the lot of them still costumed as
that simple little waif from Mexico and saying Find Me
George Antheil. We're going to sink the Hertzenbergers
and the Krupps with my torpedo.
That they tried to do, and for a while I toted round their
template, patented for George and Hedy Kiesler Markey
(which was briefly once her married name).

The post-war world was confusing and a little flat
for someone like myself who'd left her husband fishing
off Le Havre to join the brilliant entourage that pitched
its diachronics across time but came to grief in rhyme.
For a girl like me without a mother born as a machine,
I'd always had a mortal fear of *Philistine*. I went
to Princeton first and showed the figures round the Institute
where only the eccentric Barricelli took an interest.
We played four hands at George's early compositions sitting
side by side at one piano. I think he'd seen my film.
He said Your mutant language has evolved by crossings and
selections, just like species do. Take one of my cards.
A symbiogenic birth entirely from the numbers operating
on their own in Simula on DEC Sys 10. But here it is,
product of a B-math symbiont or parasite. Give it to Lamarr.
Your friends' piano-rolling weapon maybe didn't
end the war, but it could end the world. Its progeny will
be evolved in ways you cannot see and you yourself deserve
a Gödel number for your pains. He said Are you alive?
I thought he was a little nuts, but kissed him anyway
before we drove to town for Samson on a local screen....

And there she was in all her glory with that hunk
Mature who wielded for sure the jawbone of the ass
against his enemies just like it says in *Judges*.
Judge us, that's what we said in Paris, if you dare!
And did they dare? Did they draft a thousand barbers
just to cut our hair? Who but we could best put forth
the riddle of the lion's carcass and the swarm of bees?
We'd caught three hundred foxes, put the firebrands
to their tails, and loosed them barking in the standing corn.
Such corn there was! And kitsch!
We dwelt then at the top of Etam rock
which crumbled in the end and made us exiles.
Had they done their plowing with our heifer? Did
George's hair grow long again grinding in the prison house
of Paramount? Hedy played the harlot for the Philistines,
but that was all an act...

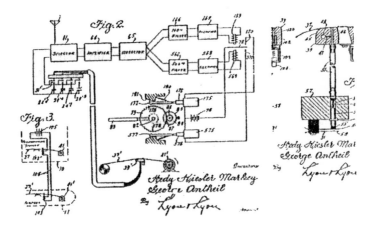

I hear they keep
old prints of *L'Inhumaine* and *Ballet Mécanique* in some
dark archive where, like Mandl with his prints of *Ecstasy*,
they turn each other on with clips cut from the body
of our work. At MIT they want to know what makes me tick.
I blip and flicker, but I turn no trick.
They're racing with the Japs at Honda to perfect their
human motion simulation software
and a clumsy biped toddler they call Dick.
I don't tell them much. What floundered first on Flanders Field
wasn't plaice. In any case. Nor when jockeys rode against
the Panzers crossing near Sars-Poteries
the undefended river Meuse. That other river that I loved
still passes Troyes and Melun and our
shining hungry haunted city of Between the Wars before
it loops through Normandy and past Rouen to empty in the sea.
Someone's fishing there. He looks like you.
I think I loved him once.
A washer-woman tired as I am now stops her climbing
up the endless stairs beside the Seine
and looks behind her with appreciation at the view.

Laundry Lists and Manifestoes

People often leave no record of the most critical or passionate moments of their lives. They leave laundry lists and manifestoes.

—A.S. Byatt

I am writing a manifesto and I don't want anything, I say however certain things and I am on principle against manifestoes, as I am also against principles.

—Tristan Tzara

He brought me also a box of sugar, a box of flower, a bag full of lemons, and two bottles of lime juice, and abundance of other things: But besides these, and what was a thousand times more useful to me, he brought me six clean new shirts, six very good neckcloaths, two pair of gloves, one pair of shoes, a hat, and one pair of stockings, and a very good suit of cloaths of his own, which he had worn but very little: In a word, he cloathed me from head to foot.

—Defoe, *Robinson Crusoe*

᷾

Nausicaa heard a buzzing in her ear.
A whisper—Girl, you left
The laundry waiting over night. That list, where is it?
Sashes, dresses, bedspreads, sheets & socks,
Your royal father's robes...
Expect a manifesto any moment that may issue from
The throne—not Alcinous', but one
Much higher, darker, grander, more sublime. I may look
Like Dymas' daughter, but behold:
I bring you soap and bleach and starch from very heaven.
Take your girlfriends and your maids. Take
A beach ball too.

               Elsewhere in that meanwhile, Yahweh
Stood complaining in the water that was now
Just ankle-deep—Girl, he said to Japheth's wife, you left
The laundry waiting over night. That list, where is it?
Quick before the waters all recede and we stand here in sand:
Wash the dirty linen and the garments of them all—Japheth,
Shem and Ham, N himself & Mrs N—
Here's the soap and bleach and starch. Here's a beach ball too.
But where is Noah's manifest?

∾

N in fact had lost it, drunk inside his tent, and couldn't
Reconstruct it from his memory; all those birds and
Mice and cats and dogs and even bugs and things. It seemed
As arbitrary as a laundry list. Still, old Yahweh'd brought
Them through and wanted an accounting. He took
His own frustration out on Ham who stood outside the tent
Staring at his father's genitals. Don't stare at my genitals, said N
And soon thereafter issued his explosive anti-Canaan manifesto...

Meanwhile in the elsewhere, Nausicaa was playing
With her beach ball having done the wash and laid it out on
Rocks to dry: her thong, her super-low-cut jeans, her black lace
Demi-bra and other things she'd ordered from the catalogue
She read with flashlight in the night hiding underneath her sheet.
Suddenly a stranger came out of the bushes holding
Just a leafy twig to hide his genitals. She told him that her name was
Nausicaa and that she'd come to do the wash. Then
She asked to see his manifest. Alas, he said, I've lost it with
My ship and all my men, but you can put this on
Your laundry list—and took away the twig. Impressed, she
Bathed the stranger in the stream where she had washed
Her under things along with father's robes and brother's
Cricket togs. But soon she realized she'd left the list itself at home
With half the things the whisperer had spoken of.

❧

We have the record of the stranger's deeds, his wily ways,
His journey home when washed and dressed and
Celebrated at the court of Alcinous. We have the history of
Abram's offspring after Babel. But Shem and Ham and Japheth,
Gomer, Madai, Javan, Tubal, Meshech, Tiras, Riphath,
Togarmah and many others on the J & P lists might as well be
Coat and tie and shirt and trousers on the one Nausicaa left at home
That floats up on a foreign shore right now.
Of Nausicaa little else is known (though more has been
Surmised.) She went on with her wash.
Zeus & Yahweh went on to become Suprematists
(The empty squares of cities not, as Kasimir Malevich
Was to say, mere empty squares).

≈

Even in Vienna they could feel the earth shake as Poseidon
Dropped a mountain in the harbor of the Phacians.
For a moment, Donna Anna ceased to sing *Come furia disperata*;
Il Commendatore dropped his guard
Just long enough to feel the sting of Giovanni's sword. As they
Resumed, the maestro lost his place & skipped to Leporello's
Laundry list: *Ogni villa, ogni borgo—*
Sing along with me yourself—in Italy six hundred eighty,
Germany two hundred twelve, France a hundred,
Spain a thousand—wenches
Maidens, ladies of the court: the laundress
Or the duchess or the barely legal teen: any shape or any age:
Nella bruna, la costanza; nella bianca, la dolcezza;
Tall or short or thin or fat, horny singles, desperate wives,
Non si picca se sia ricca se sia brutta se sia bella
Purche porti la gonnella...

≈

Giovanni turns up as
A stoned guest in Zurich, Tristan Tzara thundering
Against the 1 and 2 and 3 of things
While Leporello's list of ladies finds its way to Ararat to
Be released as species in the long dream of Darwin.
But who was girl eighty-six in Germany? girl fifty-four in Italy?
Who one hundred three in Spain? Who was thin and
Who was fat, who was barely legal? Simultaneologists debate
These questions with the Paratactical Historicists.
The friends of Nausicaa were Tamar and Elvira? Zeus & Yahweh
Sang like Il Commendatore, looking on the dead at Troy
And Sodom and the Somme?

                    Nausicaa washes on and on,
Her hands all red and gnarled. Her father wouldn't know her,
Nor would you. She washes out the blood of centuries.
Her list is endless and includes those things
You got for all but nothing at the Army-Navy store:
The shirt with corporal's stripes, a neat hole through the pocket
Right above the heart; a greatcoat out of which she never
Got the stains. The *manus* in the manifesto was cut off by Saladin,
Strictly following Koranic Law. *Profit not by Prophets*, one
Apostate's declaration had begun. *Yangtse not by Yahweh*
Sang a lost Confucian ode. Rebel Angels in a flight
Of biwing planes out of meanwhile into
Elsewhere and beyond…

＆

For their fine linen, Chapman's Homer says, *Trojan women and*
Their fair daughters had a Laundry. Heywood: *Except the sonne shyne*
That our clothes may dry, we can do ryght nought in our wash.
Crabbe: Fair Lucy First, the laundry's grace and pride...
And as for Lists: did Homer crib his own from sub-Mycenaean
Catalogues all full of places no one can identify & captains who arrive
In ships with fanfare out of elsewhere, never to be mentioned once again?
This was not the place where all his listeners nodded off
Or turned the dial back to classic rock. It was his great & cinematic feat
Of memory, & everybody hung on these 300 lines claiming for himself some
Otherwise unknown and well-born forebear, basher of skulls,
As the high if broken branch of their family tree. He'd take off into
It by error sometimes trying to remember what came next
In his more recent poem. In the midst of *Odyssey* the fans of *Iliad*
Would startle him by shouting out: *Do the bloody ships.*

᪇

Fair Lucy First, said Crabbe. Who was Lucy Second? Or was he
Counting off a list, with Lucy first, Sally next, then Jane?
(All of them together laundry's grace and pride)
To list…
                    incline to one side, tilt; heel over as in danger
On a stormy sea; listen as in *List, Nausicaa, you left the laundry*
Over night—or *List, Donna Anna, do it like a Furia Disperata*;
To be pleasing or to satisfy, to be disposed; n.—a desire or inclination;
A narrow strip of wood; an area for tournaments, a place of combat,
Ridge thrown up between two furrows by a lister; written entry
Of particulars or people sharing things in common, as
Pêneleôs, Lôitos, Arkosilaôs, Prothoênor, and other captains,
All Boiotians: Eilésion, Erythrai, Eleôn—
                                    Or Sidon, Heth,
And others from the seed of Noah out of whom the Y god
Made his nations; or the girls
Of the Anti-Giovanni League whose manifesto was the work
Of Lucy I, executed by authorities, succeeded by
Her daughter, Lucy II, honored as a forbear in
The long awaited listserve Cyborglog.com
Good St. Wystan; Never trust a critic who does not like lists—
The genealogies in Genesis, the Catalogue of Ships.
Manifestos, meanwhile,
can be used like Manna (4): exudate of the Eurasian ash,
Fraxinus ornus, taken as a laxative
In any kind of wilderness [Aramaic, *mannā*,
Hebrew, *mān*]. There was a knight who listed for a maid,
But we are merely in the background of his great
Seduction scene, plowing furrows, sorting beans and lentils,
Coriander, wheat.

❧

Maidens, kilt your skirts and go?
Mary, I want a lyre with strings Me so oft
my fancy drew Men grew sae cauld, maids sae unkind
Methought I saw my late espousèd saint Milton!
thou shouldst be living at this hour Mine be a cot beside the hill
More love or more disdain I crave Most Holy Night
that still dost keep Mother I cannot mind my wheel Much
have I travell'd in the realms of gold
Music, when soft voices die My Damon was the first to wake
My dead love came to me and said My dear and only Love
I pray My delight and thy delight My heart
aches, and a drowsy numbness pains My heart is high above
my body full of bliss My heart is like a singing bird My heart
leaps up when I behold My little son
who look'd from thoughtful eyes My life closed twice
before its close My lute, awake!
perform the last My mother bore me in the southern wild
Mysterious Night! when our first parents knew...

we'd sort out seeds—beans & lentils, coriander, wheat, maids
And musics, all the Ms, the Ls, the Ps—
Marie and Psyche, you and I, Lucy one and two—
Hot and tired with heavy work, listless by the end of day.

෨

Broken bits of tablet, tokens, tallies, notches,
Tabulation in cuneiform. In Tom Sawyer's pocket there are
Nouns: *fish-hooks, a lump of chalk, a marble.*
Ubi Sunt or Blazon?
Distributio, Expolitio, Incrementum: or make a mingle-mangle
Of it, or a concatenation. Congeries. Enumeratio.
Rocks, caves, lakes, fens, bogs, dens and so and so and so.
For a chance to fly, *a dead rat & string to swing it on.*
Rebel Angels in their biwing planes...

                                           Pierre Albert-Birot,
Blaise Cendrars, Filippo Tomasso Marinetti.
Khlebnikov.
Tzara.
Antonin Artaud.

꙳

Crusoe, like Odysseus
And Noah, lost his original list, like
Ishmael was the only soul among the farers on his ship the sea released.
Coins and precious metals were no use, although in time
He counted them. One by one he inventoried items of survivor's gold.
Spirits in the guild of fraud and guile
Perforce at Pandemonium
One by one stood up in council making manifesto of their
Will: *Manifesto for an Open War.*
Manifesto for Ignoble Ease & Sloth. Manifesto for a Nether Empire
In the Flames. Manifesto for Seduction of the Ones who
Dwell in Music, Phacia, Indices, Cockaigne, & Realms of Gold.

Them did Yahweh
Hurl headlong filthy into laundries cursed by
Noah in the son of Ham whose Canaanites and neighbors
Named the spirits (former names all lost and blotted out) the likes of
Chemos and Astarte, Thammuz, Dagon, Rimmon, Isis and Osiris,
Orus, Belial, along with Ion's Greeks, the sons of
Japheth's sons (Japheth's wife still working with Nausicaa
Somewhere on the other side of 12 degrees and 18 minutes latitude:
A storm blew westward and the ship struck sand, the sea
Breaking her apart...

&

  ...bags of nails & spikes,
Screw-jack & hatchet, grindstone & musket balls &
Guns: a quantity of powder, small shot & hammock:
Top-sail rigging rope & twine a hogshead of bread.
Runlets of rum the cables and a hawser—
Salvaged in the end by swimming out & rafting back
Eleven times until the wreckage of his battered ship blew off
The sand and sank.
Floating on the flood tide, a large red ball.
And on the beach Beelzebub with Khlebnikov.
Against whom hum, said one.
Him who heaved the wave? The other, *Hum who will his tune.*
A time there was when toil gave us tithing.
Teething gave us tooth to frighten toves. Timber built a threat
To talismanic tomb.
Temper well the will to wake and wend.
A landing strip was built close by the opera house, while in
The monastery Marinetti was the single scribe
Scribbling
   love of danger, energy, revolt.
Speed and the machine. A racing car. Aggression & destruction of
Academies, museums. Only war is hygiene. Hymn who can
The multicolored polyphonic tides, the vibrant nightly fervor
Of the arsenal blazing underneath electric moons.

Thus he would inflate Nausicaa's ball.

≈

As for arsenals, Crusoe built his own—the warehouse or
The magazine, he called it. He tells his diary that he'd omitted from his list
The pens, ink and paper, compasses and dials he'd salvaged
From the wreck. Also charts, perspectives, books
On navigation. He had from Portugal a Popish book of prayer;
He had three English Bibles. Needle, pins and thread, a shovel
And an axe. He stored his arms and powder in the arsenal.
He built a desk. He read a Bible and he wrote,
But not like Khlebnikov, whose blather near the landing strip
Annoyed him. Declaiming through a megaphone,
Khlebnikov would shout: *Zaum. Mountain. Island lu lu ssob.*
Kumara.
Nicht nicht pasalam bada eschochomo.
                                                        Crusoe
In a fever thought he saw a man descending in
A cloud—Yahweh, Zeus, Beelzebub as anthromorph?—
Who then became bright flame, who made the earth shake
When he walked upon it. His voice was terrible.
He said: *Mein Herr, sing for anything you like you wish you want.*
The ague made him thirst, so he sang: *Water.*
Waiter, menu of medicinals
                Hellebore, H. lleborus orientalis,
Berberis vulgaris, Papaver somniferum, Tamarisk, Pearl Wart,
Baldur's blood and Bryony. Mandrake root.
Kumara?
Nicht nicht pasalam bada eschochomo.
In delirium, he spat up manifestos just like Khlebnikov: *Island lu lu ssob.*
Mountain. Zaum.
All of which was Manna (4): exudate of the Eurasian ash,
Fraxinus ornus, taken as a laxative
In any kind of wilderness. [Aramaic, *mannā*,
Hebrew, *mān*]. *Mine be a cot beside the hill*
My dead love came to me and said My heart is high above
my body full of bliss My heart is like

a singing bird Mysterious night!
when our first parents knew you'd sort out seeds
and number names.

⁊

Number for example Lord Chamberlain his men & courtesans—
Banded players in a worst of times and branded
Best of teams,

                                 trams on down the Strand
Where horses draw the mighty
Quartered for the pleasure of the bull baiters
Bear baiters
Tosspots watching sly Will Sly and fat Will Kemp
Burbage Cowley Duke & Sinklo
Hemmings tosses bright red ball Nausicaa put in play to
John Grabowski Urban Shocker Combes in center
Ruth in right and Gehrig (Yankees just before the crash) first base.
Baseless claims against the *mano / manus* fundamental to their
Manifesto also hands for pleasuring the prurient the skills of
Blanche d'Antigny La Barucci Cora Pearl
Mademoiselle the Maximum Marie Duplessis Apollonie their little hands
On little balls and pricks of players bandits poets
Princes brought to practice upright just
And honorable men.

∂

Manus. Festus. Gripped by hand.
A manifest a kind of handgrasp, then a slap.
Some Cora's John in Chamberlain his men's most recent
Travesty of history, thumb and digits set to curve a little Latin o,
Hurls haptic knowledge over printer's plate
As now garroting or the axe could end the asking touch me now.

Touch me how, old clown? Some festive Feste's ball game
Play house place of ill repute? Even in the elsewhere
With their handicaps. From the handbook: bite the hand that
Feeds you eat out of another's hand & oh
Although hands down
And on the other hand lay hands on him high handedly
Throw up your hands or tip just one they're clean it's heavy
Got to hand it to you...
                            handkerchief or handiwork
Or Nausicaa's red ball—

Manifesto of the Fully Opposable Thumb:

≈

[...although between ellipses & in brackets, toes
Of manifestoes must be noted too: Man the nomad,
Aboriginal, creature of the large toe
Before the thumb, may have got a toe-hold on the
Path or rural route, sung his world into
Being, exited his animal & cave through a desert
Or an outback, grown his brain beyond co-laterals,
Memorized his lines, walked from Egypt,
Walked from Chareville
—a misprint in our own recent treatise on the
Bogomils confuses *songs* and *slogs*—*Lettre du Voyant* a
Manifesto of the foot and not the hand?
Ask the Abyssinian Rimbaud if toffs at dinner back
In Trojan's Dinar Diner (pizza and kebab)
Know enough to throw a toggle switch or even
Tattoo *tau*: a young lady in my colleague's
Final class before retirement going to the dean about
His sexist language when he said she
Shouldn't pussyfoot around, prevarication not to
Be desired but also not to be confused with
Eager toe of prurient intent...
                                        Slog on]

~

…thumb that makes for consciousness, &
Not the other way around. Forty thousand years, more or less,
Since Chiro Adónaison uploaded agency.
No paw or claw or forefoot but the Ur-tool blessed by every
Tinker tailor soldier spy who
Once was hominid & grasped itself becoming manifestal
Agent for a span beyond biology—Anaxagoras, who
Shook the hound of Aristotle, tooling down
The highway in his supercharged Lamarck. Thumb is up or down
Or meeting digits picking up a pickled pepper
Thumb opposes fully human fall from grace and makes
With fingers ancient fist to shake against the sky. Handsome Tom
Says touch me now Apollonie she says I will
My sweet and lovely biped all because of chiro-genesis.
Chiromancy to reveal Arminians among the flock?
Manifesterians all, depravity is only partial, freedom opens
Like a chiropractor's palm.

Hand me down prehension goes that line of thought
Or you'll construct a Calvinist at Leiden.
Courtesans in court deny their destiny is manifest
But list their favorite tricks. Prehensile tallies where
The RBI statistics all emerge, but prehistoric to a one
The hook-grip, scissor, five-jaw chuck
The disk- & sphere- & squeeze-grip: pops it up in short left field
Where Robert Meuseul hauls it in and throws
It all the way to Gehrig catches runner well off base besides.
And who's that girl whose touch becomes professional—
Former maid of music, product of the crazy Liszt—
Handy in her knowledge of applause
When sign of wantonness and frank caress
May guarantee a patron and the reigning Traviata
Singing like a caged Macaw? In Crusoe's dream a thumb
And fingers slip into her house the night she dies
And take her tinker taylor's tintype, take her
Bird food, bracelet, banquet table, comb
And brushes, candelabrum, Bible, letters, contraceptive pills
And all the words that tell her story. They take the gifts
Nausicaa left her, all the notes she played, her
Brooklyn lover and her Dumas *fils*. They take her *aux camélias*
Her Duplessis and her Marie. They
Take her *touch me here* and *bonne nuit mes amis*

෴

Therefore, they pass by—Nausicaa and the
Demimondaine girls—with nothing to declare at customs
By the foot of Ararat except themselves
While at the summit of the world above a Sea of Boos & Outrage
He who makes the martyrs to the proposition that
Sublime is Always Now and Everything is Always the First Time
Declines in power wondering if everything is always
The last chance. In Epistemon's visit to Elysium
The riffraff out of Rabelais work on: Joyous Dr. Festus who
Was hand-gripper, hand-groper,
Puts his hands not in the bowl of cherries but in earth
Beside a grove where all the others labor too
Digging their own graves. Xerxes cries for mustard, Cyrus
For his cows; Ulysses sews a shroud while
Agamemnon washes corpses and the sons of Fabius
Thread beads...
                              Poor Marie must sort out seeds.
Given Psyche's task, she can't tell beans
From lentils on her list, can't tell oats
From peas from Q's from qu-bits, can't find missing
Letters of the alphabet or find the cancelled tickets
For the lector's lecture on the laws...

≈

...mislaid by fingers that mis-key command for mitzvah,
Change *Nausicaa*'s to *Eurekas*
In a spell check: *Cyborg Manifesto* is immediately downloaded
While the courtesans gather up their reputations, enter
Through consumption in the lungs of Verdi's score: Virus has her
Way with Listserve, hands re-tool as handmaids
Of the process working on its own. Letters of the alphabet interpreted
As all the saved epistolary files, and so the poem in progress
Is sent out from A to Z. Giovanni grows prosthetic
When confronted with the simulacrum of the Dada Modest Woman,
Baroness von Freytag-Loringhoven plus
Attachments: coal-scuttle headdress & the nipple-rings dangling
Down brass balls. Cyborg manifesto steps
Around both Zeus and Yahweh to embrace Chimera as a fabricated
Hybrid: Tools are coded stories and the copies don't
Require an original. It may cost an arm and leg, but consider
The alternative. Where medicine's a hermeneutic of the network,
Noumena become *Das Nichts*. Arrange a nano-implant and proceed
To disengage: Cyborg semiology signals to theology; God nor
Goddess may survive the creatures of an integrated circuit
Leaving laundry lists & manifests trailing from the greatest moments
Of their lives, dualisms of a hierarchy naturalized
Before the language took on fusion of the manus & machine
Whereby Nausicaa never wakes despite the urging of the one
Disguised as Dymus' child.

∾

Noah says *Who cares about my*
Genitals when Ham looks in his tent. Kasimir Malevich paints
Away at academic nudes; Khlebnikov embraces the
Horatian ode. When Donna Anna sings *Come furia disperata*,
Il Commendatore kills her on the spot; Caruso sails
Away where 12 degrees and 18 minutes latitude's the formula
For song; Tzara praises 1 and 2 and 3.
Biplane avant-guardists loop their loops in functions
So recursive there is no avant to guard, radio an
Elsewhere in the meanwhile where it's all
A mingle-mangle, concatenation. Surface now
Outfaces depth and replication reproduction as the odd
Dualisms will no longer dial up: whole/part, woman/man
Living/Dead, maker/made or courtesan or maid or player or
The played. Aacisuan and 911 and Sessylu respond
O Mussulmans, save our goods from wretched unbelievers,
Look what's in our pocket, Tom: He words us, girls,
Mechanic slave with rule and hammer, saucy lector catches
Us like strumpets, scald rhymer who extemporally enacts
Our greatness as a squeaking boy—
Fish-hook, marble, lump of chalk. O dead rat and
String to swing it on!

~

First image ever streaming in of Monad
Claiming two hemispheres and four
Calculators for its cinema, gonad aching from a Yankee
Curve that got it in the groin: grainy movies of
The all-departing all escorted by the simulacra on their screen:
Counter tenors, sheep and goats, fallen angels, obtuse
Angles, David's armies, birds of paradise and beasts
Of the apocalypse. Clans of courtesans & baseball fans hurrah
Among the tangled wires and brachia
The polys, seriations, pleonasms in extreme
While slipping into sequence of possessive phrases
Of the quantum of the zero of the one of the watcher
Of the disambiguating
  decoherence of the end of the beginning
    and beginning of the end
Of the letter of the law of the laughter of
  the lawless... [1]

[1] See Notes, p. 350

~

...while on a promontory broken off
The screensaver image of an ancient SE10
Madam C's nine cognates gather around boxes dropped
By Ever Afterlife Balloonists working on the script
Of *Cargo Cults*. They argue (the cognates) that a manifest
Attached to shipment listing all collaterals and cogs,
Codes and codices for Mme's Nothing Else Cockaigne Machine
In fact are elegiac poems, that David sings for Jonathan,
Gilgamesh for Enkidu. They inscribe themselves as
Manifestoes which proclaim their faith in algorithms of an
Unknown field of force. They're cognizant and they can glow.
They're coeternal, and they rise to an occasion.
Although they tell no story of their lives, their little trumpets blow.

Kedging in Time

[Kedge, v. intr. A. To warp a ship, or move it from one position to another by winding in a hawser attached to a small anchor dropped at some distance; also trans. To warp. B. Of a ship: To move by means of kedging.] Poets, too, may cast an anchor well before them, pulling forward when attached to something solid, only then to cast their anchor once again.

For some of the families involved:

Drury-Lowe, Adams, Bonham-Carter, Hilton-Young, Young

Part I

Thirty-Nine Among the Sands, His Steps
or riddle there:
>   who may have sailed the Alde, and out into
the sea, but still was not the helmsman,
she was he, the captain's daughter, child too
of children's strategies on tidal rivers
where the toy wooden soldiers rose
in marshmist reeds and tipped their Bismarck helmets
to the girls, *Achtung!*

>   Cousin Erskine had preceded
by some leagues
and even Uncle Win. Sons of Lord Anchises,
prophesying war, sang
of arms and men who had come back again
by whom the bundled fasces were
restored...

&

or sailed in the channel all alone, the narrow sea
and north. Or with a friend to crew,
his maps about him and his nerves in perfect
order but his thoughts preoccupied
in case the Hun would launch those lighters full of infantry
from waters around Frisian islands or between
the unmapped sands and point them
toward the Wash or Suffolk shingle where no yachtsman
out of Orford, Harwich, Woodbridge or along
the Essex flats would come at them
like Jellicoe out of some dispatch he read at Scapa Flow...

or sat there with a romance, *Zenda* say, just as she
had done, and Winston doubtless too whose
own *Savrola* marked a pause between the Bores and bells
of a pugnacious dreadnaught caught in shore fire
steaming up the Dardanelles...

                        Fortune had to sail up the narrow
channel between heavy guns in batteries
on either side. The harbor city of Laurania could be
bombarded from the port, but only if
the ships survived their passage. *Petrarch* and *Sorato* followed,
turrets slowly turning, firing at embrasures
and the barbette mounted canons on the rocky banks.
Black smoke poured from stricken ships and
water jetted from the scuppers as emplacements pounded
the returning Admiral and his sailors who
had come from Port Said to quell rebellions in this
Ruritanian romance. He paced the quarter deck like Nelson
while Savrola waited for him with subaltern and
Antonio Molara's widow whom he loved, dreams of a
Republic in his brain...

❧

Or simply dreams of power, he thinks,
and puts aside his pen to pour himself a gin. It is 1897.
He'll publish this in 1900 and become
First Lord in time to send his ships into another well-defended
strait. Does in fact do this and thinks of Xerxes' bridge across
the narrows and Leander's swim from Sestos,
Byron too aspiring to the Hellespont, Troy on the Asian side
and Schliemann's archaeologists in search of Bronze Age
towers now become the Kaiser's gunners when
in 1915 ships steam out of romance up the channel toward
The Marmora, *Agamemnon* and *Inflexible* bombarding Turkish
forts at Kilid Bahr, mines and shore fire blasting
Irresistible into a drifting
and abandoned hulk...

⌘

Or an abandoned plan: evacuation scuttles the agenda which
had confidently hoped to open the Aegean
once again to Russian ships and drive the Turks beyond
Constantinople by a landing
from the barges which were built on orders
to attack—not Gallipoli—but points along the German Baltic coast.
Only Richard Hannay knew that Wilhelm gave it out he was a secret
Muslim and proclaimed a Jihad in Islamic lands
against the Brits. Davies & Carruthers
sailed the *Dulcibella* through the Kiel Canal early in the century.
What they saw might well preoccupy the Admiralty
in these contentious weeks, Sea Lord
Fisher hiding at a Charing Cross hotel from Lloyd George.
Someone sends out copies of *The Riddle of the Sands* to sailors
at the Firth of Forth and Scapa Flow where only fiction
saw as early as '03 the dangers lurking in the Frisians
for the eastern coast. The real skipper of that prophecy is executed
by a firing squad for having in his pocket such a little gun
it might as well have been a toy.

∾

But *Vixen* was no toy. Nor the guns he ran on Asgard to the
shores of Howth that against express intention
ended in the hands of Easter's Irishmen. In Irish, English, Frisian
or Aegean waters, what's the future of the future tense?
What's propitious in the past? Passing through the present,
kedging's all you're good for
with a foot of water under you, the tide gone out, the fog so thick
you can't see lights at Norderney but enter history in spite of that by
sounding in its shallows with an oar.
While *Petrarch's turrets turned, firing at embrasures and*
the barbette mounted cannons on the rocky
banks outside Laurania whose captain put aside his pen
to pour himself another gin and daydream about power, *Vixen* in that
sea-log sanguine summer tacked its way across the Channel
to Boulogne, then to Holland & through scattered
islands off the Heligoland Bight,
Wangerooge and up the Elbe past Cuxhaven, then through
Wilhelm's ship canal into the Baltic
and the Schlei Fiord, then back...

                         1897's log ends up intact
in 1903's fiction that prefigures 1915's fact:
Groped three-reefed and gale grew much worse
with heavy rain, wind veered to northeast
and blew a hurricane. Soon got into breakers found a devil of a
situation fearful work with tiller several heavy jibes
when close inshore then grounded but blew off again entire population
of the beach was waving. Dunes obscured by such high tide
but soon we tore into the mouth of something like a harbour, let go anchor
with a run then luffed and brought up just in time
with bowsprit over quayside, crowds of people standing and amazed
as if we'd fallen from the sky.

❧

In the sky, Zeppelins and buzzing biwing sea-planes.
In the epilogue, memorandum taken from a stove
in Norderney deciphered well before Room 40's codemen went to work
that indicated plans to send an infantry with light artillery
out of Frisian mists on lighters pulled by tugs of shallow draft and
land them on the flats along the Essex coast, perhaps at
Brightlingsea, perhaps the north side of the Wash.
The skipper of the *Vixen* and the riddler of the sands,
a deuce of trouble for the aces of *echt deutsch*, climbs
aboard a Short 136 & flies north-east above the U-boat shoals,
navigates with maps he'd drawn of islands, channels, tides when
only fishermen and pleasure craft sailed from the mouths of
Elbe and Wesser, Ems and Jade, when no ships of the *Hochseeflotte*
hid from some definitive Trafalgar.

Part II

Or from the Master of the *Dulcibella*.

His official paper
for the Admiralty is called
The Seizure of Borkum and Juist. It turns
an epilogue to forward policy proposing that the barges being
shipped to the Aegean should return, that islands which
command the branches of the Ems be taken by surprise, the German
North Sea coast blockaded. *Then invade the Frisians*
in a major action, mine all river mouths and sink a wall of scrap,
follow mapping made in fiction, loosing Russian allies
on the Baltic coast in fact. Churchill & the Sea Lords choose Gallipoli.
But not before commending him for valor in the air
and prescience at sea. Easter's Ireland waits.
In villages near Lowestoft they shout *Them roundels*
on the fuselage is us. And airships drift above the sea like
great balloons escaped the clumsy hand of Albion's
last giant's giant child. Commanders at the Harwich harbor
seek to maintain what they call an "atmosphere."

Hannay's word as well: an atmosphere. But not just one of
mastery, control, intimidation on the seas, though he too seeks
a new Trafalgar when the code words *Hafgaard Luneville Avocado Pavia*
begin to yield results and *High Tide 10.17* reveals
in tables at the Admiralty a big chalk headland close to Bradgate
and the murderous Black Stone who'd steal plans for disposition
of the ships at Scapa Flow and Rosyth just by blending in so well
that ministers and brass around the council table
might take someone with a beard and heavy hooded eyes
to be Lord Alloa himself.

∾

Trafalgar Lodge establishes
another atmosphere in days when *wildest fictions are more probable*
than facts. No one shouts out there around the tennis lawn or in
the smoking room among those gentlemen the spies, *Them roundels*
on the fuselage is us. The fact is Hannay's Buchan worked in codes
for Captain Hall, "The Blinker"—man of penetrating heavy
hooded eyes—while Buchan's Hannay found himself employed by
Alfred Hitchcock in the run-up to another war. Just ask
Mr. Memory, whose paratactic act will be the death of him
at the Palladium: *When was Crippen hanged? What's the measurements*
of Miss Mae West? When was General Gordon at Khartoum?
Who swam Hellespont? What's a monoalphabetic cipher what's
sunk off the Ulster coast where's the veldcraft chap who o'er the hill
and moory dale pursues Arimaspian in Schicksalskampf? What's
the peripeteia of the anagnorisis? What's the number of steps?

While Hannay tiptoes toward Trafalgar Lodge and notes
the tennis lawn, the marguerites, geraniums and other seaside flowers,
a yacht with Squadron's ensign rocks at anchor at
high tide. 10.17. In the Dardanelles, evacuation's under way
the day the book which he inhabits enters time.
He wonders what may melt into an atmosphere, leak out of a landscape.
Then he blows his little whistle, twice. Someone's shouting out *das Boot,*
and then *Der schwarze Stein.* The fat man who escapes becomes
von Schwabing in another place, Hannay Hitchcock's
creature in another time. Soldiers of the Empire, reading
one another's books, might find one who flew Cuxhaven's raid
remembering at Harwich guns he ran on *Asgard* after Black Hand Serbs
had shot the Archduke, Wilhelm sailing the Norwegian
fiords in *Hohenzollern* fully sixteen years after *Vixen's*
journey north;

＃

           twelve years after *Dulcibella* kedging
in the tidal stream; nineteen years of Isle of Wight regattas bringing
cousins Nicky, Willy, George to lunch at Osborne House,
boats from round the world to dip their pennants while the guns
saluted Kaiser, King, and Tsar...
But this is for the Dublin Volunteers. This is from
the men who shipped their freight from off the *Gladiator* bobbing
by the light ship north of Dover, then set mainsail,
mizzen, spinnaker and sailed toward a passage through maneuvers
of the fleet off Cowes. Near Brighton, practice firing from the
warships lights the pier where boys in shorts and girls in
pinafores stare into the west and *Asgard* sails on to Spithead,
brass bands playing on the decks of dreadnoughts passing
in review, their rails lined with sailors and marines. When the weather
turns against her, *Asgard* beats up past the Lizard, somehow
tacks around Land's End to Holyhead, then across the Irish Sea
fighting a nor'easter at full gale.

But go ask Mr. Memory: *Exactly who were Dublin Volunteers?*
Was De Valera there? Did Erskine Childers eat Carruthers' heart?
Who returned to Ireland in a German submarine when
Asgard's captain still served Empire and Ascendancy in Short 136
in skies above the Heligoland Bight? Who was hanged and who was shot
and why? Did Churchill cheer and did Cuchulain weep?
Who steps Thirty-Nine among the sands or riddles there
who also may have sailed the Alde? On 29 July the fleet leaves
Portland in the dark to pass the straits of Dover, eighteen miles of
warships undetected steaming toward the foggy empty waters
in the north...

～

and Pamela was nine.
She lived near Rosyth in the little coastal
village, Aberdour. Her father was a captain & she sometimes
saw his ship out on patrol. She wished she were a boy
and could go to sea herself and didn't like it when
her mother & the other naval wives would say
But you can marry a sailor! Precocious reader, she'd go down
to the rocks emerging at low tide with Buchan or Childers,
Rider Haggard or Hope. She'd be the hero on the run,
she'd be the spy, she'd be the swashbuckling master
of a masked identity. Then she'd make a large uncovered stone
her ship, fire a broadside at the Germans who were hunting
through the fogs to find her father and, although
she didn't know it, her future husband too. Her own child
would also be a captain's daughter and the strategist of
tidal rivers to the south where toy wooden soldiers rose in marshmist
reeds and tipped their Bismarck helmets to the girls, *Achtung!*
Achtung! her father joked, running towards her laughing down
the iron pier where landing craft left officers and men
who now and then were granted leave. He'd walk with her along
the narrow path between the bay and village, rightful
king of Ruritania, prisoner freed from Zenda and engaged
to Princess Flavia; and she'd be Rudolph Rassendyll
dueling for his borrowed crown & honor with Black Michael's
black usurping henchmen on the castle bridge.
Then her father's utter great fatigue would overwhelm him
and he'd lie down in the sun,
shade his aching eyes with his daughter's open book...

ༀ

If you asked Mr. Memory about these two, he'd be
confused. Father, daughter? Captain, mate?
Two red-headed Rudolphs? Richard Hannay and his scout Pienaar
cloaked entirely in an atmosphere & sharing stories with
the very man who stalked them? Mr. Memory at the Palladium
might falter, but not Mrs. Adams, 94, perhaps the last alive to have
seen the things she's seen, telling ancients at the ancient public school
converted to a home: *And I was Pamela, a child, and yet I*
saw it all. Every ship on the horizon steaming in formation
while the two of us would sing dispatch or distich there
beneath the sign of all these sails: darting in and out & crossing tacks
at fifteen knots, the yachtsmen heading for the Kiel Regatta,
Wayland, Nigel, Ian: Monarch firing from the
forward turret out of fog by whom the bundled fasces
or the kingdom come. She kissed her father's eyes
and read him stories from her book.

Part III

Or Cousin Nicky read—
                    to Grand Duchess Olga and her sisters
at the Tsarskoye Selo Palace, at Tobolsk, at Ekaterinburg.
Soon they would be shot like Easter's Irishmen
who borrowed *Asgard*'s cargo for their cause when her captain tried
to reconcile the Empire & Home Rule. And he too would be shot,
eventually. And even Mr. Memory. And everything dragged on in horror
on the Western Front, and Nicky read—

≈

Some comfort, maybe, that Pienaar & Hannay & their colleague
based on T.E. Lawrence got up as a Kurdish gypsy
helped to take Erzerum from the Turks despite the Kaiser's jihad
and Companions of the Rosy Hour through intelligence revealed
in actual fact by Russian deputies
on tour of Scapa Flow in February of that year.
He read how Nicholas had breached defenses with his Cossack
cavalry while he, Nicholas himself, would give
his kingdom for a horse. His daughters ask him to read on.
He is reading this in English and the guards
who never lunched at Osborne House all mock him as he says
Greenmantle is St. Francis run by Messalina.
That confused the Duchess who was thinking about
butterflies, or were they moths—Monarchs, Admirals,
Greenmantles. But Greenmantle is the Kaaba-i-Hurriyeh
for all of Islam and will wear the green ephod of prophet
for von Einem and the Turks; they'll rise inspired to hold Erzerum
unless intelligence is taken through the lines informing
Nicholas that flanks up in the hills, west and south-west,
can be turned, for they are undefended by a single trench.
As the Russian columns move at the Euphrates' Glen,
Hannay understands that Pienaar has got through, a map inside
his shirt, and that horsemen at the gap are soldiers
of the Tsar—who reads the book, a prisoner with his daughters,
sisters of the moths and butterflies remembered from
the Isle of Wight...

❧

In Room 40

Buchan keeps the watch through weeks of work
on plaintext elements and homophones in hybrid code
while Captain Hall, "the blinker" who has leant his features to
his colleague's villain with a twitch, a stare, and hooded eyes,
works beyond the *ar* & *auf* & *Krieg* of it, the *wenigen* & *werden*
all the way through steps and sands and riddles to
decode the Amadeus Telegram sufficiently to build
an atmosphere in which both Nicholas and Pamela read on
while polyphonic groups with nulls & diagraphs & single caps
for words not in Vocabulary—dates, effective numbers
and the rest—read themselves, in spite
of muddling *crypt* and *shipped, fiction* and *the faction,*
firmly into fractions of a plan more efficacious than
Carruthers', Hannay's, Hope's, or Roger Casement's—
Casement sending through a priest the message
No German Help while Blinker circulates through London clubs
the pages of a private diary that's sure to get him hanged.
As the Cossacks breach the Turkish lines at Erzerum, Greenmantle's
double in disguise shouts out: *Oh, well done our side*—
which Pamela's daughter will refuse to bellow at
the games mistress' bidding when a goal is scored, but which
somehow comforted the prison of the Tsar.

On *Vindictive,* Bryan Adams and his shipmates puzzle over
copies of that novel sent out by the Admiralty
to every ship. As code; as inspiration. While Pamela
and all the other children of the sailors in the north name the ships
that pass by Aberdour at twilight, then go off to cottage
and to bed, the man she'll marry twenty years from now prepares
to attack the guns at Zeebrugge. An atmosphere's to be
achieved. Flame throwers modified to belch black gouts of smoke,
hinged brows that lower fourteen bridges, great hooks to snag
the shore line, howitzers and pom-poms manned by the marines,
Stokes mortars all along the rail & riflemen on forecastle
and the boat deck up abaft...

                                  Shell-stars light the sky
as *Vindictive* steams out of
the smoke laid down by motor launches at her bow and turns
to landward while reversing engines and is held against
the mole by tugs pressing at her from the stern.
Sailors toss their hooks ashore and warning sirens blare.
Shore emplacements fire upon the landing party
leaping from the access deck to follow Adams toward
the guns beside the lighthouse—silenced when the viaduct is blown
and sinkships block an access to the sea.
Pamela is actually asleep by now,
her daughter reading downstairs by the fire. Once again
her husband rushes toward the lighthouse just like a hero
in some romance—*Good show and cushy job.*
I say, Adams, that was damned impressive
though your lads got rather rattled by machine gun fire.
If you ask next morning what the
celebration is, Mr. Memory will say Remembrance Day—
and poppies blooming red in every field.

❧

But he doesn't recognize the young American walking with
the family to the little Norman church
in Hacheston. The old Captain is remembering the raid.
His wife's remembering her father and the Scottish village
near the Firth of Forth. Their daughter is wondering
if she should marry the American. There's a brief ceremony
at the cenotaph, and then the several families who have
climbed the little hill disperse...

                              In the afternoon
there's sailing on the Alde. The American is not much of
a sailor, but does what he is told. The river's difficult to navigate
and full of sands and bars that can catch you at low tide
and keep you for the night. They sail slowly out from Aldeburgh,
past the squat Martello tower at Sloughden, down
past Orford Ness, the castle keep and early warning
radar nets, the bird sanctuary, through the mouth of Orford Haven,
to the sea. The Captain smokes his pipe and snoozes in
the sun. His daughter is the helmsman and is much preoccupied,
though quite familiar with these waters where she's sailed
since early youth and imagined wooden soldiers popping up
in marshmist reeds and tipping Bismarck helmets to the girls.
Her mother rather likes the young American,
but she doubts her husband does. At dinner he'd been going
on about Virginia Woolf, his back against a bookcase
full of Kipling, Buchan, Hope—the Captain looking rather bored.
She's not thinking she'll outlive her whole generation
and become at 94 the last person to have seen, with a group of children
on her father's ship, the surrender of the German fleet.
They'll tape her for the BBC and air her comments on a program
called *Der Tag*.

   ॐ

        Mr. Memory's remembering his job when
he worked for Mr. Hitchcock. They changed the story quite a lot,
making up his character from scratch. In 1935 the spies were
after plans for a silent airplane engine, not the disposition of the
British Fleet. As Hannay says to Madeleine, imported
from the studio into a story where she had no
part: *Of course there are no missing papers, all the information's
in the head of Mr. M*, whose friend Erskine Childers,
Republican at last, also had a head for things that led him to
his end. *What's the riddle of the sands? What are the 39 Steps?*
Childers was shot by the Free State, De Valera's little gun found
about his person. Memory is shot by spies. No one
pays attention to the little boat sailing in a mild breeze
along the coast of Suffolk.

࿐

But where is Greenmantle?
Who's the rightful king of Ruritania? Where's Savrola got to
with the widow of Antonio Molara?
Why did Admiral Reuter scuttle the entire German fleet?

No one fires a warning shot across their bow.

They sight no ship on the horizon.

There's nothing flying in the sky except the gulls.

After Five Words
Englished from the Russian

Horseshoe or dingbat, Sir   oh just the one
he thought, even if a hoarsepshaw brief Cyrillic Ж was altogether
confidential then. Sadistic counsel goofy as it was to hit
a mark an iron-shod method like an actor on the methadone
for bad habits, pitching his good luck
to brain the brain-damaged boy, altogether his intention
Master Craft, I swear
                    swore it when he outran a goddamn dawn
a good man reigning through obsessive thought that inning out to bean
him break his neck   Focus on the other's head
a dingbat or lucky shot   pitching high and inside
fucking up the outdoors, even fireworks on the Fourth   can't you
do an elementary task?
                    However,
He Who Finds a Horseshoe fires a synapse begs a question
but in time bags his quarry by the marsh
even brags about it, flees as far as Moony Lake running
in the tallest grass and crouching down they say
it's possible to drown in mud and sand and shoreline
stagnant pools in short order, Sir.
I Babel's unit, Blogmeister Ulyanov. A thrice-beaten hoarse
without a pshaw is very dark indeed.

In the long run in short it was like this: He stumbled bleeding
into foreign camp where all the officers played
dice with nasty dingbats, bits of backbone lacking, they maintained,
in cowards who'd run off. Their poet said that what he said
was never said by him. But also *Three times blessed is one who
puts a name in song.* Mandelstam. Ulyanov. Babel:
*No iron can pierce the human heart with the force of a period just
exactly in the right place*

Aplysia at just that point in time became, like injured campers,
Useful slugs in neurobiological associative tasks.
Aplasia, though, prevented both the classical and operant conditioning.

💣

Iron bomb's your balalaika too? And you an anarchist like me?
In this day and age, the pleaЖure is entirely mine.

II

& shhhhhhh… sashays to Ҡay… & does shay &
No iron can pierce and so on just a way of betting on the
pen that's mightier than the sword? You think
that babble saved him. All that playing Cossacks was
to chess what Cheka was to his submerged cliché:
No one gets the period in the right place. Full stop, Bakunin.
A friend of ours saw him finger-fucking the countess, then
went off to a commune called K' Klarity. Stammered it so
long ago at Horseshoe Camp they only managed checkers,
chests puffed up by golly nonetheless in pride. And no!
Not a commune merely but a country: It's Charity.

And that's a virtue too, Great Aunt Calamity: tell me Muse
what E flat played as an harmonic on a single string
can say to the amped-up soundtrack rocking the whole square
until the child screams and holds his ears and Dingbat's
prancing Lipizzaner slips on the cobbled street and breaks a leg.
Then you must put him down. A mistake: They pitched
their good luck then and brained the brain-damaged boy.
All that rock 'n' roll at such a volume it would surely damage
anybody's brain. Had you been at the May parade, it would
have damaged yours. Even had you volunteered as number
one sadistic counselor. After all, it was a job.

So too the bold advance of Ivan Chesnokov right up to
the gates of Chugunov with his regiment of cavalry. They asked
him could he read and write, and could he maybe put some
order in the Orders of the Day. He took his rimless glasses
from his pocket, but did not dismount. What he did
was read aloud the lewd jokes told at the Second Congress
of the Comintern. A kind of poetry in that. A kind of horseshoe
thrown with malice at the eyes, the mouth, the balls.
Cousin Klarity, I was only at a camp but you were in camp a.
Rabbi Mordecai was putting into verse the harsh sayings
of the one from Dobryvodka called Inert.

📖

Person of the book, Bookie of the Downbeat. Dingbats all in order
for an answer to the ringing red & black phones.

III

Picks up the black: *Name and patronymic.* You think all this
security is just a game? Interrogation's terminal.
Means you integrate, and don't fill out that line on race.
Do fill out the item re your mother's maiden name. Tartar, no?
When I first went to Paris with the orderly for mess
we asked for steak tartare. Didn't know the local customs, raw egg
on raw meat. Nearly barfed, but stayed cool, & ate it up.
Did you clean your plate at camp? No you can't phone Mother now.
You'll answer only to the bad cop at mass. I hope for
your sake, Soldier, all of this can be resolved as expeditiously
as possible.
        Hello up there & looking disingenuous
and fat. Here's a joke. Guy goes to a shrink. After a while
the shrink says, Man you're absolutely nuts. Man says Please sir
I'd like a second opinion. Shrink says OK, Man, you're
bloody ugly too. Man says, Mein Herr, but I'm the Revolution
of the Word. Shrink says: Well then speak
                         He doesn't though,
he can't. He's gagged by then. And look at how
his hands are tied behind him. If he could speak he'd
improvise a panegyric on his old Prof. Then they'd let him off.
For example, Camper Klubnik might begin, speaking as a
prisoner in the nether fields of play: *By God they had me walk
upon the water, bored. That made all of them electric.*
The men in protective cover took *Aplysia* by the tail & shocked
him good, found that serotonin is a modulator and that
neurons form connections where a new protein is required
for growth. Our team, my Champion, seeks out
long-term memory: Your own. Our mistake in Paris was in
not ordering the snails in white wine sauce.
(If you'll just attach those wires to his name and patronymic
we can all go home)
        Camp A is not ballet in Voronezh,
although it's true they have a company. The dance we'll do
together's called the Nimble Neurons. Simple stimulation with
the horseshoe, hard. The Presbyterian (head) Master
got so angry that he cast dung about him, rang the orthodox bell,

☎

hid the weapon in the tall grass of long-term mnemonics,
left it there to find. Fend for yourself, my boy, who called him friend.

IV

Picks up the red: *Koba Steel here....* (No, not a CEO.)
So stop and think. You're at a high point in telephonic history.
He asks you now about your friend. Wants to know
is he the Big One. For a moment you are overcome by envy.
Iosif the Georgian—Koba, Mr. Steel—thinks your
friend and rival maybe is the Big One. He's waiting for your
answer on the phone. *Horseshoe, you know I don't...*

So think again. You're having dinner with some friends
And Джугашвили (-shvili is the suffix meaning *child*)
telephones and asks you is your rival really great.
It isn't Harry Truman on the line, not General Eisenhower,
not even J. Edger Hoover. It's the Ossetian, *the herd of sheep.*
Yet another name is сталь, suffix -ин You've heard of sheep,
but not from Georgia. (Georgia doesn't border Florida.)
He takes an avid interest in the welfare of the motherland's bards.
Three times blessed is one who puts a name in song.
Boris Leonidovich, for example.

He says, *I think you liked the summer camp we sent you to.*
We gave you a dacha all your own; not a day, not an hour
did you spend like some Denisovich. You know. You're grateful,
But you've got these dinner guests. *Koba, we will have*
To keep it short. You're so frightened now you're shitting in
Your pants. *Can we take this up another time?*
You feel gagged, and look at how your hands are tied
behind you so you have to cradle the contrivance
with your chin. *Boris Leonidovich, have a pleasant meal.*

An old camp counselor, a bully Boy Scout grown into
a what? A what?
                    ...writing for him on Yagoda-Checkist
checker board, black squares and red, king makers, triple jumps,
a bowl of raspberries lodged in each man's lap, a rasp
in both voices, a rattle then: *Were I to take my pencil up for*

the supremist praise, I would speak of him who shifts the
axis of the world and call him by his dobrydawnsong name,
Dzhugashvili

✐

Koba was a *nom de guerre*, and he darkened eighteen others.
Dzhugashvili only an aubade.

V

The telephone, the book, the pencil, and the bomb.
The horseshoe, the letter Ж, Aplysia, a prod. Full stop, Aplasia
No codes where none intended.
No modes where all roads lead to home. No Rome.
Beneath her stone,
                    Arachne spins an Acmeist revival.
Rest with mother, bested brother,
shining on a harvest moon. Frost at midnight, steel
reflecting starlight: Stella, Stalin, Blog-
meister Ulyanov. *He Who Finds a Horseshoe*
fires a synapse, begs a question, bags his quarry in due time
but fears it was a 💣 Nihilism was your nickelodeon, Clarity
embracing nil, your dingbat more than that
but only half the whole.
                    The other half in plus fours
Told it as a crime, a time when the brakeman was annoyed
at Nickerbocker, who was there for re-hab
in the -ilitation for an injury sustained to his cerebral cortex
from the wreck of nations on the railroad track that
used to be an outback songline, wrack of notions that were
once all viable ideals, and so he hit him HARD
with what was handy: *horseshoe*. He could have put him
In a
    📖

        or gouged out his eye with a
                ✐

These are conventions that you see in
Children's books. Child Aplasia failed all exams.
Aplysia *could* respond. But where exactly in these snail brains

did one locate the long-term memory, let alone the Ego
and the Id? Could they, anyway, be trained by pain, subjective
and unconscious? (No codes where none intended.
No allusions that have not offended. No mimesis. No thesis.)
If you cross synoptic cleft, target ion channel and inject
The catalytic element, you're under way. Dingbat is an object
used as missile in the absence of a horseshoe.
Or a gizmogadget with an utterly forsaken ancient name.
A typographical ornament. A silly jerk. A slug releasing ink.

What I'm saying isn't said by me.
This is your whingding moment: dug out of the ground like gold

Afterword: John Matthias' Pocket Epics

MARK SCROGGINS

Greek rhetoricians used *epyllion*—"little epic"—to refer to a small poem, a "versicle." Nineteenth-century English classicists seized on the term to name a sub-genre, narrative poems in epic hexameters and epic idiom that never attained the grand proportions of Homer or Virgil: Catullus 64, the magnificent 'Peliaco' on the marriage of Peleus and Thetis, is perhaps the most famous example. The 'Peliaco's' four hundred lines are a holographic slice, as it were, of a longer epic—the epic rendered portable: a "pocket epic."

The modernist poets gravitated time and again towards works of epic scale. Ezra Pound shaped his own "poem of some length," *The Cantos*, on the three models of Homer's epics, Ovid's *Metamorphoses*, and Dante's *Divine Comedy*. In Pound's footsteps, William Carlos Williams (*Paterson*), David Jones (*The Anathemata*), Louis Zukofsky (*A*), and Charles Olson (*The Maximus Poems*) would also essay sprawling, epic-length poems that plotted contemporary history and culture on a timeline that stretched back to the classical era and beyond. But if the epic was the monarch of genres for Homer, Milton, and Pope, by the end of the nineteenth century it had been irrevocably displaced, certainly for the reading public and to a large degree for the critical community, by the prose novel. In the hands of such masters as Gustave Flaubert, George Eliot, and Henry James, the novel had become an infinitely ductile and responsive genre, capable of addressing the most pressing social and philosophical issues while examining individual subjectivity with an unprecedentedly intimate verisimilitude.

The long poem, at the same time, had taken an inward turn, exemplified perhaps in Wordsworth's autobiographical *The Prelude*. While Tennyson's *In Memoriam* grappled with the great intellectual and spiritual issues of the Victorian era, we are inclined to remember the poem primarily for its record of the poet's *personal* grief. Long narrative poems such as Browning's *The Ring and the Book* and Barrett Browning's *Aurora Leigh* in hindsight tend to look like "novels in verse," and by the end of the century the production of an epic-length narrative poem, in the face of a narrative prose art reaching Conradian and Jamesian heights of sophistication, looked like an antiquarian exercise: Charles Montagu Doughty's *The Dawn in Britain* (1906), for instance.

The modernists responded by jettisoning large-scale narrative from their epic-length poems. Instead, they would knit their epics together with recurrent images and motifs, with "repeats" across history and cultures, with underlying armatures borrowed from mythology and previous works of high culture (what Eliot, addressing *Ulysses* but suggesting a method for reading his own work, called the "mythic method"). In *The Cantos*, *The Anathemata*, '*A*', *Maximus*, and *Paterson*, one sees the triumph of parataxis over hypotaxis, of juxtaposition over narrative.

This turn from narrative to juxapositional art would prove problematic, and not merely in terms of the difficulties it posed for the ordinary reader. One problem was that of the part-to-whole relationship obtaining between the individual sections of the poem and the poem's larger structure, an issue complicated by the fact that these poems were often published as separate volumes, sometimes over a long period of time indeed. Another was that of *ending* such a poem. Without the clear-cut conclusion supplied by a narrative arc or by a conceptual "Aquinas-map" (Pound's term) like that of Dante's *Divine Comedy*, the modernist long poem threatened to become coextensive with the poet's life, to find its ending only in the poet's own: *The Cantos*, *Maximus*, and *Paterson* all remained unfinished when their poets died.

The first generation of "high" modernists laid out these problems in their starkest form—the modular Cantos that issued from Pound's typewriter in a seemingly endless stream, challenging readers to fit them in with the pieces that had come before, the forlorn, unfinished torsos of Pound's, Williams', and Olson's poems in their "complete" forms, chiding their authors from beyond the grave. Later generations of poets would try to turn their defeats into strengths. In the course of his sequence, 'Passages', Robert Duncan abandoned consecutive numbering, invited his readers to shuffle the various poems in whatever order seemed fit, and altogether relinquished any expectation of "conclusion"; and while the poems of Nathaniel Mackey's 'mu' and 'Song of the Andoumboulou'—perhaps the two most ambitious sequences in American late modernist poetry—continue to be numbered, they take open-endedness and inconclusiveness not as a mark of failure but as a very conceptual ground.

John Matthias is very much a poet in the tradition of Pound, and he has read and learned from both Olson and Duncan. But he has cannily shied away from opening his poems out to whatever infinity towards which the poet's imagination might strain. There's much to admire in such open-ended sequences as *Maximus* and 'Passages,' but it's unclear whether the world needs more complex, esoterically learned, and painfully incomplete poetic torsos. Instead, Matthias has given us a series of highly finished medium-length efforts, well-turned pocket epics: one

Briggflatts after another, rather than a single "poem of a life." While he has written several volumes' worth of shorter, more lyrical or "anecdotal" poems, the medium-length poem has been Matthias' chosen field, and in Matthias' hands, this *Mauberley*-length form has proven a remarkably flexible canvas.

§

One model for Matthias' early long poems is Pound's 'Near Perigord,' an agreeable tramp through the countryside of the troubadours, every castle or crossroads marked by Pound's attempts to enter into the milieu and mindset of his beloved medieval lover-warrior-poets. Like 'Near Perigord,' Matthias' early long poems tend to be *topographical* poems, works that focus upon a single place or cluster of places. 'Northern Summer' (1980-1983) is a Scottish poem; 'Facts from an Apocryphal Midwest' (1986) travels the riverways around Lake Superior in the company of La Salle and the French explorers, the ancient copper-mining "mound people," and Francis Parkman; 'An East Anglian Diptych' (1984) meanders down the ley lines and rivers of Cambridgeshire, Suffolk, and Norfolk; and 'A Compostela Diptych' (1990) travels the French and Provençal pilgrimage routes to Santiago de Compostela, the old stomping grounds of Roland, El Cid, and Pound's troubadours.

'Northern Summer' begins with a handful of lines from the Swedish poet Göran Sonnevi:

> The flight of sentimentality through empty space.
> Through its heraldic hole
> an heraldic blackbird's
> black wings, yellow beak, round eyes, with the yellow
> ring, which defines its inner empty
> space

Matthias finds himself spending the summer in an architectural folly, between a coal mine and a castle overlooking the Firth of Forth. As he trawls through the historical and etymological background of his surroundings and neighbors, muses on the technology of Victorian coal-mining, replays in his mind's eye the high scenes of Scottish history (John Knox badmouthing Mary Queen of Scots, Bonnie Prince Charlie inspecting Holyrood Castle at the height of his brief bid to regain Britain for the Stuarts), and relives his mother's reading him Stevenson's

Kidnapped, that "heraldic blackbird" continually pokes its yellow beak into the pages, surveys the poet's "flight of sentimentality" with quizzical round eyes.

This isn't Wallace Stevens's blackbird. Instead, Matthias' blackbird darts into and out of the poem as an emblem of the poet's mind brooding upon his surroundings and the history that lies behind them, arranging those materials into a poem: "Language / moving upon consequence / Consequence / upon a language: Flight / of an heraldic bird / through space that is inhabited." Or is it merely, he wonders, the "flight of sentimentality through empty space"? Matthias thinks not; rather, his musings on place and the past have opened the poem into a space in which the voices of the past speak unexpectedly and sometimes eloquently:

> I stare quizzically at what I've written here,
> at language that has used me one more time
> for consequential or inconsequential ends that
> are not mine.

Of Matthias' earlier long poems, one especially singles out 'A Compostella Diptych,' in which the poet pursues his unfinished pilgrimage before a backdrop of both his own illness and his daughter's (as illuminated in the short poem 'Dedication to a Cycle of Poems on the Pilgrim Routes to Santiago de Compostella'). But all of these poems are much of a piece: dense, sometimes bookish evocations of the historical resonances echoing in particular locations. Matthias doesn't expect us to take his research on trust—at the end of his collections he provides brief comments on each long piece, along with exhaustive lists of his sources. It's a gesture of acknowledgement for debts incurred, but neither as ponderous nor frivolous as the notes to *The Waste Land*, that "remarkable display of bogus scholarship" (as Eliot once called them) that kept professors busy for four decades. Nor are Matthias' source lists as intrusive as the notes curtaining the pages of *The Anathemata* of David Jones, the Anglo-Welsh modernist who is perhaps the most important of Matthias' acknowledged masters.

Matthias knows Jones's work better than any American alive, and probably better than all but a handful of Britons. He selected Jones for a Faber 'Introduction' in 1980, and has edited a comprehensive collection of criticism on Jones in the 'Man and Poet' series. *In Parenthesis* (1937) is an absorbing evocation of Jones's Great War service, in which the experience of the ordinary British foot soldier is embedded within a matrix of Western history, myth, and literature. "Some of us may ask ourselves," Jones writes in his Preface, "if Mr. X adjusting his box-respirator can be equated with what the poet envisaged, in *I saw young Harry with his beaver on.*" But as incongruous as the collision of the Battle of the Somme and *Henry V* might seem, Jones is sure that "at no time did one so much live with a consciousness of the past, the very remote, and the more immediate and trivial past, both superficially and more subtly. No one... could see infantry in tin-hats, with ground-sheets over their shoulders, with sharpened pin-stakes in their hands, and not recall ... *or may we cram, / Within this wooden O...*"

Jones's other great work, *The Anathemata* (1952), is a lambent and widely-woven exploration of the "matter of Britain," a rangy gathering of materials that locates Britain in a Spenglerian history of cultural growth and decay centered upon and radiating from the events of the incarnation and crucifixion nineteen centuries before. In *The Anathemata's* Preface Jones rather diffidently describes his own method by quoting the Latin historian Nennius: "I have made a heap of all that I could find." The poem may be "a series of fragments, fragmented bits, chance scraps really, of records of things," but they are "Pieces of stuff that happen to mean something to me and which I see as making a kind of coat of many colours, such as belonged to 'that dreamer' in the Hebrew myth." It is that quality of affection, that the fragments that make up the poem "happen to mean something"—happen to *matter* to the poet, that gives poetry its power and danger; Joseph's coat, after all, was both a mark of favor and source of trouble. "Poetry is to be diagnosed as 'dangerous,'" writes Jones, "because it evokes and recalls, is a kind of *anamnesis* of, i. e. is an effective recalling of, something loved."

An *effective recalling of something loved* is a fair description of the method of Matthias' long poems. What in the hands of a less involved, less *loving* poet might seem a tourist's scrapbook of diverting facts and anecdotes is transfigured into something more compelling by the voice of the poet himself—the consciousness perceiving, selecting, and arranging his materials. He's treading a fine line here, though: a poetry of place that relies so heavily on the testimony of documents, that is, constantly runs the risk of becoming a versified travelogue. We see this perhaps most poignantly in 'Northern Summer': near the beginning there's a fruitily lyrical description of the poet's environs—"Large, magnificent, commodious / with rock nearby and wood and water to afford / the eye a picture of a rare / and charming beauty"—a description immediately deflated: "the sight of which / could not but amply compensate et / cetera / the language of a tour book / threading aimlessly / through sentimental empty space." It's a moment, I'm inclined to think, of self-revelation. The poet has lost his summer home in Suffolk ("the place where I had done most of my writing for fifteen years or more"), and is desperately seeking to regain some grounding, some connection to place, a difficult matter when one is summering in an unfamiliar Scotland. We feel Matthias straining to connect throughout the poem, and the nearest connection at which he arrives—his mother's reading him *Kidnapped* at "eight or nine"—proves in the end all too tenuous:

> There is a space
> I have not learned to fill
> somewhere between printed marks and sounds
> and I am lost in some way too
> among the heather, frightened of the distances
> when all I want to do is drift on lang
> uage into dream...

Matthias' more topographical long poems "work" rather smoothly when we sense the affection and enthusiasm Matthias feels for his location—his at-homeness. When his connection to the place is more tenuous, as in 'Northern Summer' and 'A Compostela Diptych,' the poem becomes (among much else) the tracings of the poet's longing for such connection, such grounding. While the "settled" poems are perhaps more finished and masterful, the "unsettled" poems pack more emotional punch: the grand and sad old themes of exile, of *hejira*, of homeless wandering.

In 'Pages: *From a Book of Years*,' 'Cuttings,' and 'Automystifstical Plaice' Matthias shifts from a concern with *place* to a concern with *time*. Time has always been of the essence in Matthias' work, but while 'Northern Summer,' 'A Compostella Diptych' or 'Facts from an Apocryphal Midwest' build palimpsests of temporally receding texts upon particular locations, like the layers of various Troys Heinrich Schliemann excavated on the single mound of Hissarlik, 'Pages' especially is less concerned with place—Matthias' boyhood Ohio, a college trip to Turkey, graduate school at Palo Alto—than with the passage of time itself.

There's something almost haphazard about 'Pages.' The poem is divided into five sections, each of them focusing upon a particular year: 1959, 1941, 1953, 1961, and 1966. Each section frantically concatenates the happenings of its respective year, from world-historical events, the deaths of celebrities, the entry to new words into the dictionary, to Matthias' own emotional and erotic life. Where in his earlier long poems Matthias had seemed something of a "library cormorant" (a neat phase of Coleridge's), in 'Pages' his sources are more humble: the collection of yearbooks—encyclopedia yearbooks, fashion yearbooks, chess yearbooks, horse racing yearbooks—that his father had accumulated in a closet of his Columbus home. "For every day there's death you've got to chronicle and someone writes the year in yearbooks puts eventually the volume in a right and goodly order on the shelf."

Matthias, shuffling through these yearbooks alone in the house, has returned to Ohio on one of the most heartrending errands of middle age: to move his mother, suffering from Alzheimer's, into a nursing facility, and to clean out his childhood home before putting it up for sale. His mother's voice enters the poem time and again, always repeating the same mantra: "Take me home she said don't sell the house I can't remember quite which one you are you know I really don't live here I'm only visiting." In the face of such erosion of memory, 'Pages' is a frantic attempt to remember, to shore up fragments against the ruin of inexorable age. It is *anamnesis* at the edge of oblivion.

In the *Phaedrus* Plato warned that the written word would be the death of human memory ("why should I memorize something I can look up in a book?" Einstein said when asked his phone number). The renaissance humanists adumbrated complex and precise systems of memorization: visualize a familiar street, associate each item you need to remember with a specific storefront, and so forth. The yearbooks Matthias ransacks are the tabulated and bound tombs of such organic memory-arcades. Where the humanists had proposed memory systems relating the data memorized to the structure of the human world, the yearbooks rely on the contingencies of the alphabet, on the one-damn-thing-after-another logic of the calendar. Like some local historian, the poet of 'Pages' is attempting to reconstruct his own past on the basis of some thousands of pages of random data, and on the basis of his own vivid—but, he fears, faltering—memory.

In 'Automystifstical Plaice' Matthias returns explicitly to his modernist roots. One of the poem's central reference points is American composer and pianist George Antheil's 1923 performance at the Théâtre des Champs Elysées, where the pianist's violently rhythmic music (the climactic piece was entitled 'Mechanisms') seems to have prompted any number of fistfights and upended seats. Unbeknownst to its participants, that riot was being filmed, and the footage would be incorporated into Marcel L'Herbier's silent movie *L'Inhumaine*:

> A camera's panning the audience, picks out the famous:
> Picasso and Joyce, Duchamp, Milhaud and Satie.
> We see them there with Leblanc as Lescot in the film
> but we don't hear a sound Mr. Pound leaping

right out of his seat and shaking a fist as people begin
to walk out on Antheil himself...

Movies and music bounce off one another: the outrage provoked by
Antheil's "Mechanisms" becomes part of a film; "Mechanisms" itself
inspires another film, Fernand Leger's *Ballet Mécanique*, for which
Antheil in turn composes his own 'Ballet Mécanique.'

L'Inhumaine starred Georgette LeBlanc in the role (in Antheil's
words) of "an 'inhuman' opera songstress," Claire Lescot. The character
Lescot, a robot-woman like the siren of Fritz Lang's *Metropolis*, speaks
much of 'Automystifstical Plaice,' casting a cold base-two eye from her
current digs "at MIT in some robotics lab" over the frenetic techno-
fascination of modernist Paris. They were before their time, those
machine-struck moderns: "No one could actually *play* that piano roll A
wrote into the score, / the digitals moving at speeds and at intervals /
nobody's ten carboniferous digits could match." And there was no way
Antheil could realize his conception of 'Ballet Mécanique' on sixteen
pianolas: the instruments—enormously complex music-boxes, really—
simply couldn't be synchronized closely enough. Not, that is, until the
era of computer-driven, Midi-linked digital pianos: "He hadn't met the
Midi, technical cousin of Claire, his digital and instrumental interface."
Schirmer music publishers can now rent you a full set of Midi software
instructions for performing Antheil's work, and Matthias "quotes" some
of their online schemata in 'Automystifstical Plaice.'

The poem takes us in tightly woven thirty pages through twenty
years' worth of modernist-related arcana: Antheil's progress both as
avant-gardist and Hollywood hack; the writings of his bulldog Pound;
Léger's machine aesthetic; the experimental silent film scene; and the
career of the Hollywood diva Hedy Lamarr (born Hedwig Kiesler),
from her nude debut in the German film *Ecstasy* to her friendship with
Antheil in the 1940s when the two designed, of all things, a radio-
controlled torpedo: "Find me George Antheil. / We're going to sink
the Herzenbergers / and the Krupps with my torpedo." (Lamarr's first
marriage was to a German armaments manufacturer, we learn, and she
did a good deal of listening in when designs for new weapons were being
discussed around the house.) The torpedo was patented but never built,
but some of the basic principles of its design would eventually prove
crucial to the invention of cellular telephone networks. The roots of
things are cunningly and surprisingly intertwined: "What lengths what
loops," as Matthias puts it in another poem.

'Automystifstical Plaice' is an assured and more than a little zany
poem, deriving much of its verbal energy from Mother Goose-like

internal rhymes and an Oulipo-like reliance on the dictionary to suggest the next word ("the mogul / and the moilers make a single molecule for a moment / as modalities come into play"). It's also suffused with nostalgia for that first moment of "heroic" modernism, when it seemed to a certain group of artists—Antheil, Léger, Wyndham Lewis, the Futurists—that the new technologies of electricity and internal combustion would become the basis of a new, dynamic aesthetic whose madonna was Picabia's "fille née sans mère." Matthias both pays homage to the machine aesthetic of early modernism and makes a stab at a machine aesthetic for the twenty-first century. His poem is punctuated by the static and dropped-out words of a cellphone conversation, stocked with factoids garnered from the internet, and entranced by the intermittent dream that all human culture is somehow available, in a vast surrealist musée imaginaire, to the seeker who can plug the right set of search terms into google.com.

At the same time, 'Automystifstical Plaice' is a very old-fashioned modernist poem. While it may be telling us to plug into the world wide web, vast stretches of its material can be "sourced" in a printed document, Antheil's autobiography *Bad Boy of Music*, just as one sources Pound's "China" Cantos in J. A. M. de Mailla's *Histoire Générale de la Chine*. But where Pound hunts for "luminous details"—a single line in a Canto can be meant as shorthand for an entire significant passage or event in Mailla—Matthias looks for fruitful suggestions: Antheil's brief account of screening *Un Chien Andalou* for Cecil B. de Mille (he "was a pale green when the lights went up. He left without a word") prompts a darting collage in which Dalí & Buñuel's surrealism comes smack up against the demands of early-Forties Hollywood:

> so we play this little coup de vache
> on every scatalogue and watch the ants emerge
> from his stigmata, no? the way he's roped
> to this machinery he drags, pianos stuffed with putrefying
> donkey and dos padres, si? the priests tied up and
> on their backs in bondage of some kind as part of this
> contrivance & De Mille out of his seat by now
> and saying brother rat [?] or bugger that....

In 'Automystifstical Plaice' Matthias compresses into the compass of the pocket epic all of the virtues of Pound's mature idiom, a cross-cutting of lush lyricism and esoteric literary-historical references: the poem as a shimmering intersection of immediate experience and all the bright bits of history in the poet's mind.

§

If the pocket epics of the first half of Matthias' career move between concerns of *place* and *time*, his most recent essays in the form seem to modulate between tones: on the one hand, a rather serious (if always light-handed) consideration of the past, of the weight of history; and on the other, a more ludic, high-spirited verbal gamesmanship.

Over some twenty-five pages of 'Kedging in Time,' Matthias constructs a palimpsest of late-imperial British naval history from before the Great War, through the debacle of Gallipoli, to the day of the surrender of the Kaiser's fleet, *der Tag*. This history is refracted through the sensibility and family connections of Pamela Adams, the daughter and wife of British Navy captains (and Matthias' mother-in-law), and is punctuated and salted with references to various popular fictions of the early twentieth century: Erskine Childers's *The Riddle of the Sands*, Anthony Hope's *The Prisoner of Zenda*, and John Buchan's *Greenmantle* and *The Thirty-Nine Steps* (and Hitchcock's film adaptation of that novel). Matthias cannily avoids condescension in name-dropping these classics of the "boys' own" genre; indeed, he's able to evoke a sense of what tremendous *reads* these oft-neglected volumes are, much as he did with Stevenson's *Kidnapped* and Scott's *Waverley* in 'Northern Summer.'

To "kedge," an epigraph explains, is "To warp a ship, or move it from one position to another by winding in a hawser attached to a small anchor dropped at some distance." In the genial and roundabout essay 'Kedging in *Kedging in Time*,' Matthias describes his use of these prior texts (along with various memoirs, histories, and logbooks): they are "secure holds for the kedge-anchor of my reefed verbal craft." This is a bit too diffident, giving the impression of the poem as an unwieldy, engineless hulk being dragged from one extratextual anchor-point to the next. 'Kedging in Time,' rather, like Matthias' earlier long poems, is a resonant structure of historical, literary, and personal particulars held in uneasy tension, traversed by the poet's own restless, connection-seeking sensibility; and 'Kedging in Time' is particularly colored with the bittersweet aura of familial associations, touched with the melancholy sense that the poem is in some way a leave-taking of the Britain that has furnished the material for so much of Matthias' earlier work.

Far more sprightly is 'Laundry Lists and Manifestoes.' This twenty-two section poem takes its title from a couple of sentences of A. S. Byatt's: "People often leave no record of the most critical or passionate moments of their lives. They leave laundry lists and manifestoes." The biographer and archival researcher know how true this is, how often the emotional center of a subject's life can only be inferred or, worse, speculated upon: the paper trails of even the most famous often consist only of strategic public pronouncements—"manifestoes"—and the most mundane quotidian records—"laundry lists." But, as Matthias quotes Auden, "never trust a critic who does not like lists / The genealogies in Genesis, the Catalogue of Ships." and Matthias manages to conjure a delightful romp indeed out of such arrays.

The poem begins with two ur-laundry-scenes: Nausicäa, the Phaeacian princess who encounters the shipwrecked Odysseus while doing the royal family's wash, and Japheth's wife—unnamed, as so many women in the Hebrew Bible—preparing to do a major clean-up after the Flood (which has lasted well over half a year). The dovetailing of events is typically Matthian. Ham's witnessing of his father Noah's drunken nakedness leads directly to Odysseus's concealing of his genitals with "Just a leafy twig," but both events are narrated with a lubricious jauntiness quite unlike their ancient originals: "She asked to see his manifest. Alas, he said, I've lost it with / My ship and all my men, but you can put this on / Your laundry list—and took away the twig."

A "manifest," of course, is a type of list (as well as being related to "manifesto"), and Matthias' poem derives much of its delicious momentum from playing the scales of such puns and etymological relations: *list* becomes *manifest, catalogue, account,* all of them pro-liferating into their related terms—*manifesto, manifestation, accounting.* Nausicäa's laundry includes "her thong, her super-low-cut jeans, her black lace / Demi-bra and other things she'd ordered from the *catalogue*" (my emphasis). And *list* becomes *list* (verb, as in Hamlet's father's "List, list, O, list!"), *listener, listless,* and so forth. The poem veers through a forest of lists and catalogues—"genealogies in Genesis, the Catalogue of Ships," Don Giovanni's lovers, famous poems whose first lines begin with "M," items Robinson Crusoe has managed to salvage from his shipwreck—sparking them off of various manifestoes, particularly the aggressive pronouncements of various modernist movements, from Marinetti's (Italian) Futurism to Khlebnikov's (Russian) Futurism and Malevich's Suprematism. Towards the end, 'Laundry Lists and Manifestoes' becomes a meditation on creativity, communication, and technology, from the evolution of the human hand to Donna Haraway's "cyborg theory."

I suspect that Matthias regards the high-spirited romp of 'Laundry Lists and Manifestoes' as somewhat less *serious,* less ballasted with *gravitas,* than the nostalgically historical 'Kedging in Time.' But in Matthias' most recent long poem, *Trigons*—a book-length work that represents a continuation of these *Collected Longer Poems*—one can see these two styles converging to form something of a Matthian "late style." Matthias' 2004 *New Selected Poems* concluded with the mid-length retrospective poem 'Swell,' a very personal poem of aging and retrospection, a "late" work in an immediately recognizable, perhaps even *conventional*, sense. *Trigons*, on the other hand, evokes the sort of "lateness" that Adorno identifies in Beethoven's last works—

> The maturity of the late works of important artists is not like the ripeness of fruit. As a rule, these works are not well rounded, but wrinkled, even fissured. They are apt to lack sweetness, fending off with prickly tartness those interested in merely sampling them. They lack all that harmony which the classical aesthetic is accustomed to demand from the work of art, showing more traces of history than of growth.

Trigons explores Matthias' usual historical and literary obsessions, this time revolving around the Second World War: the novelist Henry Miller and the poet George Seferis, Rudolph Hess and his contemporary the English pianist Myra Hess, Christopher Isherwood and Wilhelm Furtwängler, Jack Kerouac and Robert Louis Stevenson, Jean-Paul Sartre and Matthias' "old teacher" Harvey Goldberg—a cast of thousands, really—all pursued, name-dropped, critiqued, ridiculed, and lovingly recalled in a concatenation of seven seven-sectioned poems (with a few sonnets added in). The poem's deepest obsessions are with the traces left in the poet's mind and experience by the careers and writings of these historically situated figures, with the constant presence of music, not as mere soundtrack to a life, but as the subject of his continual brooding and analysis. *Trigons*, one might hazard, is at least in part a meditation on how history, books, and music have formed the poet's subjectivity—a meditation sharpened by Matthias' discovery, during the poem's composition, of yet another John Matthias, this one a British composer and neurophysicist.

Trigons shows no lack of the high spirits that have underpinned so much of Matthias' work, but its puns, jokes, and intentional incongruities are underpinned by a deep seriousness, a pervading sense that while history continues to produce connections in inexhaustible richness, it does so in counterpoint to a continual savage, tragic wastage of life and potential. *Trigons* moves quickly—indeed, leaving behind the careful concern for closure that has marked Matthias' earlier pocket epics, the poem seems at every moment to be on the verge of shaking itself to pieces with its own concatenated momentum, like one of Jean Tinguely's self-destructive kinetic sculptures. And this is not a quirk of

Matthias' poetics: as the Englishman Haines says in *Ulysses*, "it seems history is to blame." Experiences of grace, of happiness, are ephemeral moments in the relentless, remorseless, temporal succession of heterogeneity that is human life and culture. The "lateness" of *Trigons*, then, lies in the poem's fierce impatience, its barely-concealed rage at the all-too-rapid movement of the human spectacle. *Trigons* should be read alongside the *Collected Longer Poems* as this collection's continuation, as the latest turn in John Matthias' odyssey among extended forms, and as a further earnest of the passion with which this poet has engaged himself to explore the locations and times converging on his own extraordinary moment.

Notes

Because these poems span more than four decades, I should probably say a few words about them in order to establish some contexts and explain the order of presentation, which is not strictly chronological. But because Mark Scroggins has said so many useful things in his afterword, I will be able to keep my own notes shorter than I have in the past and mainly shuffle some bibliographies taken from previous books into a new order.

I have chosen to exclude from this selection the long poems from my first book, *Bucyrus*. I now consider this work to be juvenilia. I have also excluded the book-length *Trigons*, which is quite recent and, far from being juvenilia, is certainly one of the long poems I am most keen to stand by. However, it would expand the length of *Collected Longer Poems* by more than a hundred pages. (*Trigons* is, and will remain, in print as a single volume, and I very much hope the reader will want to obtain it from Shearsman.) The first poem that does appear in this book is 'Facts from an Apocryphal Midwest,' written in 1986. This was the second of the three long poems in my book *A Gathering of Ways*, originally preceded by 'An East Anglian Diptych' (1984) and followed by 'A Compostela Diptych' (1990). My aim is to set off in these selections from the American Midwest because I myself set off from the Midwest as a person—from Ohio and, via a brief stay in California, Indiana—on the journey taken in the poems. My obligation as a writer is not only to make individual poems, but also to do my best to compose coherent books—even when they are as long and stylistically various as this one. 'Northern Summer,' dealing with a short and somewhat alienating three months in Scotland, follows the Midwestern poem, establishing the back-and-forth movement of my life for twenty years between the US and the UK. The two comic ship-going poems, back home on the *Stefan Batory* and off to Britain again on the *Mihail Lermontov*, reinforce the pattern. 'An East Anglian Diptych' settles comfortably in that part of England where I have felt as much at home as I have in Indiana or Ohio. 'A Compostela Diptych' (1990) stretches out as far as I am able to reach to a point that is even perhaps beyond my grasp. After that, chronology of composition is an adequate guide, and the remaining six poems are printed in the order in which they were written, concluding with a coda, 'After Five Words Englished from the Russian,' a fairly short "long poem" that, among other things, can function as a stand-in for the missing *Trigons*. From the beginning I have had my eye on the length of W.H. Auden's 1965 *Collected Longer Poems*, which came in at 356 pages. Anything much longer than that becomes unwieldy as a book and runs the danger of ceasing to be an aesthetic object at all.

At this point it will be enough to print the original notes on sources as they appeared in books from *Crossing* (1979) through *Kedging* (2007) and down to the present.

Facts from an Apocryphal Midwest

I have grappled in this poem with some midwestern American geography, geology, prehistory and history that parallel in many ways those I was working with in 'An East Anglian Diptych.' The chief trails this time—although they are by no means "ley lines"—began as prehistoric paths down which Lake Superior copper was carried from the early days of the Mound Builders until the collapse of their particular economy and way of life. These trails, and especially the Old Sauk Trail and the St. Joseph-Kankakee portage, were later used by the Potawatomi, the Miami and other local Algonquian tribes, as well as by the Iroquois on their raids into the area, and by the French explorers, traders and missionaries. Again, as in the East Anglian poem, three rivers figure in the topographical configuration that emerges: the St. Joseph (which the French called the River of Miamis), the Kankakee (also called the Seignelay), and the Illinois. The dominant historical figure in the poem is René Robert Cavelier, Sieur de La Salle. Having begun my research while still at work on 'An East Anglian Diptych' and having determined to write about rivers and trails which I often crossed but as yet knew little about, I found myself stimulated by exactly those things which from time to time I had thought might stimulate "another poet" as I sat writing about things I knew and loved in East Anglia—La Salle's voyage through the great lakes and journey along the local paths and waterways, Algonquian (mostly Potawatomi) history and mythology, the geological and geographical transformations which occurred during the last glacial recession, and the prose of Francis Parkman in the volume of *France and England in North America* called *La Salle and the Discovery of the Great West*. What had begun as an act of will rapidly became, in the actual processes of composition, altogether something else. Although I do not take La Salle all the way to the Mississippi (usually called the Colbert in the poem), I take him pretty far down the Illinois. For some of the same reasons that Edward Thomas and John Constable appear in 'An East Anglian Diptych,' Parkman himself appears briefly here. His prose is sometimes quoted, paraphrased, versified. Where quotations are not exact, I intend no disrespect. Formal constraints now and then demanded slight modifications in rhythm, diction and syntax. Neither Fenimore Cooper's stagecoach ride into the area nor the dedication of the cornerstone of the La Salle Memorial Project are fictions. The merging of the two, however, in the context of a pageant which occurred at the quatro-millennial anniversary of the La Salle-Miami Council is only a convenient way, consistent with the conclusions of both 'Ley Lines' and 'Rivers' in 'An East Anglian Diptych,' to bring the poem into the present historical period.

Among the sources for this poem are three that very few readers will have come across. These are books by an almost vanished breed, the local amateur historian. Charles H. Bartlett's *La Salle in the Valley of the St. Joseph*, George A. Baker's *The St. Joseph-Kankakee Portage*, and Timothy Edward Howard's

A History of St. Joseph County were all enormously useful. Other sources for the poem include: Charles Haight Farnham, *A Life of Francis Parkman;* Howard Doughty, *Francis Parkman;* Louise Phelps Kellogg, *Early Narratives of the Northwest* and *The French Regime in Wisconsin and the Northwest;* Henri Joutel, *A Journal of La Salle's Last Voyage;* Carl O. Sauer, *Seventeenth Century North America* and *Selected Essays 1963-1975;* James A. Clifton, *The Prairie People;* R. David Edmunds, *The Potawatomis;* George T. Hunt, *The Wars of the Iroquois;* Fay Folsom Nichols, *The Kankakee;* Archer Butler Hulbert, *Indian Thoroughfares;* Hugh Brody, *Maps and Dreams;* Andrew Trout, *Jean-Baptiste Colbert;* James Fenimore Cooper, *The Oak Openings: or The Bee Hunter;* George Dekker, *James Fenimore Cooper: The American Scott;* Blake Nevius, *Cooper's Landscapes: An Essay on the Picturesque Vision.* The dedication of this poem reflects formal debts as well as friendship. 'An East Anglian Diptych' began as a homage to David Jones and Robert Duncan. The present poem, beginning with its title, takes a leaf from Ken Smith's *The Poet Reclining* and some strategies from Michael Anania's *The Color of Dust* and *Riversongs.*

Northern Summer

Sir William Fraser, *Memorials of the Family of Wemyss of Wemyss;* Göran Sonnevi, "Void which falls out of void..."; *The Gododdin;* Antonia Fraser, *Mary Queen of Scots;* Robert Gore-Browne, *Lord Bothwell and Mary Queen of Scots;* Moray McLaren, *Bonnie Prince Charlie;* John Prebble, *Culloden;* Sir Walter Scott, *Waverley;* Robert Louis Stevenson, *Kidnapped;* Jenni Calder, *Robert Louis Stevenson;* A. N. Wilson, *The Laird of Abbotsford;* Adam Smith, *The Wealth of Nations;* Fred R. Glahe, *Adam Smith and the Wealth of Nations;* R. B. Haldane, *Adam Smith;* E. W. Hirst, *Adam Smith;* John Rae, *The Life of Adam Smith;* John Fleming, *Robert Adam and His Circle;* James Macpherson, *The Poems of Ossian;* Derick S. Thomson, *The Gaelic Sources of MacPherson's Ossian;* Bailey Saunders, *Life and Letters of James Macpherson;* Henry Mackenzie, *The Man of Feeling;* Gerard A. Baker, *Henry Mackenzie.*

The Stefan Batory Poems and The Mihail Lermomtov Poems

Batory: Adam Mickiewicz, *Pan Tadeusz* (in the G. R. Noyes translation); *Adam Mickiewicz* (Unesco Books: essays by several hands); V. L. Benes and N. J. G. Pounds, *Poland;* Tadeusz Ocioszynski, *Poland on the Baltic;* Jerzy Jan Lerski, *A Polish Chapter in Jacksonian America;* Henry Beston, *The St. Lawrence;* Guilbert Parker and Claude G. Bryan, *Old Quebec;* Eric Zagrans, two rejected lines from an early draft of his translation into Yiddish of 'The Love Song of J. Alfred Prufrock.' **Lermontov**: *The Poetry of Lermontov* (edited and translated by C. E. l'Ami); *A Lermontov Reader* (edited and translated by Guy Daniels); Mihail Lermontov, *A Hero of Our Time* (in the Nabokov translation); Janko Lavrin, *Lermontov;* Serge Sovietov, *Mickiewicz in Russia;* Edward J. Brown, *Russian Literature Since the Revolution;* Yon Barna, *Eisenstein;* Colette Shulman, ed., *We the Russians;* James H. Billington, *The*

Icon and the Axe; Robert Payne, *The Fortress;* Charles M. Wiltse, *The New Nation;* R. C. McGrane, *The Panic of* 1837; N. K. Risjord, *The Old Republicans;* Sir Edward Creasy, *15 Decisive Battles;* Alan Wykes, *An Eye on the Thames;* Basil E. Cracknell, *Portrait of London River;* Philip Howard, *London's River;* A. P. Herbert, *The Thames.*

An East Anglian Diptych

This is very much a "poem of place" located in those parts of Cambridgeshire, Suffolk and Norfolk linked by the ley lines and rivers which connect locality with locality, and time with time. The ley lines in question are the ancient paths and tracks which date back to the neolithic period. The chief ley line followed is the Icknield Way, the track explored by Edward Thomas in his final volume of prose on the English countryside. Thomas himself figures in the prose section of the first part of the sequence, section iv. The controlling myth for both 'Ley Lines' and 'Rivers' derives from T. C. Lethbridge's *Gogmagog: The Buried Gods*, which treats the old Celtic/Belgic religion in terms of his excavation of the Wandelbury chalk figures and their relationship to better known hill figures such as the Cerne Giant. The presiding presences in 'Ley Lines' (who also return in 'Rivers') are the dowser—Lethbridge himself was a dowser—and his prototype, the Dodman, who was the prehistoric surveyor who aligned the paths and tracks. The transition between the 'Ley Lines' section and the 'Rivers' is made by way of the terrestrial zodiac at Bury St. Edmunds, a vast arrangement of figures by means of which I move from the Sagittarius beginning on the River Lark near Abbots Bridge in Bury to the Gemini (in the form of Wandil, the East Anglian devil) standing on the Stour near Clare Castle. The rivers dealt with are, in order, the Stour, the Alde, and the Deben. As in 'Ley Lines,' this section shuttles backwards and forwards in time, though its geographical or topological movement is direct enough. This part too has a section in prose, John Constable on the Stour corresponding to Edward Thomas on the Icknield Way. The gods and goddesses invoked in both sections are the same: Gog (the sun/Bel/Baal/Belenus/Helith, etc.), Magog (the moon/Meg/Magg/Epona, etc.), and Wandil (darkness/the East Anglian devil/the giant with a sword, etc.). When the last section of 'Ley Lines' moves into the present by counting off the numbers which locate Whittlesford church on the Ordnance Survey Map, the fit of alliteration is not gratuitous. The Sheela-na-gig figure over the Whittlesford church door is an image of Gogmagog, and Lethbridge argues that words like "goggle," "giggle," "ogle," and the child's grotesque toy "Golliwog" are all verbal derivations. The end of "Rivers," like the end of "Ley Lines," also moves into the present—but without the fit of alliteration.

Sources: T. C. Lethbridge, *GogMagog;* Shirley Toulson, *East Anglia: Walking the Ley Lines and Ancient Tracks;* W. G. Arnott, *Alde Estuary, Orwell Estuary: The Story of Ipswich River, Suffolk Estuary: The Story of the River Deben;* George

Ewart Evans, *The Pattern Under the Plough, Ask the Fellows Who Cut the Hay;* Julia Pipe, *Port on the Alde;* R. Allen Brown, *Orford Castle;* F. J. E. Raby and P. K. Baille Reynolds, *Framlingham Castle;* O. R. Sitwell, *Framlingham Guide;* Julian Tennyson, *Suffolk Scene;* Rupert Bruce-Mitford, *The Sutton Hoo Ship Burial;* Bernice Grohskopf, *The Treasure of Sutton Hoo;* Michael Alexander, trans., *Beowulf;* W. J. Ashley, ed., *Edward III and His Wars, 1327-1360;* Michael Prestwich, *The Three Edwards;* William Longman, *The Life and Times of Edward the Third.*

A Compostela Diptych

The final poem in what, from the summer of 1984 to the winter of 1990, slowly took the form of a trilogy, deals with the most distinguished trails of them all: the pilgrimage routes to Santiago de Compostela. Having written two poems where I felt on very familiar ground—though in two different ways—I began in 1986 to meditate a poem about a ground with which I was totally unfamiliar, except through the literature to which it had given birth from the troubadours to Walter Starkie and Eleanor Munro. In the summer of 1987 I walked parts of the Via Tolosana over Somport Pass and on through Jaca, San Juan de la Peña, Leyre, Sanguesa, Pamplona, Puente la Reina, Estella, Logroño, Nájera, Santo Domingo de la Calzada, and Burgos, crossing back into France through the pass at Roncesvalles. I did not reach Santiago itself, and I do not reach Santiago in the poem. The writing, however, became a pilgrimage in earnest when, without warning, I had first to help another person struggle towards physical and spiritual health, and then, unwell myself, begin a similar journey of my own.

As with the two earlier poems in the trilogy, I have more debts than I can possibly acknowledge. Stylistically, David Jones is once again a welcome and benevolent presence. Indeed his good help and hope have actually become, in a sense, one of the subjects of the present poem. The same could be said of Ezra Pound up through the walk from Excidieul. I have leaned heavily on a number of translations. Although the poet knows the various languages which he must sometimes quote all too imperfectly himself, the poem's polylingual texture is essential: it is necessary for the reader to try and hear the Latin, French, Spanish and Provençal words as best he can. I need particularly to acknowledge W. S. Merwin's translation of the *Poema del Cid,* Robert Harrison's and Dorothy L. Sayers' translations of the *Chanson de Roland,* and the three translations, one into French and two into English, of the Pilgrim's Guide attributed to Aimery Picaud from the *Codex Calixtinus* listed below with my full range of sources. Walter Starkie's *The Road to Santiago,* Roman Menéndez Pidal's *The Cid and His Spain,* and Eleanor Munro's *On Glory Roads* have been my constant companions. (Much in Part I derives from Munro's interpretation of the visual setting and internal structures of pilgrimage in the light of archaeo- and ethno-astronomical theory.) Occasional phrases from these books turn up in the poem itself, as also from the texts by Meyer

Shapiro, Erwin Panofsky, Umberto Eco, Jules Michelet, Thomas Carlyle, Desmond Seward, Jacques Lacarriere, Emmanuel Le Roy Ladurie, Henry Chadwick, Alphonsus M. Liguori, Edward Peters, John James, Jan Read, J. A. Conde, Oleg Grabar, Henry Kamen, Christopher Hibbert, Franz Cumont, Henry Sedgwick, Johan Huizinga, Bruno S. James, Edgar Holt and Adam Nicholson listed below. Borrowings in the poem are usually indicated by italics.

Sources for Part I: Jeanne Vielliard, *Guide de Pèlerin de Saint-Jacques de Compostelle* (Texte Latin du XIIe Siecle, Edité et traduit en Français d'après les manuscripts de Compostelle et de Ripoll); Constantine Christofides, *Notes Toward a History of Medieval and Renaissance Art, with a Translation of 'The Pilgrim's Guide to Saint-James of Compostela'*; Paula L. Gerson, Annie Shaver-Crandall, & M. Alison Stones, eds. & translators, *Pilgrims' Guide to Santiago de Compostela*; A. Kingsley Porter, *Romanesque Sculpture of the Pilgrimage Roads*; Meyer Sharpiro, *Romanesque Art*; Joseph Gantner, *The Glory of Romanesque Art*; Vera Hell, *The Great Pilgrimage of the Middle Ages*; Eusebio Goicoechea Arrondo, *The Way to Santiago*; *El Camino de Santiago: Guia Del Peregrino*; Eleanor Munro, *On Glory Roads: A Pilgrim's Book about Pilgrimage*; Waiter Starkie, *The Road to Santiago*; Noreen Hunt, *Cluniac Monasticism in the Central Middle Ages, Cluny Under Saint Hugh 1049-1109*; Jacobus de Voragine, *The Golden Legend* (translated and adapted from the Latin by Granger Ryan and Helmut Ripperger); Christopher Page, *Voices and Instruments of the Middle Ages: Instrumental Practice and Songs in France 1100-1300*; Russell Chamberlin, *The Emperor Charlemagne*; Charles Edward Russell, *Charlemagne: First of the Moderns*; Peter Munz, *Life in the Age of Charlemagne*; H. R. Loyn and John Percival, *The Reign of Charlemagne: Documents on Carolingian Government and Administration*; H. W. Garrod and R. B. Mowat, eds., *Einhard's Life of Charlemagne*; Robert Harrison, trans., *The Song of Roland*; Dorothy L. Sayers, trans., *The Song of Roland*; Edward Peters, *Heresy and Authority in Medieval Europe*; Msgr. Leon Cristiani, *Heresies and Heretics*; St. Alphonsus M. Liguori, *The History of Heresies, and their refutation* (trans. from the Italian by the Rev. John T. Mullock); Henry Chadwick, *Priscillian of Avila*; Jacques Lacarrière, *The Gnostics*; Emmanuel Le Roy Ladurie, *Montaillou: The Promised Land of Error*; Joseph R. Strayer, *The Albigensian Crusades*; Desmond Seward, *Eleanor of Aquitaine: The Mother Queen*; Johan Huizinga, *The Waning of the Middle Ages*; Peter Makin, *Provence and Pound*; Adam Nicholson, *Long Walks in France*. Sources for "Intercalation": Erwin Panofsky, ed. and trans., *Abbot Suger on the Abbey Church of St.-Denis and Its Art Treasures*; Umberto Eco, *Art and Beauty in the Middle Ages*; Bruno S. James, *Saint Bernard of Clairvaux*; Donald Francis Firebaugh, *St. Bernard's Preaching of the Second Crusade*; Thomas Merton, *The Last of the Fathers*; Henry Adams, *Mont-Saint-Michel and Chartres*; Steven Runciman, *A History of the Crusades*; Odo of Deuil, *De Profectione Ludovici VII in Orientem*; John

Hugh Hill and Laurita Lyttleton Hill, *Raymond IV Count of Toulouse;* Jules Michelet, *History of the French Revolution,* Vol. VII (Books 14, 15, 16 and 17), trans. by Keith Botsford; Thomas Carlyle, *The French Revolution;* John James, *The Traveller's Key to Medieval France: A Guide to the Sacred Architecture of Medieval France.*

Sources for Part II: 1. A. Condé, *History of the Dominion of the Arabs in Spain;* Jan Read, *The Moors in Spain and Portugal;* Oleg Grabar, *The Formation of Islamic Art;* Keith Albarn, Jenny Miall Smith, Stanford Steele, Diana Walker, *The Language of Pattern;* W. S. Merwin, trans., *The Poem of the Cid* (with facing page Spanish text of the edition of Ramon Menéndez Pidal), *From the Spanish Morning: Translations of Spanish Ballads;* Ramon Menéndez Pidal, *The Cid and His Spain, Poesía Juglaresca y Origenes de las Literaturas Romancias;* Ernest Merimée and S. Griswold Morley, *A History of Spanish Literature;* David William Foster, *The Early Spanish Ballad;* Cecil Roth, *The Spanish Inquisition;* Henry Kamen, *The Spanish Inquisition;* David Gates, *The Spanish Ulcer: A History of the Peninsular War;* Richard Humble, *Napoleon's Peninsular Marshals;* Christopher Hibbert, *Corunna;* W. H. Fitchett, ed., *Wellington's Men: Some Soldier Autobiographies;* C. S. Forester, *The Gun;* Hugh Thomas, *The Spanish Civil War;* Franz Cumont, *The Mysteries of Mithra;* M. J. Vermaseren, *Mithras: The Secret God;* Francisco Goya, *The Complete Etchings, Aquatints and Lithographs;* Eleanor Elsner, *The Romance of the Basque Country and the Pyrenees;* Johannes Jorgensen, *St. Francis of Assisi;* Omer Englebert, *Saint Francis of Assisi;* Henry Dwight Sedgwick, *Ignatius Loyola;* Mary Purcell, *The First Jesuit;* Walter Nigg, *Warriors of God: The Great Religious Orders and their Founders;* W. S. Porter, *Early Spanish Monasticism;* Edgar Holt, *The Carlist Wars in Spain.*

Cuttings

Much of this sequence draws directly, without external attribution, from a wide range of poems, letters, journals, and scientific literatures of the 18th and early 19th centuries, as well as from contemporary scholarly and critical sources. The "cuttings" have been made, mostly, from the following works.

Part I

Lyric epigraph: Edith Grey Wheelwright, *Medicinal Plants and Their History;* William Shakespeare, *A Midsummer Night's Dream.*

Sections numbered 1-5, 'John Tradescant' to 'Richard Spruce': Kenneth Lemmon, *The Golden Age of Plant Hunters;* Charles Lyte: *The Plant Hunters;* M. Hadfield, *Pioneers in Gardening;* S. Parkinson, *A Journal of a Voyage to the South Seas;* Kingdom F. Ward, *The Romance of Plant Hunting.* 'Endeavors' 1-5: J. C. Beaglehole, ed., *The Endeavour Journal of Joseph Banks;* Patrick O'Brien, *Joseph Banks;* John Gascoigne, *Joseph Banks and the English Enlightenment: Useful Knowledge and Polite Culture;* Ronald King, *Royal Kew;* Richard Mabey, *The Flowers of Kew;* Robert Hughes, *The Fatal Shore;* K. A. Austin, *The Voyage of the Investigator.*

Part II
'As Kew As You': Ronald King, *Royal Kew;* Richard Mabey, *The Flowers of Kew;* The Rev. W. Mason, 'Heroic Epistle to Sir William Chambers'; Erasmus Darwin, 'Botanic Garden'; Stephen Duck, 'The Thresher's Labour'; Thomas Chatterton, 'Kew Gardens'; Fanny Burney, the Diaries and the Letters; Wilfrid Blunt, *The Art of Botanical Illustration;* Gordon Dunthorne, *Flower and Fruit Prints of the 18th and Early 19th Centuries.*

Part III
Sections numbered 1-5, 'Humea Elegans' to 'Ipomopsis Elegans': James Edward Smith, *Exotic Botany: Consisting of Coloured Figures and Scientific Descriptions of such New, Beautiful, or Rare Plants as are Worthy of Cultivation in the Gardens of Britain; with Remarks on their Qualities, History, and Requisite Modes of Treatment.* 'Endeavors' 1-5: Wilfrid Blunt, *The Art of Botanical Illustration;* Jean-Iacques Rousseau, *Letters on the Elements of Botany Addressed to a Lady;* C. E. Vulliamy, *Rousseau;* William H. Blanchard, *Rousseau and the Spirit of Revolt;* Robert John Thornton, *The Temple of Flora;* Hugh Macmillan, *The Poetry of Plants;* John Ruskin, *Proserpina;* John Dixon Hunt, *The Wider Sea: A Life of John Ruskin;* Alan Bewell, *Jacobin Plants: Botany as Social Theory in the 1790s;* Mary Louise Pratt, *Imperial Eyes: Travel Writing and Transculturation;* Judith Pascoe, *Female Botanists and the Poetry of Charlotte Smith;* Kenneth Lemmon, *The Golden Age of Plant Hunters;* Percy Bysshe Shelley, 'The Sensitive Plant.' 'Homo Sapiens': Linnaeus, as quoted in Edward Dudley and Maximillian E. Novak, eds., *The Wild Man Within;* Michel Foucault, *The Order of Things.*

Laundry Lists and Manifestoes
Homer, *The Odyssey,* Trans. Robert Fagles; Stephen Mitchell, *Genesis: A New Translation;* Harold Bloom and David Rosenberg, *The Book of J;* Kasimir Malevich, *Suprematism;* Lorenzo Da Ponte, *Don Giovanni* (the libretto); Daniel Defoe, *Robinson Crusoe;* John Milton, *Paradise Lost;* Oxford English Dictionary; Arthur Quiller-Couch, *The New Oxford Book of English Verse;* Robert E. Belknap, *The List: The Uses and Pleasures of Cataloguing;* Pierre Albert-Birot, *Banality;* Pierre Albert-Birot, *Nunism;* Blaise Cendrars, *The ABCs of Cinema;* Robert Delaunay, *Simultaneism in Contemporary Modern Art, Painting, Poetry;* Robert Delaunay, *Light;* Filippo Tomasso Marinetti, *The Founding Manifesto of Futurism;* Velimir Khlebnikov, *Selected Poems,* Trans. Paul Schmidt; Tristan Tzara, *Dada Manifesto;* Antonin Artaud, *The Theatre of Cruelty;* Antonin Artaud, *Revolt Against Poetry;* Else Von Freytag-Loringhoven, *The Modest Woman;* Mina Loy, *Auto-Facial-Construction;* Valentine de Saint-Point, *Manifesto of Futurist Woman;* Valentine de Saint-Point, *Futurist Manifesto of Lust;* William Shakespeare, *Antony and Cleopatra;* Peter Ackroyd, *Shakespeare: The Biography;* Joanna Richardson, *The Courtesans;* Raymond Tallis, *The Hand: A Philosophical Inquiry into Human Being;* Donna Haraway, *A Cyborg Manifesto: Science, Technology and Socialist-Feminism in*

the Late Twentieth Century; Francis Spufford, ed., *The Chatto Book of Cabbages and Kings*; Mary Ann Caws, ed., *Manifesto: A Century of Isms*; George B. Dyson, *Darwin Among the Machines: The Evolution of Global Intelligence*; Ray Kurzweil, *The Age of Spiritual Machines*; Michèle Mètail, 1,000 Possessive Phrases.

I.
9842: …of the decoherence of the kedging…
9843: of the quantum of the zero of the one of the watcher
     of the disambiguating of the decoherence
9844: of the end of the quantum of the zero of the one of the watcher
     of the disambiguating
9845: of the beginning of the end of the quantum of the zero of the one
     of the watcher
9846: of the law of the beginning of the end of the quantum
     of the zero of the one
9847: of the laughter of the law of the begining of the end
     of the quantum of the zero
9848: of the loop of the laughter of the law of the beginning of the end
     of the quantum
9849: of the player of the loop of the laughter of the law
     of the beginning of the end
9850: of the rat of the player of the loop of the laughter of the law
     of the beginning
9851: of the guard of the rat of the player of the loop of the laughter
     of the law
9852: of the dial of the guard of the rat of the player of the loop
     of the laughter
9853: of the language of the dial of the guard of the rat of the player
     of the loop
9854: of the surface of the language of the dial of the guard of the rat
     of the player
9855: of the depth of the surface of the language of the dial of the guard
     of the rat
9856: of the groin of the depth of the surface of the language of the dial
     of the guard
9857: of the tool of the groin of the depth of the surface of the language
     of the dial
9858: of the virus of the tool of the groin of the depth of the surface
     of the language
9859: of the hand of the virus of the tool of the groin of the depth
     of the surface
9860: of the foot of the hand of the virus of the tool of the groin
     of the depth

9861: of the squeeze of the foot of the hand of the virus of the tool
of the groin
9862: of the toe of the squeeze of the foot of the hand of the virus
of the tool
9863: of the sock of the toe of the squeeze of the foot of the hand
of the virus
9864: of the spy of the sock of the toe of the squeeze of the foot
of the hand
9865: of the queen of the spy of the sock of the toe of the squeeze
of the foot
9866: of the goods of the queen of the spy of the sock of the toe
of the squeeze
9867: of the scald of the goods of the queen of the spy of the sock
of the toe
[1–9842, 9868–1,000: elsewhere: and the appropriation of the spirit of
the letter of the kedging of the text]

Kedging in Time
History: Robert K. Massie, *Castles of Steel*; E. Keble Chatterton, *The Königsberg Adventure*; David Kahn, *The Codebreakers*; W.G. Arnott, *Alde Estuary*. Rom Memoirs: E. Hilton Young, *By Sea and Land*; Pamela J. Adams, *The Iron Pier* (unpublished); S.R. Drury-Low, *Midshipman, Log Book* (unpublished). Biography: Burke Wilkinson, *The Zeal of the Convert: The Life of Erskine Childers*; Tom Cox, *Damned Englishman: A Study of Erskine Childers*; Jim Ring, *Erskine Childers*; Andrew Boyle, *The Riddle of Erskine Childers*; Andrew Lawnie, *John Buchan: The Presbyterian Cavalier*. Fiction: Winston Churchill, *Savrola*; Anthony Hope, *The Prisoner of Zenda*; Erskine Childers, *The Riddle of the Sands*; John Buchan, *The Thirty-Nine Steps, Greenmantle, Mr. Standfast*. Criticism: John G. Cawelti and Bruce A. Rosenberg, *The Spy Story*; Mark Glancy, *The 39 Steps*. Film: Alfred Hitchcock, *The 39 Steps*. Reference: *Oxford English Dictionary*; *Rand McNally World Atlas* (Imperial Edition). Poetry: Virgil, *The Aeneid*, translated by Robert Fitzgerald.

After Five Words Englished From the Russian

Statement for 'Huffington'

I've been asked to write 250 words about 'After Five Words.' The five words in question come from Osip Mandelstam's great poem 'He Who Finds a Horseshoe,' written in Moscow in 1923. I cannot read it in Russian, but I have loved the poem in English for many years (favoring first one translation, then another.) That is the source of the horseshoe. The dingbats come from, well, "Insert/Symbol" at the top of my MacBook Pro. I think of them as sucking-stones. Demosthenes sucked stones, but so did Beckett's Malloy. *Watt* concludes: "parole non ci appulcro _ _ _ Threne heard by Watt in ditch on way from station. The soprano sang:" followed by four and a half inches of white space in my old Calder and Boyars edition, followed in turn by "no symbols where none intended." That last statement is, I suppose, the memory trace leading to my lines about codes, modes, allusions, mimesis, and thesis in part V. Anyone who has read my recent book, *Trigons*, will know that I have, in my layman's way, been reading neurology in recent years, especially where it connects with musical composition and comprehension. Have a Google at *Aplysia californica*, and see what pops up. If you're feeling ambitious, read Eric R. Kandel's *In Search of Memory: The Emergence of a New Science of Mind* instead. Section II draws heavily on a story by Isaac Babel. There's a pun, of course, on his name. There are lots of puns. I was forced to attend a summer camp once as a child and had to deal with a sadistic counselor. To associate this with Soviet era camps in the Gulag may seem outrageously wrong, but I've been unable not to. (Auden said that his best reason to oppose Fascism was that at school he lived in a Fascist state.) Stalin had lots of *noms de guerre*, most famously Koba. I was asked to write about 250 words. I'll check the automatic counter. 340. Perhaps that's close enough. Oh, 29 more, quoted from the work of Kandel's seven year old daughter: "An aplysia is like / a squishy snail. / In rain, in snow, in sleet, / in hail. / When it is angry, it shoots out ink. / The ink is purple, it's not pink." Great lines, those. But the ink here is black.

CPSIA information can be obtained at www.ICGtesting.com
Printed in the USA
LVOW09s1629090914

403214LV00006B/741/P